M
IN SPANISH GOLDEN
AGE LITERATURE

Analysis of Burlesque Representation

Kimberly Contag

University Press of America, Inc.
Lanham • New York • London

Copyright © 1996 by
University Press of America,® Inc.
4720 Boston Way
Lanham, Maryland 20706

3 Henrietta Street
London, WC2E 8LU England

Library of Congress Cataloging-in-Publication Data

Contag, Kimberly Elizabeth.
Mockery in Spanish Golden Age literature : analysis of burlesque
representation / Kimberly Contag.
p.   cm.
Includes bibliographical references and index.
1. Spanish literature--Classical period, 1500-1700--History and
criticism. 2. Burlesque (Literature) I. Title.
PQ6066.C57   1996   867'.309--dc20   96-8239 CIP

ISBN 0-7618-0373-4 (cloth: alk. ppr.)
ISBN 0-7618-0374-2 (pbk: alk. ppr.)

TABLE OF CONTENTS

AKNOWLEDGEMENTS

When I began my investigation of the historical and social functions of burlesque mockery in Spanish Golden Age literature, the questions I posed outweighed the answers I found. Many people guided my work either through their scholarship, their formal or informal discussions about my topic, or through persistent inquiry into various aspects of historical burlesque. I am particularly grateful to those who have valued my on-going project by funding the research, preparation and publication of the manuscript: the University of Minnesota Doctoral Dissertation Fellowship (1986), Fulbright-Hayes (1986-87), the University of Oklahoma Junior Faculty Fellowship (1990), Mankato State University Arts and Humanities Mini-Grant award, and the Program for Cultural Cooperation between Spain's Ministry of Culture and United States' Universities grant (1996). I am especially indebted to Anthony N. Zahareas for his helpful comments in the preparation of the project, and to the professors at the University of Minnesota who read several versions of the early text, and to Larry Bratsch for preparation of the final manuscript. I could not have completed the project without my husband, Jim Grabowska, whose generous gifts of time, support and editorial comments allowed me to complete the project to my satisfaction.

I dedicate this study to my students. Hark, I have found the answers; the questions are now multiplied.

CHAPTER ONE:
BURLESQUE AND THE LITERATURE OF THE "GOLDEN AGE" OF IMPERIAL SPAIN

Introduction

To define the nature and art of burlesque and to discuss the central aspects of Spanish cultural burlesques, both aesthetically and ideologically, is to chart the many ways in which burlesque art developed as the social history in which it was rooted was changing. It is not the purpose of this study to provide an exhaustive account of the many situations of the burlesque but instead to outline and explore the forms and functions taken by burlesque. In seventeenth century Spain the burlesque mode of representation was a means to transfer notions, ideas, sentiments and expectations concerning established literary, political, religious, judicial, social, and moral canons to seventeenth century readers. In particular, it was a way of pointing out what sorts of things seemed absurdly misconstrued and ill-adapted in society. Thus, analysis of the burlesque mode suggests the playful concretization of ambiguous relationships among writers, translators, and readers. Through analysis of burlesque art scholars can identify the role(s) of burlesque discourse in the transformation of literary history in terms of the cultural age of the Baroque.[1]

The intention of this study is to exhibit the peculiar travesties brought about by burlesque art as an integral part of culture during the zenith of the critical perception of

Spanish decadence. More particularly, the aim is to analyze burlesque during the years of Philip III's reign (1598-1621), also the time specified as *baroque*. What the investigation of the nature and function of the burlesque mockery and a humorous mode of representation indicates is that the burlesque mode of representing critical issues is one of the most available indices to contemporary perceptions of (im)morality, and (ir)rationality, to list only two examples. The burlesque mode is both a jesting manner of expression and a product of an age when frivolity in cultural expression thrived in the midst of social, political, and economic decline. The burlesque way of representing reality in literary texts has much to do with contemporary attitudes, perspectives, tones and moods. It is unfortunate that until recently the burlesque as a literary category has been denied the attention it might otherwise have been afforded by its role in Spanish literary history. Evidence shows that the amusing nature of the burlesque destined it to be labeled and classified as frivolous and immoral. Only recently have scholars begun to investigate the potentially serious dimensions of burlesque cultural manifestations.

Any definition of seventeenth century Spanish literary burlesque is only an approximation to those etymological, social, and linguistic factors which informed its nature and function in contemporary Spanish texts. Concrete records of contemporary Spanish definitions of burlesque exist in a myriad of documents such as contemporary dictionaries, popular adaptations, imitations, translations, "festive" and "burlesque" texts, and contemporary commentaries concerning these burlesque cultural manifestations. The most reliable source of data concerning the phenomenon of the burlesque are these manifestations themselves.

An investigation of burlesque mockery in representative burlesque texts by Góngora, Cervantes, and Quevedo highlights the key interests of burlesque in 17th century Spain, and also has implications for a more general theory of burlesque and its historical significance for societies that use it as a cultural form of expression. For it seems that while burlesque is never kind or lenient, its criticism is directed less against morality, nobility, excellence, self-control, justice, and exemplarity than it is directed against defective and counterfeit representations of these virtues. In fact, the key interest of burlesque is to mock the outrageous and absurd pretense of everyday individuals who, through bogus subscription to commonplace ideologies, wittingly or unwittingly, make fools of themselves. Such is the historical bond between mockery and ideology.

The implication of the reappraisal of burlesque in Spanish *Golden Age* cultural manifestations is that the investigation influences the taxonomy of cultural historiographies.[2] Despite the global agreement of the burlesque presence and dominance in Golden Age literature, wherever was there a single burlesque situation sufficiently explicated without debates and controversies regarding its art or, perhaps, its social or historical function? Most scholarly work on the burlesque of Golden Age texts is usually suggestive only, indicating therein possibilities or tokens, not definitive explanations. While the technical and methodological manner of burlesque mockery is not necessarily time bound, its particular mockery certainly is. There have been many other historical instances when honorable subjects have become a laughable matter. The historical inquiry into the uses and abuses of burlesque, the diverse contents of burlesque, the "common denominator" of burlesque, and the historical conditions of burlesque illustrates that an effective way of testing burlesque is its specific application in distinct historical ages. The test case of the Spanish Baroque is an appropriate and effective model because it spans centuries of difficulties in interpretation and categorization but is never divorced from the particularly puzzling age of the *perceived* Spanish crisis.[3]

Burlesque and the Meaningful Coincidence of Brilliant Letters and Miserable Realities

All problems concerning burlesque art, however diverse, have their origin, at least potentially, in serious elements. It is an instructive paradox, then, that the grimmest spiritual and economic period in Spanish history was also the period in which the most richly distinctive burlesques appeared in Spanish literature. Because of its entertaining critical nature and ambiguous laughter, festive literature in general and burlesque art in particular are suitable for expression of contemporary controversial issues, albeit in an apparently harmless and authorized manner.[4] There is no doubt that burlesque, because of its humorous manner of representing literary, judicial, religious, social, political, and economic issues, became a successful means of expression for many of the major writers of the Imperial Spanish decadence. Literary historiography shows that Góngora's humorous verse, Quevedo's satirical burlesque poetry or his *Sueños*, and Cervantes's *Don Quixote* were no less appreciated by these writers' contemporaries than their more serious writings.

The ubiquity of "festive" literary art in the early seventeenth century is unquestionable. A representative sampling of all the major Spanish writers of the time indicates that most wrote successful festive literature. Witness a sampling of the variety of texts of a "festive" nature that appeared during the first half of the century: Mateo Alemán's *Guzmán de Alfarache* (1598); a chapbook by Francisco de Medina called *Cuento muy gracioso que sucedió a un arriero con su mujer* (1603); Cervantes's *Don Quixote* (1605 and 1615) and *Entremeses* (1615); López de Ubeda's *La pícara Justina* (1605); Gaspar Lucas Hidalgo's *Diálogos de apacible entretenimiento* (1606); jocose examples of festive popular stories in Covarrubias's *Tesoro de la lengua castellana* (1611); Salas Barbadillo's *La hija de Celestina* (1612); F. de Avellaneda's apocryphal second part to *Don Quijote* (1614); Juan de Luna's *Diálogos familiares* (1619); Carlos García's *La desordenada codicia de los bienes ajenos [Antigüidad y nobleza de los ladrones]* (1619); Quiñones de Benavente's *Entremeses* (1621) and *Josocseria. Burlas veras, o reprehensión moral y festiva de los desórdenes públicos. En doce entremeses representados y veinticuatro cantados* (1645); Fernández de Ribera's *Epitalamio en la boda de una viejísima viuda* (1625); Gracián's *Agudeza y arte de ingenio* (written about 1627 and published in 1642); Quevedo's *Juguetes a la niñez y travesuras del ingenio* (1631); and Calderón's *El mayor encanto, amor* (1635), are just some of those texts which were considered both festive and entertaining.[5]

There is little doubt that the purpose of such festive literature was to create laughable situations and thus amuse a contemporary reading and viewing audience. However, particularly in periods of political, economic and social crises, festive images help to build an historical awareness and a critical consciousness of crisis. Many have noted the unusual paradox between comicality and the historical perception of crisis. Mikhail Bakhtin argued convincingly in his study of *Rabelais* that "All popular-festive images were made to serve this new historical awareness. . .These images saturated with time and the utopian future, reflecting the people's hopes and strivings, now became the expression of the general gay funeral of a dying era, of the old power and old truth" (99). While the intention of carnivalesque laughter was to make a laughing stock of anachronism and to refocus and invigorate the worn-out images of familiar traditions and ideals, the ambiguity inherent in the laughable situations brought forth a social awareness of how things were and should be. Bakhtin's pioneering study of the history of laughter points directly to the meaningful relationship between comicality and history, and an investigation of burlesque which answers theoretical and practical questions about historical incidences of burlesque must begin at the juncture of laughter and society.

Many scholars in a variety of disciplines have attempted to tap the amusing nature and social function of comicality. The extensive bibliography of humor studies ranging from the anthropological investigation of humor and laughter or theoretical and practical applications of play and fantasy to studies which focus on humor and amusement in literature gives testimony to the diversity and breadth of the investigations and queries surrounding the broad and general category of "humor."[6] What this diverse body of thinkers on humor have in common is their attempt to demonstrate that humor is multifaceted and complex. No matter what their particular focus on humor, all have been concerned for one reason or another with what humor conveys about what people find funny and why. It seems that the preoccupation with humor has really been a preoccupation with people's attitudes toward the most pressing issues of their time. Throughout the ages humor seems to have functioned as an index to crisis. That is, historically, laughter and seriousness seem to coincide.

If "The best jokes are usually made by people who have long had a deep need for things to laugh at," there are several important aspects of festive literature to be identified (Galligan 16). Jests have a specific social function to "cut through layers of stale assumptions to reveal a fresh truth," and comicality and festivity are most often employed during particularly difficult historical situations (Galligan 12). Jokes have long been a common means of dealing with difficult situations, real or potential. Many joke with infidelity and death, for example. Laughter becomes a means of sharing the absurdities of tragedies and a way to handle the fears associated with them. Amusement is not a product of insensitivity to tragic situations, but instead a result of an acutely critical awareness of the implications of tragedy.

Clinton-Baddeley stressed the social importance of festive literature. He argued that to laugh at important and puzzling issues was "to save them from the canker of sentimentality" (13). He concluded that festive literature, and burlesque art in particular, did not only appear when a historical crisis developed, but specifically "in the warm atmosphere of tolerance" (14). This specific atmosphere of tolerance made it possible for people to "laugh obliquely at sacred things--not laughing in reality at the things themselves, but at those enthusiasts who make a noble thing undignified by the warmth of their admiration" (13). Don Quixote's burlesque representation of heroic knights-errant of chivalric romances is a good example of such an atmosphere of tolerance. Chivalric romances were already out of fashion in Spain, but the ideological baggage associated with these idealistic stories was still given lip-service (Russell).

Festive literature may have been one of the ways for Spanish writers of the early seventeenth century to deal with and comment on the puzzling factors of their age, but it was only one of the many available cultural forms through which the awareness of the Spanish Imperial crisis was exposed. The memorials, discourses, allegations and manuals or *arbitrios* sent to King Philip II, and to his heir Philip III, by social, political and economic analysts for the restoration of the health of the Spanish Republic reflected a growing general consciousness of a Spanish Republic in decline (an impoverished Monarchy) and a social, political, and economic structure which seemed to be coming apart at the seams.

The discourses of several of these political and social advisors demonstrate their concern with a Republic in crisis.[7] Baltasar Alamo Barriento, and Pedro Calixto Ramirez wrote treatises on the art of governing. Francisco de Aragón y Borja was concerned with Catholic discourses and the education of the prince. Philip II and Philip III's physician Pérez de

Herrera, who was preoccupied with the state of poverty in the Spanish Republic, wrote the *"Discurso del amparo de los legítimos pobres y redención de los fingidos y de la fundación y principio de los albergues de estos reinos y amparo de la milicia de ellos."* Esteban de San José Sumiter wrote a discourse on the (in)tolerance of prostitution. Much of these "serious" writings had to do with the development of changing attitudes toward a growing sense of social crisis.

Other more well known *arbitristas* such as F. de Navarrete, G. de Cellorigo, and Sancho de Moncada wrote specifically on the economic, political and social decline of the Spanish Republic, and offered the King what they felt might restore the Republic's social, economic and political well-being. Luis Cabrera de Córdoba chose another means to chronicle the changes in the Spanish Republic in his *Relaciones de las cosas sucedidas en la corte de España desde 1599 hasta 1614.* At the turn of the seventeenth century contemporary thinkers tried to increase the Spanish Court's awareness of what seemed to be a troubled Republic. Their intention was to identify the diseases of the Body Politic so that a remedy might restore the health of the Spanish Republic. The apparent crisis was not a Royal secret, however, and the Spanish public was well aware that they were surrounded by social and moral corruption.

Public sermons by well known preachers also attacked the discerned social and moral corruption among the citizens of the Imperial Spanish Republic. Sermons by contemporary preachers such as Alfonso de Aragón, Pedro Anas, Francisco Alberto de la Cueva, Cristóbal de Fonseca, Felipe Godinez, Angel Manrique, Agustín de Rojas Villandrando, for example, provided an outlet for communicating moral and spiritual ills. These treatises, studies, and sermons constituted a somewhat official evaluation of the ills of the perceived Imperial decline. The perception of Imperial Spanish crisis was handled in a variety of ways. The above list is only a small collection of some of the more *serious* and official attempts to approach the crisis (J.P.S.P.).

The cultural sphere of the manifestations of crisis in early seventeenth century Spain was broad. It is well known that all the major writers wrote both serious works and works which are particularly festive in nature. Jesting both in art and in life was a common means of expression for the seventeenth century Spaniard. Mockery was a pleasant and amusing way to criticize someone or something that seemed to deny the real nature of things. The mad hidalgo, Don Quixote, is perhaps the most predominant literary figure who comes to mind when we seek a comic character whose madness lead him to deny the real nature of things and to suffer the burlesque mockery of those about him.

Jesting in everyday life was certainly a contemporary pastime for seventeenth century Spaniards. In a rare study of the possible authors of the apocryphal *Quixote*, J.S.B.P. pointed out that the playwright Ruiz de Alarcón was one of the most envied writers of his time yet he was badgered and mocked by most of his contemporaries for his physical deformity. Ruiz de Alarcón suffered from a deformed upper torso acquired in a fall. He was called *"jorobado"* (hunchback) by Lope de Vega, *"sabandija y simio"* (bug and simian) by Suarez de Figueroa, and Quevedo remarked that from the side he appeared to be a D (*"dijo que D era su medio retrato"*) (75). He was called the Muses' tortoise (*tortuga de musas*) by some, and the poet between two plates (*poeta entre dos platos*) by others. The point of this historical example is to indicate that jesting with ugliness and the unusual was a popular contemporary pastime. Mockery was a peculiar but efficient means of highlighting the comic and absurd essence of imperfection.

Imperfection and the ugly seemed ridiculous to contemporary seventeenth century Spaniards because it deviated from accepted preconceived notions about how things *should* be. Essential deviance from the quintessential norm of those social, political, religious, economic, judicial, and literary categories held inviolable is the foundation of burlesque: the discrepancy between an ideal concept and its second-rate material interpretation was worthy of mockery's ambiguous praise and admonition. The ridiculous and illogical fusion of an ideal concept and a bogus representation of that concept did not deny the essence of the ideal but merely critiqued, humorously and in an extravagant way, how those ideals might be misused in everyday social situations. Festive literature thus provided a distorted self-referential image of an ideal society for the amusement of its contemporaries. Burlesque was only one of the particular modes that festive literature took in the first twenty years of the seventeenth century in Spain.

Burlesque mockery as a cultural phenomenon in seventeenth century Spain is indisputable. It is the analysis of its nature in texts and the interpretations of its historical function that have raised perplexing questions and difficulties. What is historically significant is that the amusing manner of burlesque brings to a jovial surface many authorized preconceptions about the familiar but illogical ideological notions that often cloaked miserable and sordid realities. The burlesque way of representation is a bonafide literary category which often stresses in an absurd manner the meanings, values, and attitudes which many seventeenth century Spaniards considered inviolable yet, when practiced, were not only insufficient to the charge, but entirely ridiculous and inadequate. What stands out in this literary category (especially when handled by skillful manipulators of language like Cervantes, Góngora, and Quevedo is the formal strategy which systematically critiques the ideological formations that recreate the key social relations between writers and their historical audience.

The Artifice of Burlesque

Certain seventeenth century cultural and historical discourses were commonly shared by the writers and readers. Many of these shared ideas and concepts are routinely burlesqued in the texts studied here in the following chapters. The burlesque texts provide counterfeit versions and absurd material representations of familiar discourses. The reader recognizes or "decodes" the resulting "cheap" counterfeit and laughs. Burlesque discourses expose the idea of *counterfeit* and *original* for the purpose of eliciting an amusing paradoxical situation: neither the counterfeit nor the original seem acceptable and readers are encouraged to laugh at what might be, in any other instance, an alarming situation.

Individual burlesques of specific discourses concerning chivalry, honor, virtue, morality and justice, for example, are framed by an overall burlesque mode of representation in each text. Even when specific cultural codes familiar to a particular group are unfamiliar to certain underinformed readers, these codes also fall prey to the larger burlesque frame. In the case of *Don Quixote* the chivalric codes are unfamiliar to some twentieth century readers, but readers are still amused by the hidalgo's representation of these codes. Twentieth-century readers of *Don Quixote* may find odd, archaic, and seemingly ridiculous the mad hidalgo's explanation of the ornate way with which the storyteller of his adventures should relate his first sally even if they are not familiar with the code specified in chivalric fiction. Technically, the historical reader cannot ignore the burlesque of the chivalric literary tradition in spite of unfamiliarity with the chivalric tradition in literature because familiarity with the essentials of the literary and historical traditions is inscribed in the narrative. Readers of the *Quixote* are "in on the joke" from the burlesque title (Part I) to the final sonnets at the end of the Second Part.

Burlesque in *Don Quixote* or in other burlesque texts is not merely the mockery of isolable common discourses, but rather a mode of representation that has the qualities of a joke. The burlesque mode of representation is a joking, frivolous manner applied to, or characteristic of, certain texts that may be literary, dramatic, painted, or musical. Burlesque is playful mockery of codified forms of culture. Its mockery depends on reversals, inversions, contradictions, incongruities, jokesters, joke victims, joke targets, inversions, irony, satire, parody, quotation, travesties, grotesque, imitation, and caricature, but any of these alone do not effect burlesque.

Burlesque's mockery ridicules the absurd practices and ludicrous representations of pretentious fools who use standards of behavior to defend their counterfeit ideals. In this strict sense burlesque debunks faulty practices and ridiculous material representations of standard discourses (i.e. false virtue, exaggerated honor, ignobility, disloyalty, infidelity) in order to lay bare possible perspectives, ambiguities and preconceptions concerning the historical practices of those familiar ideals and standards in everyday society. This "working definition" of burlesque differentiates it from satire, travesty, parody, and irony. If it is true that burlesque mocks less than ideal representations of familiar discourses with the intention of exposing both the most obvious and least obvious possibilities of that discourse for the purpose of amusement and raising a critical awareness of things gone awry, then there are perhaps no transhistorical definitions of burlesque--unless this is a transhistorical definition in itself. What would necessarily be true, then, is that a thematic, topic listing of what burlesque burlesques would be difficult if not impossible for motifs change with the times. But analysis of burlesque would thus be an adequate means of approaching the startling controversies of the age in which it appears.

Burlesque is an aesthetically enjoyed experience which can occur in response to either artistic or non-artistic representations. However, it is in its textual form that burlesque can be analyzed as a mode of representation. The major components of the burlesque mode include mockery, the seriousness of what is mocked, the manner and techniques and patterns of mockery, and the effects of the resulting amusement. Mockery relies on techniques and patterns and its success or failure is determined by willing receivers and an artful mocker. Mockery is determined by and bonded to the perceived seriousness and lightness of the objects, notions, or persons being mocked. While the list of components is lengthy and complex analysis of the empirical evidence concerning burlesque cultural manifestations indicates that the functional interrelationships between these diverse components provide clues to historical responses toward burlesque. Analysis leads to the identification of what the attitudes and preconceived notions behind those attitudes were, and provides historical clues to what comprises the nature of amusing representations of cultural patterns and conventions.

The laughter elicited by reading or viewing burlesque representations is akin to, but not the same as, laughter elicited by other means. The comprehension of burlesque requires, in particular, the ability for abstract thinking. To appreciate burlesques or to be amused by them we must be rational beings who are able to transcend both the practical and immediate considerations of any critical situation. Readers must be disposed to humor to appreciate the jesting disposition of a burlesque text. Without the psychological distance from practical and immediate considerations readers might otherwise be moved to empathize as in tragedy. Philosophical studies on humor and laughter point out specifically that to appreciate something mocking (this implies a representation of contrasting concepts which momentarily--and only seemingly--come to a ridiculous and incongruous union) one must rely on intellectual representations of categorical concepts.[8] Familiarity and intimacy with systems of literary, social, judicial, religious, political, economic and popular-traditional categories is essential to successful burlesque, but amusement is also key to burlesque's effectiveness.

Burlesque has been used by writers, poets, playwrights, actors and film producers throughout history as a mode of representing notions, ideas, and sentiments concerning serious issues in a playful and mocking fashion. The burlesque text might well be that unit of interrelating discourses that makes up a filmed burlesque strip-tease show of the 1930's or the lengthy narrative of Cervantes's *Don Quixote* (1605, 1615). The task for both literary critics and cultural historians is to investigate those instances in which certain writers or cultural producers chose the burlesque mode as a preferred mode of expression.

Studies of the burlesque have taken diverse paths. Those interested in the social and historical function of humor or even those who have taken an anthropological or psychological approach toward humor studies have investigated the relationship between humor related modes and its relationship to particularly volatile historical situations (Foucault, Freud, Kern, Hume, Morreal, Larsen). The aims and objects of burlesque have been the concern of those interested in theoretical and social aspects of burlesque. Studies of the quarries of burlesque have led to the classification of social targets as well as to the distinction of burlesque from parody, travesty, satire and extravaganza. Some have researched of the targets of burlesque (Iffland, Legman) or the taxonomy of types and categories of humor-related modes like parody, satire and travesty (Karrer, Highet, Kerr, Rey-Flaud, Rickonen, Hutcheon, Worcester). Others have attempted to distinguish between whimsical and biting burlesques or "high" and "low" burlesque (Jump, Wilson) or to establish a definition of the more modern hard-boiled burlesque and detective fiction (Newlin). There are, of course, surveys of burlesque works that provide insights into the nature and function of burlesque (Clinton-Baddeley, Bar, Flögel, Kitchen, Schlötke-Schroer, Sobel, Trussler).

There has been some effort on the behalf of literary critics and seventeenth century specialists to identify the practical function of burlesque, but few studies have balanced theoretical assumptions with empirical evidence. Even fewer studies provide the technical vocabulary and methodological tools for the analysis of the burlesque mode of representation in literature. An effort has been made here to establish the necessary technical vocabulary and methodological tools for working with the burlesque by providing sufficient empirical evidence of contemporary seventeenth century usage in Spain. Any definition of the burlesque as a mode of representing critical issues in the literature of seventeenth century Spain must include its etymology and significant social and linguistic factors in seventeenth century Spanish texts.

Burlesque Modes of Representing the Critical Issues of Imperial Spain

Much of early seventeenth century Spanish burlesque discourse mocks certain absurd practices of the most familiar discourses concerning fidelity, honor and sensuality, for example, in order to lay bare possible perspectives, ambiguities, and preconceptions about the social function of common attitudes surrounding established codes for behavior. The burlesque way of representing these discourses involves decoding one cultural code after another and requires familiarity with moral, religious, literary, economic, juridical, political, and especially popular, entertaining or folkloric patterns and expressions of the sixteenth and seventeenth centuries. Because the art of burlesque involves deflating ideals and lampooning immoderate nostalgia of a glorious Imperial past, the writers of burlesque in Spain induced readers to critique what seemed grotesquely idealized and out of proportion, and what was amusing about the miserable state of their everyday reality. Young girls foolishly mistake lasciviousness for true love, old men mistake youth and beauty for punity, fidelity and stability.

If burlesque mocks illogical representations of familiar discourses with the intention of exposing both the rational and irrational orders surrounding those discourses, then systematic analysis of the burlesque mode is one of the most telling means of approaching the particularly touchy controversies of any cultural age in which it becomes a legitimate means of expression. Just as a joke defines itself on its own terms within a particular social context, the burlesque mode of representing critical issues can best be defined according to the unique historical circumstance in which its mockery is rooted.

Burlesque is not a manner which is exclusive or unique to the seventeenth century or to seventeenth century Spanish cultural manifestations. Burlesque, in a variety of forms--dramatic, literary, musical, pictorial, etc.--has appeared in a variety of countries in a variety of ages. In the United States, for example, burlesque shows made their mark in the 1930's and 1940's with strip-tease acts and stand-up comics. Some of Shakespeare's plays use the burlesque mode even though burlesque as a term was not known in England until the middle of the century (c. 1640). Clinton-Baddeley claimed that "burlesque. . . in its simpler forms, was well known on the English stage at the beginning of the seventeenth century: but not by that name" (20). Some critics of medieval texts, like Pierre Bec, claim that medieval cultural manifestations also used elements of the burlesque. Many medievalists would agree that the Juan Ruiz's *Libro de buen amor* uses burlesque techniques and some might even argue that he uses a burlesque mode of representing the critical issues surrounding celibacy and the priesthood. The overall framework of the *Libro de buen amor* is not burlesque, however, and cannot be consitered a burlesque work. The challenge is not only to identify what the burlesque mode of representation was for seventeenth century Spaniards but also what patterns and techniques burlesques might share from age to age.

The specific theoretical and practical problems of the burlesque mode of representation are introduced in Chapter Two. Some historical aspects of burlesque are discussed and with the intention of locating the common denominator of all functional meanings of burlesque and the meaningful coincidence between brilliant burlesques and sordid historical realities. The formulation of a theory that would account for the complex phenomenon of burlesque cannot be abstracted from the historical conditions which informed the specific writers who preferred the burlesque mode of representation over other available modes of expression.

Writers of burlesque were aware of its economical means of dramatizing the discrepancy between appearance and reality. To understand the burlesque mode of representation consists in going beyond, within or beneath the burlesque appearance to the serious realities of the historical situation and laughing at the awareness of a distortion of ideals. A new interpretation of the burlesque mode of representing critical issues is an indispensable element in the study of Spanish Baroque culture, because it is one way for modern readers to approach this age of perceived crisis. An interpretation of burlesque is, however, only one element. In layers below it lie other forms of literature and popular culture, while in layers above it the histories of culture, law, *arbitrismo*, and religion.

Analysis of the burlesque in representative Spanish literary texts highlights the key central layer between learned and popular literature. Such a study provides the general framework within which future specialized studies on the burlesque can be elaborated. Because of the complex instance of burlesque the range of a study on its nature and function must include the conventionally separate fields of poetics, literary criticism, cultural history, and to some degree, the sociology of literature. The challenge, of course, has been to analyze burlesque works in terms of the cultural expression of the time.

Burlesque and the Modern Battlefield of *Literary Theory* and *Cultural Historiography*

One of the major difficulties in dealing with burlesque is the treatment burlesque has had in terms of literary theory and cultural historiography. Burlesque cultural manifestations are rude by nature, and burlesque's irreverence toward the establishment has greatly influenced its categorization in or exclusion from cultural historiography. In fact, a major study of its theory and practice indicates that the historical classification of this pedigree of festive texts charts the changing attitudes toward textually inscribed comicality on the one hand, and also helps to investigate the attitudes which informed how festive texts were categorized in or marginalized from cultural historiographies. In the last ten years it seems that there has been an effort to reappraise burlesque comicality in literary texts. The reappraisal of comic literature has touched Spanish Golden Age studies in particular. Some of the reasons for this increased interest in "low" or burlesque humor and its relation to Spanish studies of the sixteenth and seventeenth centuries are pertinent to this investigation of burlesque.

In *The Absolute Comic*, Edith Kern suspected that "Our own age, vehemently anti-authoritarian, has regained, it would seem, not only a healthy tolerance for comic outrage at all that is pompous and overbearing and a joy in toppling what is too high and mighty, but also a sense of the therapeutic value of such outrage and joy in a world in danger of losing all sense of proportion vis-à-vis individual life and death" (114). Kern targeted the shift in the perception of humor as one which benefits its critical and therapeutic value, and blamed the shift in perception on the historical challenge of authority. Perhaps no category challenges absurd representations of authority more effectively than burlesque. While Kern's suspicion may be accurate in general, another more reliable explanation for the shift toward a reappraisal of humor in cultural literary manifestations is that the analysis of comicality in literary texts has earned a greater place in literary studies following a general trend toward critical approaches which value and evaluate what some have termed popular-traditional elements. The writings of Russian literary theoretician Mikhail Bakhtin, and in particular his study on the way Rabelais subverted official culture with the mockery of carnivalesque laughter, provided different analytic strategies for approaching literary texts or discourses that have formed the canon. Bakhtin's studies of unofficial or popular culture have been instrumental in directing a score of those ideas which are most pertinent to the investigation of the role of burlesque and its function in the radical transformations of modern literary history. Bakhtin's *Rabelais and His World* offers telling arguments concerning the history of laughter--a key ingredient of burlesque.

Many literary critics have already begun applying Bakhtin's theory and methodology to canonized literary manifestations as well as to various other cultural manifestations. The trend has been to scan a trove of available cultural materials while zeroing in on what is now a very complex notion of "text." Due, in part, to such reappraisals and rereadings, there is no doubt that current research continues to challenge the concepts most have of "literature," "literary history," and "cultural historiography."

Oddly enough, much of the current research influenced by Bakhtin's pioneering studies--written years ago and available only recently--has been done in the area of the Spanish "Golden Age." In part, this is due to the make-up of the Spanish literary canon and in part, to "the fact that the very project of literary history as it came to be formulated in German Romanticism relied upon a construct of literature that, it was claimed, had actually been achieved in Spain and was yet to obtain in Germany."[9] Spanish Golden Age literature has, thus, become a test case and some believe that "more is to be gained at this time from studies focused on specific national traditions than from broadly comparative ones" (Spadaccini and Godzich xi). Anthony Close's arguments concerning *Don Quixote*, for example, highlight the importance of examining all literary categories within their specific national traditions.

Anthony Close's provocative rejection of most *Don Quixote* studies as "untrue" to the author's plans and intentions leads to some stark implications for the Spanish literary canon and Spanish historiography. In *The Romantic Approach to Don Quixote* Close provided a historical survey of radical changes in reading (and understanding) the burlesque narrative about a local madman from its publication to modern times. He charted the ways in which readings of the *Quixote* changed as the history of ideas in which the readings of literature are rooted were changing. He suggested that the modern ways in which readers have read the *Quixote* have profoundly influenced the interpretation of the work. Modern readings are, in fact, diametrically opposed: Is the *Quixote* a funny burlesque or a tragic view of lost illusions? The contradictions among *Don Quixote* experts are of significance to literary criticism and historiography.

Research into burlesque modes enriches the historical record by exploring various "texts" which had been previously labeled as "trivial" and "frivolous," for example, or those texts which, for a variety of other reasons, were not deemed worthy of study. In Spanish Golden Age studies this has led to theoretical investigations of learned and popular culture especially in terms of the *género chico*, and of proverbs, sermons, tales, chapbooks, satirical and burlesque sonnets and romances, and satirical exemplary novels, and other works previously classified as "low" or trivial literature. The modern battlefield of literary theory and literary history is necessarily challenged by these investigations of *low* genres.[10]

In a theoretical discussion of *Parody / Meta-fiction* Margaret Rose points succinctly to the empirical difficulties of dealing with cultural manifestations which had been categorized as frivolous or humorous: "the use of the term burlesque might also be said to have made it easier for parody (of both ancient and modern kinds) to be banished from the canon of 'serious' and 'acceptable' literature at that time" (40). It seems that the role of burlesque and cross-over terminology including parody, travesty, caricature, satire, extravaganza, and grotesque in the transformations of literary history has much to do with the current discussion dealing with categories, the literary canon and the "marginalization" of certain texts. Many representative burlesque examples have not yet entered standard histories of literature. An investigation of the theory and practice of burlesque may aid in identifying how and why the burlesque, a well-documented cultural phenomenon, has been so marginalized in terms of European cultural history.

Because of the disreputable categorization of burlesque cultural manifestations in particular, and most festive works in general, until recently there had been little development of a technical vocabulary for defining the variants of festive literature. While major studies by sociologists, socio-anthropologists and social psychologists have compiled a technical vocabulary concerned with humor, their working definitions and theoretical contributions, have, in general, not been applied to, or tested in, festive literary texts by students of literature. Modern textual editions and recent publications of varying quality are now beginning to provide such a vocabulary for festive works. In Spanish Golden Age studies, for example, ompilations such as *Cancioneros de obras de burlas provocantes a risa* (Jauralde Pou and Bellón Cazabán) or the recompilation of erotic poetry by Pierre Alzieu, Robert Jammes and Ivan Lissorgues in *Floresta de poesías eróticas del siglo de oro* and specific studies of known authors such as Ignacio Arrelano's *Poesía satírico burlesca de Quevedo* or Jauralde Pou's collection of Quevedo's *Obras festivas* and

Robert Jammes' chapter on parody and burlesque in his very recent book on Góngora's *Obra poética* are pioneering efforts in this area.

Robert Ford's dissertation on the "stylistic and semiotic reappraisal of Góngora's humorous verse," García Lorenzo's investigation of the seventeenth century *comedia burlesca* , Forcione's study of Cervantes's satirical *novelas*, H. Bergman's critical editions of Quiñones de Benavente's interludes, Chevalier's examination of the *cuentos jocosos*, and the series of diverse studies in *Risa y sociedad en el teatro español del Siglo de Oro* indicate that critical trends have strived to include a deep concern for the popular-traditional areas of laughter, carnivalesque and the comic spirit (Gorfkle, Durán, Soons, Joly).

To illustrate the point, Monique Joly's philological study *La bourle et son interprétation,* which investigates the strategic motivating force of joke relations on which narrative plots of picaresque and para-picaresque texts rely, is primarily concerned with the seventeenth century Spanish vocabulary of jokes and suitable places for deception. Her study provides a survey of jokes and hoaxes in Spanish picaresque and para-picaresque literature and their relationship of jesting to narrative paths (*le voies du récit*) and paths of reality (*les chemins de la réalité*). Joly's investigation of the joke--like other broader cultural studies which discuss Golden Age cultural manifestations within those specific historical conditions which surrounded them-- emphasizes that festive literature was a successful artistic phenomenon in the Spanish seventeenth century and that its study can enrich modern readers' understanding of the time of Mateo Alemán, Cervantes and Quevedo. Maravall's thesis regarding the picaresque novel in *La literatura picaresca desde la historia social* and Joly's study of the joke both support the argument that Spanish jesting or burlesque representations of contemporary Spanish ideologies brought to the surface the concerns of writers who were puzzled (and amused) by their fellow countrymen and the times.[11]

What some critics have discussed is that Spanish festive literature of the Golden Age is more than a historical development within a classical tradition of humorous works. Joly, for example, attributes the ubiquity of festive literature to the Spaniards' *"particularité nationale"* or *"caractère national,*" and insists that the Spanish sense of causticity is unparalleled in other literary traditions (3, 5). Joly explains that while the term *burlesco* was imported to Spain from Italy, *burla* was a particularly Spanish creation: "*C'est un fait connu que burla est passé du domaine espagnol au domaine italien...L'italien a rendu à l'espagnol l'adjectif burlesco*" (23). What cannot escape consideration is that burlesque was a bonafide literary category in the Spanish Republic during the first half of the seventeenth century.

There is little need to rely on the confusions surrounding the term burlesque in modern times although some comparative analysis is useful in determining a common denominator for burlesque across the ages. There are meaningful definitinos of the term *burla* and *burlesco* which span history, but certainly the most representative for the Spanish Baroque are included in Covarrubias's *Tesoro de la lengua española* and the later *Autoridades* and in literary texts of the period. The definitions offered in literary texts are extensive and provide accurate seventeenth century limitations for the usage of burlesque. One could certainly argue that the burlesque texts themselves provide a theoretical discussion of the strategies of burlesque. *Don Quixote* is certainly one of the most complete registers of burlesque and the exchange of satirical-burlesque sonnets between Quevedo and Góngora provide other excellent examples of seventeenth century usage.

Response definitions of Spanish burlesque and comicality are offered in a variety of documents. Contemporary adaptations of Cervantes's *Don Quixote* for dramatic and prose texts, letters to the King concerning certain burlesque literary productions, Clemencín's comments on the *Quixote* and Avellaneda's apocryphal sequel are some of those documents which have been consulted here to determine more accurately the scope of the burlesque as a cultural phenomenon in the seventeenth century. Some of these diverse documents like Lope's novella *Guzmán el Bravo* which, according to Mariana Scordilis Brownlee, was "a miniature chivalric novel in which Don Quixote the character, the book written about him, as well as Cervantes, both the man and the author, are the object of a detailed parody" attest to contemporary attitudes toward comicality in general and burlesque in particular (*The Poetics* 165). The attitudes of readers toward comicality in the case of the *Quixote* for example, is textually inscribed. Thus reader reception can provide a gauge for determining just how Spanish contemporaries classified and used burlesque, and also a gauge for determining how literary historians across the centuries have dealt with the so-called *"literatura de pasatiempo."* A theory of burlesque for literary production characterized as frivolous and "burlesque" in Spain during the reign of Philip III (1598-1621) and, by extension, to 1640 and part of the reign of Philip IV, is an effort to evaluate the ideology of mockery and outline its social significance.

Arguments for a Model of Burlesque Literature: A Case for *Don Quixote*

The key to a study of burlesque as a mode of representation is to balance certain theoretical problems about the burlesque as a literary category with some concrete analysis of works classified as burlesque. Necessarily, then, there are references made to modern critical polemics regarding the interpretation of texts that, one way or another, involve key aspects of the burlesque. *Don Quixote*, despite its dominant position in the Hispanic and Comparative canons, is a paradigm of such polemics. Anthony Close has stoked the fires of all polemics regarding literary interpretation by boldly and defiantly doing a critical slum-clearance of a good majority of *Quixote* studies--all in the name of the burlesque. The main objective of Cervantes's critics, he has argued, is to ascertain just how the burlesque functions in the narrated episodes, a task which, he keeps on claiming, has not been pursued adequately the last one hundred and fifty years even though the burlesque, especially if the *Quixote* is read in terms of its age, is the one indispensable factor for any large-scale interpretive criticism or critical theory about narrative, quixotism or ideology. Both the canonized *Quixote* and the polemics of Anthony Close are good illustrative examples of the need for concretization of theoretical arguments.

Generations of readings demonstrate that while Cervantes's *Don Quixote* was read in its own time as a comic book intended to entertain, for nearly two centuries it has been read as some kind of tragic story of lost ideals. Yet parts I and II are rich examples of the mockery of familiar authorized discourses including erudition, chivalric and pastoral romance, love sonnets, picaresque fiction, Italian novellas, proverbial discourse, sermons, and so on. Concrete analysis of the amusing nature and pragmatic function of burlesque in the *Quixote* alone provides a marvelous example of how burlesque straddles both the learned and the popular traditions in literature in the cultural age of the Baroque. It is a curious irony that the burlesque as the principle mode of representation in Cervantes's *Don Quixote* has been denied the attention it might otherwise have yielded by its role in literary histories and cultural historiographies. Yet, as P.E. Russell confirms, "Gaiety, more than disillusion, is, despite what some have suggested, still the prevailing impression it communicates to the open minded reader, specially if the latter can read the book in Spanish" (*Cervantes* 55). Until recently, few have analyzed the *Quixote* as the *comic*, entertaining storytelling that Cervantes's contemporaries read, commented, and imitated.

The downplay of the *Quixote's humorous disposition* seems to reflect the interests of historical ages. Anthony Closes critical history of literary criticism concerning the *Quixote* is the most persuasive argument for reappraising the burlesque as the cogent mode of representation in the *Quixote*. His appraisal of what he calls the "Romantic Approach" traces the specific historical circumstances which conditioned critical readings that encouraged investigations of the *Quixote* as some kind of tragic story of lost ideals. Through the diachronic and systematic study of *Quixote* criticism he concluded that historical objectives forced *Quixote* scholars into different directions where arguments regarding the book's symbolic and historical importance seemed more important than its pervasive *humorous disposition*.

The shift to over-serious interpretations of the *Quixote* can be attributed to the influence of historical trends in reading, to modern readers' continued inability to appreciate the burlesque satire of chivalric romance (Martín de Riquer), to a changing perception of what is funny (Francisco Ayala, P. E. Russell), and to a disregard of authorial intentions and the "age" of Cervantes (Russell). Those critics who take into account the reactions of contemporary readers in terms of the declared intentions in the prologue to *Don Quixote* offer an instructive critical alternative. The textual questions proposed by Martín de Riquer, Anthony Close, and P.E.

Russell about the parodic or satiric intentions and the mechanism of the burlesque need to be examined.

In *The Romantic Approach to Don Quixote* Close charted the subtleties of the shift to "oversolemn" trends and pointed out the inadequacies of much of *Quixote* criticism since the pioneering "romantic" critics (the Schlegel brothers, F.S.J. Schelling, Ludwig Tieck, and Jean Paul Richter). He argued that the romantic critics' inability or refusal to read Cervantes's comicality initiated the "Romantic tradition" of *Quixote* criticism. This tradition yielded a "serious, sentimental, patriotic, philosophical and subjective" investigation of Cervantes's "funny book" (239). He concluded that the Romantic tradition has remained strong in its influence and has directed much criticism away from questions that the text itself suggests.

The result is that *Quixote* readers have been trained to read the form and meaning of the two-part narrative burlesque on two planes of understanding: there is the plane of the "textual" or "literary" sense of the burlesque in the *Quixote* as revealed, commonsensically, by the author's declared intentions concerning the parodic (or invective) aspect of the burlesque. There is also a series of interpretations of that same textual or literal reality that, simultaneously, expose the supposed deeper "meanings." The deeper "meanings" and "interpretations" have been produced (maybe even "invented" or "imposed") within Cervantine studies and expostulated repeatedly in hundreds of ways by some of the most respected scholars in the field. Now, these two readings of the same burlesque narrative are so far removed from each other that the diametrically opposed interpretations derived from them--"funny" or "serious"--appear to be those of wholly different burlesque modes.

Close pointed out that critics who have read the *Quixote* as a satire or as didactically corrective--or as a burlesque "funny" book--have remained on the periphery of the traditional *romantic* criticism of *Don Quixote*. They have been considered marginal to the tradition or are excluded from it. The various diverging critical paths taken by critics such as Martín de Riquer, A. A. Parker, Otis Green, Erich Auerbach, and P. E. Russell offered alternative critical strategies for approaching the bothersome humorous elements of the *Quixote*. They do not claim to know the "real" *Don Quixote* but they do insist that the pervasive comicality of the *Quixote* cannot go unexamined. These alternative critical readings are key to Close's study since those steeped in the "Romantic tradition" do not provide a convincing or concrete means for dealing with the comicality of burlesque misadventures or Cervantes's declared intentions regarding invective and laughter. Close singled out the absence of investigations of the comic elements in the *Quixote* and sketched an argument for burlesque parody which relies on burlesque patterns. He argued that these burlesque elements have been scantily appraised. What Close recognized was that modern criticism had somehow assumed that readers felt compassion and sympathy for the mad hidalgo and his apprentice-squire, Sancho Panza. Modern readers were thus incapable of accepting the constant joking manner as harmless since they dealt with the hilarious situations as serious matters for philosophical speculation.

In the *Romantic Approach* Close builds a brief but persuasive argument for reading the *Quixote* as a satiric burlesque novel. Close is not the first to tie *Don Quixote* to the burlesque, however. In fact, critics have long suggested that the burlesque tradition itself was legitimated in Cervantes's *Don Quixote* (R. F. Wilson, Murch). Close's diachronic investigation of the development of over-serious trends is attractive to *Quixote* scholars since he arrived at the suggested reading for burlesque parody only after a systematic analysis of over-serious historical trends in *Quixote* criticism.

The *Quixote* is an appropriate test case because it is one of the most read books in history and because it has been read both as a tragic and as a funny book. It was characterized by contemporaries as a "frivolous" book, one meant to please adults and children, and for several centuries as a "serious" book worthy of philosophical speculation. In addition the readership of *Don Quixote* is broad. While the *Quixote*, for one reason or another, has retained its privileged position in critical investigations of theoretical, methodological, literary, cultural, and historical import, today the *Quixote* is still considered an entertaining book for the European youth.

It is not surprising that the *Quixote* has lent itself to diverse disciplines for a variety of critical purposes.

Ironically, to date there is little evidence that these critical reviews provide a convincing and concrete means for dealing with the pervasive and consistent comicality in the *Quixote*. To focus on the burlesque mode of representing critical issues is to highlight the meaningful game of the prologue where the author's "friend" suggested that the mockery of chivalric romances was the intention of such a book, and to give evidence to the mirthful reception of this hilarious counterfeit history by Cervantes's seventeenth-century contemporaries.

Cervantes provided his readers with a vocabulary of comicality[12]. The *Quixote* also defines, re-defines, encodes and decodes *burla, burla pesada, burla pensada, burlón, burlador, burlado*, and even takes the possibilities of joking to its ultimate and logical consequences. The *Quixote* is an excellent test case for the burlesque mode of representation because it is a seventeenth-century registry of spoofs, comic stories, mockery, counterfeits, jokes, hoaxes and word play.

The focus on the relationship of specific burlesque elements or parody, travesty, irony and jokes, for example, to the overall narrative burlesque provides a more comprehensive reading of Cervantes's serio-comic text. The reading of the overall narrative burlesque avoids to a great extent, the serious, straight reading of the mad hidalgo's mis-adventures which the narrator mocks in his "history." Such a reading also facilitates the "recuperation" of the *Quixote* as a "funny book" by pointing out the relationship between over-serious readings and comicality. Close analysis of oversolemn trends tells us a great deal about how this book was read historically and pinpoints the specific problems associated with the *Quixote*'s comicality. The long reappraisal of *Don Quixote* in terms of the burlesque is not an end but a pretext. The intention is to highlight the *Quixote* as a paradigm of what burlesque is and what diverse functions of the burlesque mode might be. It also follows, then, that if critics are to reexamine the literary canonand other orthodox interpretations it is necessary to consider the *foundations* of burlesque in other Golden Age literary texts.

Examination of the *foundations* of burlesque in burlesque sonnets by the rivals Luis de Góngora and Francisco de Quevedo, in the lengthy burlesque romance *La fábula de Píramo y Tisbe*, Salas Barbadillo's *Fiestas de la boda de la incasable mal casada*, and in Cervantes's theatrical interlude,

El Retablo de las Maravillas and *Don Quixote* opens ways of solving problems concerning burlesque laughter and serious concern. The analysis of representative Golden Age texts in chapters three, four and five focuses on the double-edged function of burlesque: the intertwining of the serious and frivolous and the historical dimensions of the conversion of one form to another. The investigation of the sonnets, romance, theatrical interlude and lengthy *Quixote* are meant paradigms for the interpretation of the burlesque mode of representing critical issues in seventeenth century Spain.

Now, the theoretical and practical parameters of the burlesque mode need some discussion before solid examples of representative Spanish burlesque texts can be analyzed. The concept of burlesque as a mode of representation is still unfamiliar to critics. Yet it has been subject to sweeping verdicts and confusing interpretations. The *strategies* toward burlesque suggest both lines of development and consolidation of theoretical and practical parameters of burlesque. The plan is to find a common denominator for burlesque, uncover the innermost layers of burlesque representation, define the historical and cultural uses and abuses of burlesque, and provide the strategies for analysis of selected representative texts.

CHAPTER TWO:
STRATEGIES TOWARD BURLESQUE

Introduction

Over the last three or four centuries the term burlesque has accumulated such broad connotations and a multiplicity of meanings or parallel references that it is now difficult to construct a working framework suitable for analyzing burlesque modes of representation without providing room for other related modes as well. One way to proceed is to formulate a model of sufficient generality to encompass at least certain types of texts or discourses carrying the label of "burlesque," as well as non-burlesque but related modes incorporating the notions of travesty, parody, satire, extravaganza, imitation and wit. Clearly, this is an extremely risky task, especially in view of past and recent attempts, and failures, to do so. In what follows, various attempts to deal with the burlesque are explored in order to flush out the common denominator for all burlesques. The understanding of a common denominator of all burlesques aids in the analysis of concrete Spanish Golden Age burlesques.

The purpose of this chapter is to develop a statement of what a burlesque mode in art is and how it can best be researched and studied. Since the concept of burlesque as a mode of representation is still unfamiliar to critics the first order of business is to clarify the label "burlesque." Generally, and particularly when burlesque is compared to related nouns like caricature, parody or travesty, burlesque refers to a bizarre imitation of something. As a verb, burlesque means to make a travesty of whatever is imitated in an absurd manner. The key to understanding burlesque includes an evaluation of the process of imitation, the thing imitated and the manner of imitation. Burlesque implies mimicry (especially of words or actions in the theater) that almost always arouses laughter and amusement. Thus, amusement is a basic component of any serious analysis of the burlesque mode of representation for it implies both reception and what goes with it: timing, place, context, etc. The term *burlesque* suggests distortion. Sometimes the distorted imitation is palpably extravagant and often grotesquely debased. The result might be disquietingly hilarious, like a travesty. There is ludicrous exaggeration of features as in caricature for the sake of ridicule. Burlesque might begin with a trifling subject and treat it in a mock-heroic vein, or it might start with a serious subject and give it a frivolous or laughable turn. In most burlesques the trifling and the serious are both separate and entwined threads. Both the most frivolous and the most grave can work for the sake of the *comic effect.*

The problem of studying a subject as diverse and dynamic as the burlesque is apparent in the evidence of its nature, its function and its treatment throughout history. Historically, the burlesque has been subject to sweeping verdicts and confusing interpretations. Not much knowledge surrounding a difficult concept, like burlesque, can be taken for granted. To begin, there needs to be an illustration of where the ambiguities lie in traditional or historical and modern uses and abuses of burlesque. Since the aim is to flush out the common denominator for all burlesques a "modern" example of burlesque--American Burlesque of the 1930's--is reappraised. Armed better with the historical aspects of burlesque and burlesque's overall functions, short works like a burlesque sonnet or romance, or a lengthy and complicated text like Cervantes's *Don Quixote* can be analyzed more effectively. The *strategies* toward burlesque include both lines of development and consolidation of theoretical and practical parameters of burlesque. The strategy is to determine the original meanings of burlesque and its diverse functions and critical uses or abuses, and to develop a theory for burlesque that fits more effectively--and more systematically--cultural manifestations of burlesque throughout history.

Toward a Common Denominator

Attempts to define and explain the nature and function of dramatic and literary burlesques tell a great deal about how the burlesque as a mode of representation has been categorized throughout history. A review of some attempts to classify burlesque indicates what difficulties this mode of expression has caused literary and dramatic critics, cultural historians and readers. The purpose of scanning available critical inquiries into the historical nature and use of burlesque to demonstrate that the history of burlesque is long, complicated and unnecessarily confusing.

At one end of the spectrum of modern studies, those who study the burlesque as a literary genre often rely on John Jump's brief study of *Burlesque*. For Jump literary burlesque is a generic category divided into four species: travesty, *hudibrastic*, parody, and the mock-epic. Travesty and *hudibrastic* make up "low burlesque" while parody and the mock-poem or the mock-epic constitute "high burlesque." Jump includes a separate discussion of dramatic burlesque which he considers distinct from the purely literary burlesque. Jump's divisions and categorizations not only reflect the eighteenth century classifications of "high" and "low" style burlesque but they needlessly obscure the pertinent boundaries between burlesque and parody.

Jump relies on Richard P. Bond's definition of burlesque: it is through incongruous imitation that the serious subjects identified by audiences are made amusing. Although this broad definition could be applied to burlesques across genres and historical generations, Jump specifically refuses any significant relationship between the literary burlesque he studies (Butler's *Hudibras*, Pope's *Rape of the Lock*, Fielding's *Shamela* and *Joseph Andrews*, and Byron's *Vision of Judgment*) and other historical burlesques (e.g. Francis Beaumonts's *The Knight of the Burning Pestle*, Scarron's *Virgile travestie*, George Villiers's *The Rehearsal*, Boileau's *La Lutrin*, Sheridan's *The Critic*, Henry Carey's *Chrononbotonthologos*, Swift's *Baucis and Philemon*, Fielding's *Tom Thumb* and his *Historical Register for the Year 1736*, Gay's *The Beggar's Opera*, Gilbert and Burnand's nineteenth century burlesques of opera, and William Rhodes's *Bombastes Furioso*). He denies any relationship between such literary burlesques of old and the modern burlesques enacted on the stage in American theaters in the 1930's. He is quite clear about the parameters: "For many Americans today, a burlesque is a kind of variety show with a heavy emphasis upon sex, featuring broad comedians and strip-tease dances. This is not the sense that concerns us here" (1). Jump's definition is so restrictive that he has difficulty accommodating it even to the few selected representative works chosen to illustrate his investigations of the subject matter. He offers no common denominator of the functional uses or meanings of burlesque and avoids any definition of burlesque which might link, however cautiously, his separate categories of literary and dramatic burlesques to the ages in which they were produced.

The task of seeking out the commonplaces of burlesque has been carried out most unsuccessfully by many critics. Jump was only one of many who, for better or worse, sought out a working definition of burlesque through models whose composition and reception always seemed to outgrow the narrow definition. Perforce, many of the mechanisms, techniques and patterns of burlesque can and have been identified. Burlesque uses the techniques of caricature, slapstick, parody, grotesque imitation, word play, reversals and travesty. Yet many critics have failed to provide a convincing argument for burlesque precisely because they attempted to distinguish burlesque from all the other cross-over terminology: satire, irony, farce, grotesque imitation, extravaganza, parody, travesty, and so on, instead of focusing on the inclusive nature of the burlesque manner of representation itself.

Shepperson's study of prose-burlesque in *The Novel in Motley: A History of the Burlesque Novel in English* is an attempt to give burlesque greater independence over parody. His definition of burlesque for eighteenth and nineteenth century novels confuses parody and burlesque by forcing the distinction to rest on the proximity of parody or burlesque to the original and on the intention to ridicule content but not form. He argued that burlesque:

> carries the suggestion of grotesqueness and extravagance, and includes the idea of parody, which is actually one of the devices, one of the forms of burlesque writing. It is conceivable that a burlesque work might be written

without the aid of parody; but every parody belongs to the general class of burlesque literature (6).

Shepperson's argument is not off the mark here. He distinguishes parody and burlesque (and suggests parody as a subgenre of burlesque) but confuses them again when he specifies that his definition concerns "novels written against other novels, rather than with novels of social, political, or philosophical burlesque" (6). He argues that the distinction between burlesque and parody has to do with close imitation:

> Burlesque is the more independent of the two and is not obliged to follow, as strictly as parody must, the lines of its original; it ridicules not so much the form as the spirit or aim of another work. Lastly,burlesque usually attacks a group of works by different authors, or by the same author, which have a common character; parody, on the contrary, attacks one work only (6).

Burlesque definitely involves close imitation--for comic effect and laughter--of another author's language, style, and manner. Like parody, burlesque debunks and degenerates through distortion. Shepperson's earnest attempt to distinguish burlesque and parody underlines the commonplaces of burlesque and parody: burlesque and parody are often aimed at an august object and imitation (absurd, grotesque or straight) implies a good understanding of that object. He did not, however, establish commonplaces for the burlesque.

Shepperson is particularly interested in the history of the burlesque novel. He argues that burlesque novels were that

> "form of fiction which incorporates the salient features of some type of novel, by one author or by several different authors, and holds them up to ridicule or criticism by presenting them in an absurd, grotesque manner, incongruous with the serious intention of the original work" (7).

Burlesque novels are different from what he labels parody-burlesque then, since a burlesque novel was "written against a particular work rather than a type, and it employs parody as the principal means of burlesque" (7). These are cumbersome distinctions because while a pattern or model may be followed closely, there can be significant variations from the targeted original of parody or burlesque. Burlesques, for example, are often laughable representations of *something* in another medium.

Just as Shepperson attempted to define burlesque in relation to parody, others have tried to define burlesque in relation to satire, humor, wit, lampoon, extravaganza, and the grotesque. Those whose aim was to provide a working definition of burlesque often spent more time arguing differences between the cross-over terminology than arguing convincingly for the definition of the nature and function of burlesque. Fortunately, those whose intention was to provide working definitions of satire, travesty, lampoon, parody, caricature, irony, and extravaganza, for example, often found burlesque an obstacle and attempted to define it as a matter of contrast. Some of these definitions are useful in determining the borderlines between burlesque and other related terms.

Margaret Rose, for example, draws attention to the relationship between parody and burlesque in her theoretical study on parody as a form of meta-fiction. In her discussion of parody she explores the often cited symbiotic relationship between parody and burlesque. The symbiotic relationship is certainly prevalent in the representative seventeenth century texts we study here, and especially in the *Quixote.* Rose argues that parody is "in its specific form, the critical quotation of preformed literary language with comic effect, and, in its general form the meta-fictional 'mirror' to the process of composing and receiving literary texts" (59). Her distinction of parody from cross-over terminology including burlesque, persiflage, plagiarism, 'pekoral,' the literary hoax, pastiche, satire, quotation, and irony, is historical but often too general to provide a working definition for practical application. Her extended discussion of burlesque primarily draws attention to the harmful relationship of parody and burlesque. She highlights the effects of the historical confusions between parody and burlesque and stresses that the consequence of such confusions influenced the authorization of entertaining literature for incorporation into literary histories. Thus, her discussion of parody and burlesque also touches on the institutional issue of literary and cultural historiography.

According to Rose the role of burlesque in "transforming literary history" is clear: "the use of the term burlesque might also be said to have made it easier for parody (of both ancient and modern kinds) to be banished from the canon of 'serious' and 'acceptable' literature at the time" (40). Rose claims that the burlesque label was often responsible for the undervaluing and misrepresentation of *festive* works. She does not offer her own working definition of burlesque but instead includes Henryk Markiewicz's significant definition which seems broader than Jump's, and is much more useful in terms of its application to Spanish Golden Age literature.

Markiewicz defines burlesque as "grotesque, rank or flat comicality, extravagence (sic) of imagination or style (especially using vulgar or extraordinary language), no matter to what literary genre the work belonged; in its more narrow sense, the word was applied to travesty or to the mock-heroic poem, or as the name for a category including these last two."[13] Markiewicz introduces the telling characteristic that burlesque functions throughout a variety of genres. He liberates the burlesque from limited uses by stressing burlesque's categorical relationship to travesty and the mock-heroic poem.

Linda Hutcheon also provides a useful delimitation of the parameters of burlesque in *A Theory of Parody*. She isolates parody from burlesque and travesty for the purpose of discussing the role of each in modern art. She argues convincingly that "Both burlesque and travesty do necessarily involve ridicule, however; parody does not" (40). Hutcheon's statement is correct in terms of the burlesque: close analysis of the burlesque mode of representation in Spanish Golden Age literature indicates that mockery is a key element of the burlesque. Her distinction underlines the startling fundamental difference between parody and burlesque which is often disregarded or overlooked.

A definition of burlesque which avoids puzzling comparisons and frustrating distinctions between burlesque and the cross-overs is offered by Kenneth Burke in *Attitudes toward History*. Burke explains briefly but pointedly that burlesque involves a particular attitude on behalf of the writer of burlesque. The burlesque attitude focuses on, or systematically selects, the "externals of behavior" which, when taken to their (il)logical conclusion, appear ridiculous. The key passage concerning the abnormal narrowing of *what* is represented burlesquely and *how* it is presented to an audience through the burlesque mode highlights not only the formal role of stricture, but more importantly proposes a structural relationship between a writer's attitude and method. Burke clarifies that burlesque involves character types who are more memorable for their appearance than for the complexities of their *psyche*.

> The writer of burlesque makes no attempt to get inside the psyche of his victim. Instead he is content to select the externals of behavior, driving them to a "logical conclusion" that becomes their "reduction to absurdity." (54).

The *victims* of the burlesque mode of representation become flat characters because the burlesque writer systematically distorts the victims' critical perception. That is, the position of attitudinal superiority directs the method of grotesque distortion.

> By program, he obliterates his victim's discriminations. He is "heartless." He converts every "perhaps" into a "positively." He deliberately suppresses any consideration of the "mitigating circumstances" that would put his subject in a better light. . . . (54-55).

Burke's discussion of burlesque is right on the mark when applied to concrete examples. Cervantes is "heartless" with Don Quixote, and all the mad hidalgo meets on his misadventures. Similarly, the storyteller in Góngora's *Píramo y Tisbe* never gets away with convincing readers that he is anything more than a vulgar *juglar* who wants to discredit Ovid's heroic account of the star-crossed lovers on the basis of sensualism. Burke attends to the characteristic skewed perspective that distorts the readers' or spectators' angle on the subject of the burlesque:

> Hilariously, he converts a manner into a mannerism. The method of burlesque (polemic, caricature) is partial not only in the sense of partisan, but also in the sense of

incompleteness. As such it does not contain a well-rounded frame within itself; we can use it for the ends of wisdom only insofar as we ourselves provide the ways of making allowances for it; we must not be merely equal to it, we must be enough greater than it to be able to "discount" what it says. (54-55).

The method of burlesque involves a distorted perspective which readers and spectators recognize as such. Readers are amused by *Don Quixote*'s burlesque representation of fictional chivalric heroism because they recognize the madness of anachronism for what it is.

What Burke also confirms in his key passage is that burlesque requires the exercise of the rational faculties yet the effect of burlesque is to affirm apparently irrational orders. An excellent test case is, again, the *Quixote*. The obvious notions, sentiments and appearances or the "externals of behavior" which under other circumstances might be taken for granted are mocked in the mad hidalgo's burlesque representation of heroism. What burlesques expose with this teasing manner of baring the external essentials are the false sentiments concerning virtues which have become ridiculous through extravagance and false pretense. Burke recognized earlier than most that burlesque is a programmatic affirmation of irrational orders for sport (burlesque laughter), and that burlesque shows systematically that order is hilariously undone (serious concern).

If Burke's definition is taken a bit further, the purpose of burlesque is to teasingly strip the controlling hidden clockwork of familiar representations of ideal discourses, laying bare by means of distant--and therefore, heartless--mockery both rational and irrational cultural orders which perpetrate, and are perpetrated by, the ideological baggage governing attitudes toward specific human relations. Burke captured the functional essence of burlesque mockery: mockery and ridicule involve hierarchies of social relations. Burlesque is a mode which employs caricature, travesty, grotesque distortion, extravaganza, and other methods and techniques of mockery for "purposeful" amusement. The task of burlesque amusement is to entertain idle readers or spectators by making them laugh at joking images of things of importance to them.

Amusement and laughter require both psychological distance and emotional intimacy with what is being burlesqued. The particularly *heartless* attitude used by the writers of burlesque implies distance, and the built-in familiarity with what is being treated heartlessly implies intimacy. Therefore, the distanced attitude and interpretive role demanded of burlesque's audience is also important. The more familiar readers are with the notions, feelings, and social codes normally associated with whatever is being mocked, the more fully they lay themselves open to amusement and the more aware they become of extreme attitudes, ideas, images, and experiences that lie behind, within, and beyond the ambiguity of the jest. Ironically, then, burlesque enlightens because of its *perspective* through incongruity.

The Intimacy of Burlesque

Writers of burlesque must prepare readers for proper and full appreciation of jesting mode within which they will encounter critical issues. The jesting relationship must be established through intimacy. Readers are guided to share in the demiurgical perspective of the writer and in the absurd perspective of the agent (storyteller or strip-tease artist) of the burlesque mode. A "modern" example of burlesque, the American Burlesque Show of the 1930's, introduces the role of intimacy within burlesque's overall functions. The controlling hidden clockwork of mockery is tied to this intimacy.

Intimate burlesque is a statement of an invitation to burlesque amongst friends. *Intimate burlesque* was the billing for a burlesque show produced at the Republic Theater on 42nd street at Broadway beginning May 11, 1931. The word *Intimate*, both verb and adjective, probably conjured up a variety of notions and sentiments for theatergoers or passersby of the Republic Theater. Intimacy suggested friendly and familiar experience with private activities and close personal encounters which, carried out between unfamiliar parties, might be labeled illicit affairs. Intimacy also evoked inviting and friendly thoughts of potentially steamy or perhaps even *seamy* activities which are best carried out among consenting adults.

Intimacy also brought forth the notion of essence. The Republic Theater billing suggested that all that pertained to the natural composition of burlesque was intimated in the show. In essence, the intrinsic constituents of burlesque were to be stripped of dispensable externalities and bared in front of close friends. *Intimate* burlesque is the sort of burlesque that interested producers of burlesque shows in the 1930's in the United States. It is the sort of burlesque representation that is of interest here since the suggestiveness of *intimacy* draws a crowd while also prescribing a consensual contract for spectators. For all practical purposes, burlesque is best among consenting adults.

The review of the *modern* example of burlesque, and in particular, the example of American Burlesque shows which included strip-tease and stand-up comics, for example, may still seem only remotely related to the reappraisal of Spanish Golden Age burlesque. However, American Burlesque shows and Golden Age Spanish burlesques--like Cervantes's *Don Quixote* and Góngora's burlesque romance *Píramo y Tisbe*– have a great deal in common. What John Jump did not realize, or refused to recognize, when he divorced his study of literary burlesque from American burlesque shows is that the American Burlesque show shares a number of diverse elements common to all burlesques.

Gypsy Rose Lee was the belle of burlesque shows fashionable on American stages in the 1930's and 40's.[14] Gypsy had a rare talent for making nudity witty. She stripped prudently fashioned transparent gowns revealing a teasingly nude net sprinkled with discreetly positioned leaves. Show after show she bid farewell to a smiling and applauding audience who was still busy wondering if good sense had been outraged or not. The producer, production crews, dancers, singers and actors of burlesque were well aware of the fact that a well produced burlesque show straddled the fuzzy boundaries of seemliness and unseemliness, and rode cautiously--although confidently--on the edge of good judgment. Overdone burlesque brought in the censors. Underdone burlesque was meaningless nonsense.

American burlesque survived on what was left to draw on in depression-ridden America. The actors and actresses were run-off talent from moribund vaudeville. Burlesque turned unemployed and hungry dance girls into strip-teasers and replaced magic acts with stand up comics who toyed with familiar, although already worn-out glorious ideals of the prosperous 20's. These ideals, while still given lip-service in depression-ridden America, seemed quite inappropriate and hilarious when played out seriously on stage by clever frauds.

Gypsy and others like her stripped pretentiousness (yards of lavender net skirts and matching velvet jackets reminiscent of better days) on stages which had earlier housed both operas and vaudeville acts. These theaters probably resembled the Old Opera in *The G-String Murders*, Gypsy's fictional account of unusual homicides behind stage in a burlesque theater. She wrote: "The Old Opera wasn't exactly the show place that Moss had affectionately called it, but it was one of the choice burlesque theaters. In the nineties, when only opera was performed there, it must have been considered elegance personified" (7). The Old Opera was a preferred theater for burlesque shows precisely because of its woebegone days.

The description of its deteriorated externalities echoed the golden years while invoking its current deplorable state:

> "The façade was gray marble, the lobby long and spacious. To the right, there was a wide staircase that led to the balcony and loges. The red carpeting was frayed and worn, the gold leaf peeling symbolically enough from the cherubs that decorated the ceiling. In places, the marble had cracked and had been repaired clumsily with plaster" (7).

The Old Opera was a shambles that barely got by as a theater. The theater which had once produced grand operas characterized by classy, serious and tragic performances and elevated musical pretensions was now an appropriate and proper spot for the cheap counterfeit burlesque shows.

Burlesque shows of the 1930's and 40's were widely acclaimed as *girlie shows* and *nudies*. A telling portrait is offered by Gypsy:

> "Full-length, hand tinted pictures of girls in various forms of undress graced the walls. The one of me, wearing a sunbonnet and holding a bouquet of flowers just large enough to bring the customers in and keep the police out, was third from the left" (7).

The suggested *intimacy* drew an audience. However, as Gypsy Rose Lee recorded in *A Memoir*, the nature and meaning of her *art* was in the tease not in the strip: "June St. Clair, for instance, complained to the Associated Press that I was a fraud. 'Gypsy's work isn't art,' she was quoted as saying. 'She's fooling the public. Why she doesn't even strip'" (308) The tease is suggestive and significant.

Whenever familiar ideals about modesty, virtue, self pride, and righteousness are contaminated by (un)familiar staged counterfeits and these (un)convincing counterfeits are contaminated by convincing familiar ideals, intimate burlesque has significantly exposed an array of contemporary preconceptions and ambiguities concerning the most familiar topics and critical issues. There is no doubt that a certain amount of teasing and amusing stripping of intellectual pride, sententiousness, false decorum and pomposity occurred on these run down American stages as well. In the run down second-rate theaters second-rate actors were able to make meaningful commentaries on life in America. These commentaries were as valuable and telling as anything found in other cultural manifestations of the same period.

The discussion of American Burlesque shows is pertinent to an analysis of the burlesque mode of representation in Cervantes's *Don Quixote*, Góngora's burlesque sonnets, Quevedo's burlesque sonnets, Lope de Vega's *Gatomaquia*, and to most literary or dramatic burlesque in any age. Nevertheless, John Jump, and countless others have denied American burlesque any place in serious studies of cultural burlesque. Because it was a variety show which emphasized sexuality, featured broad comedians and strip-tease dancers Jump rejected any meaningful common denominator between these *sleazy* shows full of *adult* entertainment and other ages of dramatic or literary burlesques (1). There is ample evidence to indicate otherwise. Literary burlesque, for example, borrows a great deal from spectacle--which, pertinently, seems to be a concern of most *Don Quixote* studies, and especially of Bakhtin's study of the carnivalesque in *Rabelais and His World*. When burlesque is viewed as a mode of representation (filmic, pictoral, literary or dramatic) which consistently mocks those familiar but often absurd practices and material representations of discourses which have public approval, but seem to deny the real nature of the very discourses they imitate, there is a common denominator among burlesques of different ages. Burlesque's derisive laughter is reality, entertainment, and make-believe. Perhaps burlesque best comes under an overall umbrella of various nouns meaning a grotesque or bizarre imitation of quintessential cultural ideologies or of verbs meaning to make such an imitation of these ideologies. Specifically, burlesque implies mimicry of someone else's speech patterns, gestures or attitudes by aping them amusingly and making a spectacle of it. Burlesque relies on (and implies) dramatic distortion: to test a trifling matter in a mock-heroic vein or to give a frivolous and laughable turn to a serious matter implies an already distorted subject matter. Clearly there are shared operations among all burlesques. Now, before any analysis of the burlesque mode of representation in concrete Spanish texts, it is necessary to review historical aspects of burlesque to place the discussion of Spanish burlesques of the "Golden Age" in a meaningful, historical frame.

Toward a History of Burlesque and its Labels
A preliminary scan of the historical aspects and traditional usage of burlesque provides the following information: *burlesque* as a noun in everyday life or rhetoric is akin to satire, lampoon, farce, spoof, caricature, extravaganza, irony, cartoon, parody and travesty. As a noun in literature it is related to mock-heroic, mock-tragedy, mockery, imitation, exaggeration and fake-off. As a noun in American theater the word *burlesque* conjures up its affiliation with the peep-show, strip-tease, girlie show, nudie, slapstick, follies and harlequinade. As an adjective *burlesque* is akin to farcical, travestying, parodic, mocking, mimicking, ludicrous, ridiculous, comic, overdone, sarcastic, derisive, bizarre, grotesque, bawdy, indecent, off-color, and risqué representations of otherwise serious matters.
A serious study of the burlesque cannot rely on just a collection of interesting or pertinent definitions, but instead it must develop a statement of what a burlesque mode of representation in art is and how it can best be researched and studied. In this sense, the term "strategies" heading the chapter is somewhat prescriptive: the problem of studying a subject as diverse and dynamic as the burlesque is to strike

a balance between the existing consensus of literary scholars, however fragile and ever-changing in recent times, and the developing potential of the burlesque mode--especially if tested out and advanced in terms of major learned and popular works of the Golden Age. The burlesque mode, though often overlapping with travesty, imitation, and irony, is an identifiable, elaborated and vital means of discourse within the literary corpus of Golden Age culture.

To determine the contemporary seventeenth century meanings of burlesque and its diverse functions and critical uses in Golden Age cultural manifestations is key to developing a theory for burlesque that fits Spanish burlesques of the period and also informs how a theory of burlesque might fit more effectively and more systematically all burlesques. For a definition of the term *burlesque* and its diverse contents one must consult general background studies concerning the burlesque in several literary and dramatic traditions. The historical perceptions of burlesque are indispensable in exploring limited and broad definitions which lead toward the common denominator of all functional meanings of burlesque and provide a working definition of the burlesque mode for seventeenth century Spain.

There are a variety of general studies concerning the burlesque in several literary and dramatic traditions. Particularly fine studies are available on the burlesque tradition in English theater and prose fiction, for example. Clinton-Baddeley's "Introductory" to *The Burlesque Tradition in the English Theatre After 1660* is a useful study of the nature of burlesque and its origins before becoming a dramatic category for the English stage during the Restoration. While his main concern was burlesque in Britain, Clinton-Baddeley's insights provide important markers for forging a theory of burlesque which fits more effectively and more systematically all instances of burlesque. George Kitchin's *Survey of Burlesque and Parody in English*, Robert Wilson's *Their Form Confounded*, Jump's *Burlesque*, Shepperson's *The Novel in Motley*, E. A. Richards's *Hudibras in the Burlesque Tradition*, and Francis Bar's *Le genre burlesque en France au XVIIe siècle* are a few of those studies which have been useful in delimiting the pragmatic functions of burlesque.

Studies which debate burlesque in terms of other divisions of comicality (satire, travesty, parody, irony, farce, extravaganza, lampoon, caricature, and mock-heroic) afford useful distinctions and limitations which press toward common denominators and a working definition of burlesque for the seventeenth century as well as for modern times. I have already mentioned Hutcheon's *A Theory of Parody*, Margaret Rose's *Parody//Metafiction*, and Galligan's *The Comic Vision in Literature*. Wolfgang Karrer's *Parodie, Travestie, Pastiche*, David Worcester's *The Art of Satire*, Christiane Stoltz's *Die Ironie in Roman des Siglo de Oro* are others.

There is no doubt that many studies on burlesque humor exist. The focus here is on the peculiar travesties brought about by burlesque art as integral parts of culture during the national decadence of the Spanish Empire; that is, both as literary techniques and as an effect of the age when burlesque art flourished and when Spaniards perceived their Republic to be in a serious state of spiritual, moral and economic decline. Only a few relevant studies are available for seventeenth century Spanish literary burlesque and many pay particular attention to the instance of comicality in a specific author's work. Investigations such as Anthony Close's introductory essay *Don Quijote as a Burlesque Novel (Romantic Approach)*, Maurice Bardon's "*Don Quichotte*" *en France au XVIIe siècle*,[15] Ignacio Arrellano's *Poesía satírico burlesca de Quevedo*, and James Iffland's *Antivalues in the Burlesque Poetry of Góngora and Quevedo* stress the complex nature of the burlesque and its historical fortunes and misfortunes. None of these studies provides the necessary methodological tools or theoretical foundation for analysis of the burlesque. For this reason theoretical and methodological sources beyond the seventeenth century phenomenon must be tapped as well.

Historical Uses and Abuses of Burlesque

The burlesque mode of representation is made up of a complex system of interrelating verbal and non-verbal joking patterns. Ironically, in working definitions offered by those interested in the tradition of the burlesque, the original etymological and functional basis of the term is often overlooked, taken for granted or simply lost within comparative definitions of cross-over terminology. There is nearly a general consensus concerning the etymological root of the word burlesque pointing to its origin in the Italian word *burla*. But the word *burla* itself has an uncertain history.

In the *Autoridades* Corominas explained that *burla* is limited to deception: *"la acción que se hace con alguno, à la palabra que se la dice, con la qual se le procúra engañar."* He also pointed out the kinship between *burla* and the Latin *deceptio, derisio*, and *illusio*. He specified that the basis of *burla* was mockery: *"la acción, además, ò palabras con que se hace irrisión y mofa de alguno, ù de alguna cosa."* And moreover, he highlighted the ancient relationship between *burla*, mockery and spectacle: *"Convocaron a toda la cohorte, para que asistiessen a este espectáculo, y à la burla y farsa que pretendían hacer de Christo."* Corominas did not believe the italianism *burla* or *burlare* to be ancient since his source, Crusca, found no examples of these words in Italy before the sixteenth century.

It is quite well known that the term *burla* was widely used in Spain before the sixteenth century. Juan Ruíz's *Libro de buen amor* is full of *burlas*. Corominas recognized that the Spanish usage of *burlar* is much older than the Italian. He acknowledged its first use in the Castillian language in the writings of Juan Ruiz, in Portuguese writings from 1446, and in Catalán writings from the fourteenth century. In fact, he suggested that the earliest usage of *burlar* was more a peninsular phenomenon than an Italian one. One of the most recent attempts to define *burla* historically and especially for seventeenth century Spain was carried out by Monique Joly in *La bourle et son Interprétation*.

One of the greatest set clues to the uses and abuses of burla in the seventeenth century Spain is Cervantes's *Don Quixote*. The *Quixote* provides a wealth of examples of the contemporary use of *burla* and the players involved in jesting. Cervantes identified the, *sabidores de la burla, consabidores de la burla, inventores de la burla, burlador, amigo de donaires y de burlas, engañador, discreto, burlón*, and *socarrón* as those who masterminded all sorts of jokes and hoaxes. These jokes and hoaxes might have been *burlas pensadas, burla[s] pesada[s] y muy barato el precio, burla pesada y costosa, burla risueña, burlas que alegran sin enfado, mala burla, pasatiempo, burlería, traza, trampa, trómpogelas, encantamiento, disparate, cosa contrahecha y de burla, fraude, embeleco,* and *cátalo cantusado.*" Those who were the victims of the jokes and hoaxes *por modo de fisga* became the *engañado, burlado, escarnido, defraudado,* and *embaído.* The joke victim's reactions were also inscribed by Cervantes: *no sentirse la burla, no parecerle bien la burla, parecerle mal la burla, no saber de burlas, tener a burla, caerse en la burla, sacar malas veras de sus burlas* or *ser engañado* were all possible reactions to being mocked. The effect on jokesters was also defined: jokesters were either amused by the results of the jest *(ponerse ahínco en burlarse)* or their jokes occasioned more seriousness than they expected *(sacar malas veras de sus burlas)*. Indeed what this list shows is that in *Don Quixote* Cervantes provided a record of many of the diverse seventeenth century meanings and usage of *burla* and the common implications of the complex process of jesting and joking with the intention of providing amusement. Jokes and hoaxes in the *Quixote* are part and parcel of the framework of the burlesque mode of representing critical issues.

The origins of *burlesco* are much more obscure and its usage throughout history has caused much more difficulty than its apparent progenitors *burla* and *burlar*. There seems to be little doubt that *burlesco* was a much later derivation of *burla* and that its origin was Italian and, more specifically, its use can be traced to the sixteenth century works of writers like Francesco Berni. According to A. Martin, Francesco Berni was "the culminating figure of the burlesque sonnet tradition in Italy" (59). Although the term *burlesco* was widely used by Cervantes, Góngora, Quevedo, and other writers of the early seventeenth century, the term was not included in Covarrubias *Tesoro de la lengua castellana* (1616). And, while there is ample evidence of the usage of *burla* in the *Autoridades*, only two entries are provided concerning the term *burlesco*:

> **BURLESCO,** *CA adj. Equivále à jocóso, lleno de chanzas, chistes y graciosidades. Comunmente se dice, y aprópria à los escritos que tratan las cosas en estilo jocóso y gracioso: y assi se llaman Comédias, Romances, Sonétos burlescos, aquellos en que las matérias se tratan por modo jocóso y festivo.*

BURLESCO. *Se dice también de los sugétos, ò las Persónas: y se llaman assi los que son amigos de burlas (719).*

The *Autoridades* specified that the common application of the term was as an adjective which described written works that employed a specific style, manner or mode which was festive and jesting, astutely witty and entertaining. Something of a burlesque nature was jocose (*jocoso*) filled with *chanzas* (witticisms meant to entertain the rational faculty;[16] *chistes*, (subtle quips spoken as in a snicker) (*Tesoro*); and entertaining quick-witted pleasantry or *graciosidades* (*Autoridades*). The definition also highlighted the use of burlesque as a noun which labeled a literary category which comprised several different genres that employed a burlesque mode: there were burlesque comedies, romances and sonnets. The definition in the *Autoridades* could well have listed as examples Góngora's *Fábula de Píramo y Tisbe*, Lope de Vega's *Gatomaquia* or Quevedo's burlesque sonnets. While the definition from the *Autoridades* includes burlesque comedies they have not been selected for this study because most of the *comedia burlesca* were written later than the other texts studied here (Serralta).

It is important to note that until recently there were few studies on the burlesque comedies. Frédéric Serralta studied the phenomenon of the burlesque comedy in *Risa y sociedad en el teatro español del Siglo de Oro* (99-125). He identified the burlesque comedies as a *"género olvidado, cuando no despreciado por los estudiosos"* (114) and argued, if not for their reassessment, at least for their categorization as one of the *"géneros menores"* in Spanish cultural historiography.

> *La comedia burlesca no maneja elementos nobles, conceptos, ideas ni significados. Es precisamente la negación del significado. Lo cual no quiere decir, por supuesto, que la existencia del género carezca de significación y no se pueda enmarcar en tal o cual perpectiva crítica o ideológica. . . Para nosotros la comedia burlesca es algo así como la celebración de un culto pagano, el culto de una diosa, la Risa, y de su profeta, la Palabra; su principal interés es que al mismo tiempo aprovecha y enriquece un fondo de cultura plasmado en el idioma, fondo que, mediante un fenómeno*

*de transmisión esencialmente oral, se viene repercutiendo
incluso en las generaciones actuales* (114).

While Serralta de-emphasized and denied the burlesque
comedy any consequence in terms of significant serious
meaning or intention, he did salvage the genre on the basis of
its place in cultural historiography. His list of thirty-three
known burlesque comedies included comedies written by or
attributed to Vicente Suárez de Deza, Juan de Matos
Fragoso, Alonso de Olmedo, Jusepe Rojo, Francisco Antonio
de Monteser, Fernánez de León, León Marchante, Rodrigo de
Herrera, Calderón, Francisco Bernardo de Quirós, Pedro
Francisco Lanini Sagredo, Mosén Guillén Pierres
[pseudonym], Felipe López, Moreto, Juan Maldonado,
Jerónimo Cáncer y Velasco, Luis Vélez, and Martín Lozano,
and several anonymous burlesque comedies. His study
indicates that the burlesque mode of representation was
indeed a bonafide means of expression for later seventeenth
century writers as well. There were, during the Golden Age,
parallel discourses of the burlesque. The works of Quevedo,
Cervantes, and Góngora turned out to be among the most
effective--hence their importance in a historical study of the
burlesque.

The second entry for burlesque in the *Autoridades*
indicates that *burlesco* was also an adjective applied to an
agent who was partial to jokes. In this sense *burlesco*
described the nature of a jesting person or joker rather than
the nature of a text belonging to a particular category of
literature. Someone with a burlesque disposition was also an
amigo de burlas. An *amigo de burlas* was irresponsible,
reputably worthless in important matters and lacking in a
serious disposition. This *hombre de burlas* is described in the
Autoridades: "*Se llama el que tiene poco assiento y maduréz en
su modo de proceder, y reputado por inútil para cosas de
entidád*" (717-18). The definition of the *hombre de burlas* is
important for understanding the jokes in *Don Quixote* and
the variety of reactions to them. The Duke and Duchess are
extremely partial to jesting with the mad hidalgo. However,
their amusement is condemned by an ecclesiastic who refuses
to jest along with the others (*Don Quixote* II:31). The *amigo*
or *hombre de burlas* is thus contrasted with a person who

lacks a sense of humor, one who is responsible and respectful of important matters:

> *No es hombre de burlas, ò Amigo de burlas. Se dice del hombre mui sério, y ajénò de chanzas: y tambien del que está acostumbrado à cumplir lo que promete, ò à tratar de veras aquello en que se empeña (Autoridades 717-3).*

One who does not have a humorous disposition treats things in an entirely different manner. His manner of treating things is responsibly or *de veras* and not irresponsibly or *de burlas*. Cervantes provided a clear example of such a fellow lacking a sense of humor (*no hombre de burlas*) in the ecclesiastic who was a visitor at the Duke and Duchess's palace and a witness to the tomfooleries that went on there. The scandalously harsh words of the overly serious ecclesiastic condemn the Duke and Duchess for playing into the hidalgo's madness. He questions their morality and suggests that there will be a hefty price to pay for their amusement.

> *Vuestra excelencia, señor mío, tiene que dar cuenta a nuestro Señor de lo que hace este buen hombre. Este don Quijote, o don Tonto, o como se llama, imagino yo que no debe ser tan mentecato como vuestra excelencia quiere que sea, dándole ocasiones a la mano para que lleve adelante sus sandeces y vaciedades. (Don Quixote II:31 281-2)[17]*

The ecclesiastic is incapable of being amused by the mad hidalgo's crazy antics and silly imitation of the language of chivalry because he refuses to operate the hidalgo's representations of literary and historical ideas in a manner that is either impractical or non-theoretical. The ecclesiastic does not find any humor in the hoaxes and jests. He is a man without a sense of humor. Even the Duke and Duchess who are classic examples of *amigos de burlas* and Don Quixote and Sancho who are agents of the just are unable to humor him. The ecclesiastic disapproved of the Duke and Duchess's devotion of time, energy, and money to earthly frivolities and trivial pleasures as it was his job to secure the Duke and Duchess's devotion and perhaps wealth to religious duties and practices.

The ecclesiastic's even harsher words to Don Quixote reveal that the priest wanted to impress practicality and social responsibility on the hidalgo who, in his eyes, had lost sight of the duties of the social rank of an hidalgo. He tells the pretentious and crazy hidalgo to return to his social responsibilities:

> *Y a vos, alma de cántaro, ¿quién os ha encajado en el celebro que sois caballero andante y que vencéis gigantes y prendéis malandrines? Andad en hora buena, y en tal se os diga: volveos a vuestra casa, y criad vuestros hijos, si los tenéis, y curad de vuestra hacienda, y dejad de andar vagando por el mundo, papando viento y dando que reir a cuantos os conocen y no conocen.* (II:31 282)

The priest cannot get beyond the impracticality of the hidalgo's assumed pretensions. In this case, he was one who could not appreciate the *humorous disposition* of the situation. It is important to remember that the mad hidalgo did not take the situation lightly either. One could argue that, like the overly serious ecclesiastic, Don Quixote was not an *hombre de burlas*, although he did snicker at Sancho's blanket tossing at Juan Palomeque's inn. Nevertheless, the mad hidalgo was perceived by others to be a jokester because of his madness. The role of the burlesque agent or the *hombre de burlas* and the *amigo de burlas*, or the observer with a sense of humor are fundamental to amusement because without an individual's willingness to appreciate the humorous representation of an idea or concept, the jest loses it humorous disposition and becomes serious.

The burlesque agent or jokester was also studied by Monique Joly in her lengthy study of *La Bourle* even though the phenomenon of the jokester was not her main focus. Her definition of the burlesque agent was telling in any case since it outlined *burlesco* in relation to *burla* and its derivatives. Joly relied on contemporary dictionary definitions as well literary examples for her evaluation of the term *burlesco* for the seventeenth century. She explained that in its original usage *burlesco* did not characterize a person directly but instead it characterized the person's spirit (89-90). Joly illustrated her point with the particular *burlesco* employed in Cervantes's *Don Quixote* which was used to label the Duke's *mayordomo*. ("*Tenía un mayordomo el duque, de muy burlesco y desenfadado ingenio*" II:36 320). In this particular case the adjective *burlesco* was a means of informing readers of this practical jokester's witty style and sense of humor. Joly's definition of *burlesco* points specifically to its relationship with *burlón* and brings into question the problem of cross-over terminology concerning pranksters, again a key to the hoaxes in *Don Quixote*.

The many available labels for describing tricksters, pranksters and jokesters were useful for Joly's establishment of a glossary concerning the ubiquity of gaming and playful folks in Spanish literature, and they are of interest to us here. However, the meaningful dissimilarities between *burlesco* and *burlón*, *socarrón*, *taimado*, *bellaco*, *bufón*, *gentilhombre de la bufa*, *chancero*, *pícaro*, *embaidor*, *embustero*, *embeleco*, *mofador*, *trazador*, or *tretero* are unnecessarily avoided when the meaningful correspondences divorce the functional relationship between the humorous disposition and its creator. By giving burlesque's individual agent priority over considerations of the overall impressions of witty discourse within which that individual agent functions, one ushers in an inappropriate set of critical questions which might be useful when dealing with the tragic mode of representation where individuality is foremost, but misleading when dealing with a burlesque mode of discourse where the humorous nature of the representation of that individuality is what matters most.

Joly pursued the individual agent of burlesque in two other examples: the *Vida y hechos de Estebanillo González hombre de buen humor* and Gracián's *El Discreto*. On the basis of three choice examples from these texts she historicized her definition of burlesque by suggesting that by 1646 the term *burlesco* had already lost its original meaning of entertaining jokester in good humor and argued that it had degenerated to signify a fellow with a bufonesque character or a fellow who was little more than a clown (90-91). Joly completely disregarded any other common seventeenth century usage of burlesque. Yet there is no question that writers and editors used the term *burlesco* to classify specific literary pieces. In *Don Quixote* the cousin-licentiate who guides the mad hidalgo and Sancho to the Cave of Montesinos alluded to this contemporary usage when he described one of the entertaining books that he had written:

> *Otro libro tengo también, a quien he de llamar*
> *Metamorfoseos, o Ovidio español, de invención nueva y*
> *rara; porque en él, imitando a Ovidio* a lo burlesco, *pinto*
> *quién fue la Giralda de Sevilla y el Angel de la Madalena,*
> *quién el Caño de Vecinguerra, de Córdoba, quiénes los*
> *Toros de Guisando, la Sierra Morena, las fuentes de*
> *Leganitos y Lavapiés, en Madrid, no olvidándome de la del*
> *Piojo, de la del Caño Dorado y de la Priora; y esto, con sus*
> *alegorías, metáforas y translaciones, de mode que alegran,*
> *suspenden y enseñan a un mismo punto* (II: 22 206, my
> emphasis).

The licentiate did not offer parodies but burlesques. He
was not only quick to deflate excesses of nostalgia about a
glorious pseudo-historic past but he also called attention to
the critical intention and entertaining effect of the
mischievousness. In the licentiate's own burlesque of writing
histories he maintained a pretense of not being funny at all,
although readers suspect the shadow of a grin upon his less
than innocent face. He made a mockery of writing histories in
the presence of a very enthusiastic hidalgo who made the
notions concerning noble chivalric and historical endeavors
undignified by the intensity of his admiration for fictional
versions of them, and by his religious fervor to physically
reproduce them on a daily basis for unsuspecting Spaniards.

The licentiates's outrageous mockery and abuse of
erudition is a hilarious representation of how bonafide
scholarly activities can be made absurd:

> *Olvidósele a Virgilio de declararnos quién fue el primero*
> *que tuvo catarro en el mundo, y el primero que tomó las*
> *unciones para curarse del morbo gálico, y yo lo declaro al*
> *pie de la letra, y lo autorizo con más de veinte y cinco*
> *autores: porque vea vuesa merced si he trabajado bien, y si*
> *ha de ser útil el tal libro a todo el mundo.* (II:22 206)

The licentiate's burlesquing of writing histories, carrying
out scholarly research, and following a long tradition of
erudition guides readers toward laughter and amusement.
Readers do not laugh uproariously at these activities in
themselves but instead they smile at serious activities as
they become an outlandish and overtly ridiculous religious
exercise through burlesque representation. The licentiate's

history is a bogus history, his scholarly research is conjecture, and his erudition is fraudulent. With these few quips to Don Quixote's initial questions concerning the licentiate's writings the witty licentiate clearly and humorously uncovers the fundamental weaknesses of writing histories, carrying out scholarly research, and providing erudite authorities. The powerful burlesque of false erudition is larger than the agent of burlesque who, in this case, is the licentiate. The burlesque prods the weaknesses of many writers who, like the licentiate and because of their false pretensions, ridicule themselves by distorting the function of scholarship and erudition. Such is the critical potency of burlesque.

Analysis of literary samples indicates that the creator of burlesque minimalizes the sovereignty of the individual agent. One must therefore look to a broader framework of mockery to identify elements and patterns of burlesque which capture the essence of the contemporary instance of *burlesco* within the vast geography of usage by writers and readers of the Spanish seventeenth century. Seventeenth century Spanish dictionaries and examples from contemporary literature offer the most accurate working definitions of burlesque for this time period. These definitions identify what later ones often take for granted: these seventeenth century definitions do not confuse the term burlesque with satire, parody, or travesty, nor do they categorize burlesque, as many modern theorists do, only in relation to the various cross-over terminology.

The Ages of Burlesque

One basic premise underlines this investigation of the burlesque mode: there is no doubt that the ages of burlesque have to do with the specificity of regional or national situations and their time. An effective way of testing the burlesque is its historical age. Because there is the danger of abstraction if analysis of the burlesques is removed from the historical conditions that produced and consumed them, specific examples of Spanish burlesque are studied in terms of the cultural age of the Baroque. There is some agreement that there are ages when burlesque works flourished (eg. American Burlesque in the 1930's and 40's, English Burlesque in the eighteenth century, and French burlesque in the seventeenth century, to name a few). There is even some general consensus concerning a set of works that might be labeled burlesque even though, in many instances, the term burlesque was not originally used to categorize them. Burlesque has been associated with the plays of Aristophanes. And, in fact it would be difficult to deny that the satyr plays were a form of burlesque.

There is ample evidence of Western European works that might be labeled *burlesque* outside the confines of Spanish literary history. A list of such works might include Shakespeare's *Pyramus and Thisbe* performed by rustics in *A Midsummer Night's Dream*, Francis Beaumonts's *The Knight of the Burning Pestle*, Scarron's *Virgile travestie*, Samuel Butler's *Hudibras*, George Villiers's *The Rehearsal*, Boileau's *La Lutrin*, Sheridan's *The Critic*, Henry Carey's *Chronon-botonthologos*, Pope's *The Rape of the Lock*, Swift's *Baucis and Philemon*, Fielding's *Tom Thumb* and his *Historical Register for the Year 1736*, Gay's *The Beggar's Opera*, Gilbert and Burnand's nineteenth century burlesques of opera, and William Rhodes's *Bombastes Furioso*. On the basis of this short list we can already gather evidence for several ages when burlesque flourished.

Future research in the area of burlesque as a mode of representing critical issues will eventually tackle some of the nagging questions which surround those works labeled as burlesque and the historical situation in which they were produced and read or viewed. Are there historical times that are more appropriately suited for burlesque? Are there social, political, and economic factors that conduct writers toward using the burlesque mode of discourse as a more immediate but harmless means of getting at difficult issues? These questions cannot be answered easily. The Spanish model posed here may provide a means of probing the essentials of these queries in other disciplines and time periods.

In Spanish Golden Age examples burlesque was the most efficient, ambiguous and safest way to lay bare the contradictions, preconceptions, preoccupations, ideas and notions of perceived Imperial decadence and moral decline. In Spain, seventeenth century writers used the burlesque mode of representation to explore the accepted ideological baggage of their time. To broach the essential and inviolable moral, spiritual and ethical preconceptions in an entertainingly didactic and critical manner was to draw ties between history and fiction. To do so during the culture of the Baroque was to avoid the canker of sentimentality and nostalgia of better days which was escalating and growing out of proportion.

It happens that the serious dimension of the burlesque lies in the very mode of burlesque representation. Burlesque representation produces a contrast by going beyond the superficial appearance of things imitated, thus the ridiculed externalities of burlesque heroism, for example, and the commonly accepted essence of heroism coincide through contradiction. The following chapter is dedicated to burlesque laughter and serious concern in a variety of texts. The first section is devoted to two burlesque sonnets (Luis de Góngora's *Entrando en Valladolid, estando allí la Corte* and *Melancólica estás, putidoncella*, an obscene burlesque sonnet attributed to Quevedo). Both sonnets dramatize, hilariously, the discrepancy between burlesque representation in history and myth in fiction thereby pointing up the precarious borderlines between appearance and reality or *burlas* and *veras*. The discussion of burlesque laughter and serious concern involves an analysis of the burlesque representation of serious motifs which are mockingly burlesqued in these sonnets. The analysis of burlesque laughter and serious concern in two sonnets is followed by a study of the burlesque articulation of serious issues (the *language* of burlesque) in Góngora's burlesque *romance*, *La fábula de Píramo y Tisbe*, and in Salas Barbadillo's *El descasamentero*, a short burlesque interlude in *Fiestas de las bodas de la incasable mal casada*. Chapter Three concludes with the study of the artistic function of the burlesque in Cervantes's theatrical interlude *El Retablo de las Maravillas*. Cervantes's *entremés* is appraised as a *blueprint* for burlesque representation. The patterns and techniques of burlesque representation discussed in terms of the variety of short burlesque works in Chapter Three are then applied to the *Quixote* in Chapters Four and Five.

The application of a theory of burlesque to *Don Quixote* as well as a variety of Golden Age literary genres yields discussions which appear to be highly abstract. They are ultimately meant to be relevant to the analysis of concrete works. In order to analyze such concrete burlesques as Quevedo's burlesque sonnets, Góngora's burlesque *romance*, Salas Barbadillo's burlesque theatrical interlude, the theory of the burlesque mode of representation must be developed through various levels of abstract discussion until it may ultimately grasp the complexities of a burlesque work like *Don Quixote*.

CHAPTER THREE:
Burlesque Literature of the Spanish Baroque

Si yà no es, que de las simples Aves,
Contiene la República bolante
Poëtas, ò Burlescos sean, ò Graves.
              Luis de Góngora[18]

Burlesque Laughter and Serious Concern
The central point of any study about the burlesque mode of representation concerns burlesque laughter and serious concern. Every serious motif of Western civilization has been mockingly imitated in burlesque sonnets and *romances*, theatrical interludes (*entremeses*), *loas*, *jácaras* and *mojigangas*, or burlesque life stories called *vidas* or *picaresques*. Writers like Luis de Góngora, Francisco de Quevedo, Salas Barbadillo, Miguel de Cervantes, D. Antonio Hurtado de Mendoza, and Quiñones de Benavente used mockery as one mode of articulating matters of serious concern. There are, of course, many disputes over how far and with what result the burlesque articulation of serious matters is carried out artistically. The problem is a key issue in this investigation of representative burlesque texts by several well-known Spanish writers who wrote during the first part of the seventeenth century. Just what modern readers are to understand by the burlesque mode of representation (and related modes) is explained and

illustrated throughout the representative Spanish texts chosen for analysis.

The number of burlesque works written in Spain during the first twenty years of the seventeenth century by major and minor writers is overwhelming. The diverse texts labeled as burlesque, for example, include a variety of literary genres. The intention is not to expose any one author's particular use of the burlesque or to study the use of the burlesque within one genre, but rather to discuss some pertinent problems involving the varied aspects of the burlesque, and its social function in the cultural age of the Spanish Baroque. The focus of this chapter is, then, on the functional relationship which straddles burlesque *laughter* created by texts and *serious* concerns that, paradoxically, determine laughter.

The representative texts selected for analysis here highlight the laughable representations of traditional values of chivalry and heroism, nobility and virtue, for example. In each text, idealistic messages are mocked for their pretentiousness or inauthenticity in history. What analysis of the burlesque mode of representation in these texts illustrates is that the artistic function of burlesque is, ironically, to preserve the historical, the finite, the perishable, the dross, the ephemeral and the sweaty from the efforts of idealism to transcend them.

The burlesque mode of representing critical issues was one of the dominant modes of cultural production during the Golden Age. Yet many literary accounts of the period do not examine the burlesque reactions which shaped much of the seventeenth century critiques. This gap will have to be addressed in the future: there is a need for a historical survey of the burlesque from the early *pasos* of Rueda to the surprising *entremeses* of Calderón, charting the ways in which the burlesque mode of criticism was developing as the Spanish society in which it was rooted kept on changing. Such a task cannot be done as yet. For now it is enough to discuss various aspects of the burlesque in light of a few representative examples. The theoretical discussion and concrete analysis in representative texts can serve as preparation for the analysis of the burlesque mode in the lengthy *Don Quixote* and, together, as models for future, more sweeping surveys of the problem. The works chosen are by major authors who knew how to mingle effectively the lowest and highest aspects of culture. Their burlesques are highly entertaining but simultaneously encode contemporary ideologies because the situations burlesqued were, at that time, representations of the values by which Spaniards were experiencing--consciously or not--their "declining" society.

In order to analyze concrete burlesque texts (say, Góngora's burlesque sonnets or Cervantes's *Don Quixote*), the theory of the burlesque mode of representation must be developed through several levels of abstract discussion until it can ultimately grasp the complexities of a work like *Don Quixote*. During the last two decades, theories of literary modes of discourse have been at the highest level of abstraction. Yet, there is a need for the practical application of such theories to difficult texts. Cervantes's *Don Quixote* will serve as a benchmark in appraising the theory and practice of the burlesque as a literary category. This does not mean that conclusions based on Cervantes's burlesques are incontrovertible, but that all interpretations of the *Quixote* must be judged in the light of the burlesque.

Since the nature of burlesque is paradoxical in the sense that the "trifling" and the "serious" seem separate yet are intertwined threads, the challenge is to expose how the frivolous and the serious work together and against each other for the sake of the *comic effect*. The task is to expose the burlesque optic which provides a hilarious view on the two extremities ("trifling" and "serious") of any important issue.[19] The burlesque mode of representation is akin to a distorted eyepiece through which readers view the fabric and stuff of the text. The burlesque lens might quite properly be named "cheaters" since the lens provides a telling look at what is often cloaked behind the showy, but thread-bare, appearances of idealizations. The burlesque employs a perspective through a warped magnifying glass which, for the sake of sport and building a critical awareness of things gone awry, augments, exaggerates and articulates material imperfections.

The notion of using a warped lens as a means to transform learned, traditional or popular standards is not unique to seventeenth century burlesque. The awry perspective can be traced to the prominent Spanish writers of the early seventeenth century. In fact, Don Ramón del Valle-Inclán, a twentieth century Spanish writer, did just that. Valle-Inclán highlighted the "distanced" artistic perspective of Cervantes and Quevedo (and later, Goya) as precursor to his unique literary genre which he called *esperpentos*. Valle-Inclán explained that the skewed angle of looking at realities (a demiurgical one) is a particularly Spanish perspective used by some of the major Spanish artists:

> *Y hay otra tercera manera, que es mirar a los personajes de la trama como seres inferiores al autor, con un punto de ironía. Los dioses se convierten en personajes de sainete. Esta es una manera muy española, manera de demiurgo, que no se cree en modo alguno hecho del mismo barro que sus muñecos. Quevedo tiene esta manera. [Cervantes, también. A pesar de la grandeza de Don Quijote, Cervantes se cree más cabal y más cuerdo que él y jamás se emociona con él.] Esta manera es ya definitiva en Goya. Y esta consideración es la que me llevó a dar un cambio en mi literatura y a escribir los esperpentos, el género literario que yo bautizo con el nombre de esperpentos.* (Cardona 237)[20]

The perspective from above, or the writer's superior and therefore distant position as a demiurge, underscores the premise that the *stuff* of the writer's creation is, by nature of the perspective, inferior and imperfect. Valle-Inclán described how this alternative perspective differed from the two other perspectives known to him:

> *Hay que estudiar a los autores en sus tres maneras Primera, el personaje es superior al autor. La manera del héroe, HOMERO, que no es de sangre de dioses. Segunda, el autor que se desdobla: SHAKESPEARE. Sus personajes no son otra cosa sino desdoblamientos de su personalidad. Tercera, el autor es superior a sus personajes y los contempla como Dios a sus criaturas. GOYA pintó a sus personajes como seres inferiores a él. Como QUEVEDO.* (Cardona 237)

While the demiurgical perspective implies burlesque imperfection and absurd inferiority in the rough raw materials involved in the (re)creation, it does not imply at all imperfection or inferiority of artistic composition. On the contrary, for Valle-Inclán the demiurgical perspective was the means by which artists have been able to make ugly or burlesque realities aesthetically pleasing. In *Luces de Bohemia* his blind poet theorized about the use of a concave mirror to transform classical norms into grotesque spectacle (Cardona and Zahareas 35). For Valle-Inclán, the concave mirror was a code for distorting the reality of historians with the mathematical precision of artists. The malformed mirrored image was a filter that provided a perfectly formed deformation.

Valle-Inclán's notion of the concave mirror and the grotesque is, by his own confession, akin to the notion of a skewed optic that distorts and perverts an image. The notion of the "cheaters" clarifies the function of the distortion: the "cheaters" either magnify the image or *correct* the perception of an image so that the exaggerated details of the image can be perceived clearly. The corrective lens does not change reality but an individual's already distorted perception of reality. When writers choose a burlesque lens or a burlesque mode of expression, reality is necessarily filtered through a transparent but distorted eye-piece. It is important to remember that the *corrected* perception of reality is unexpected, uncanny and amusing (and possibly unsettling) to the perceiver who is accustomed to accepting the original distortion as an undistorted and authentic image.

The Case of Two Burlesque Sonnets:
Burlesque Distortion of Social Criticism: Góngora's "Entrando en Valladolid, estando allí la Corte"

Burlesque mockery relies on caricature, that is, the deliberate exaggeration and grotesque distortion of the most manifest features of a recognizable object or concept.[21] The importance of caricature to burlesque mockery is evident in the burlesque caricature of the seventeenth century Royal Court at Valladolid offered by the professional poet Luis de Góngora. This burlesque sonnet is an urgent, economical and laughable reaction to the topsy-turvy court life that the poet witnessed during his visit to Valladolid in 1603.

[Entrando en Valladolid, estando allí la Corte]

Llegué a Valladolid, registrè luego,
Desde el Bonete al Clavo de la Mula,
Guardo el Registro, que será mi Bula
Contra el cuidado del Señor Don Diego.

Busqué la Corte en el, y yo estoy Ciego,
O en la Ciudad no esta, o se disimula,
Haziendo Penitencia vi à la bula,
Que Platón para todos está en Griego.

La Lisonja hallé, y la Ceremonia,
Con luto, idolatrados los Caziques,
Amor sin Fe, Intereses con sus Bigotes.

Todo se halla en esta Babilonia,
Como en Botica grandes Alambiques,
Y mas en ella Titulos que Botes.[22]

In the first quatrain the poetic speaker, in a first person
narrative, complains of the ridiculous and excessive
inspection of his person and personal belongings upon
entrance to the city of Valladolid. The complaint about the
bothersome inspection at the Court in Valladolid has
historical significance. As Antonio Carreira explained in his
anthology of Góngora's poetry, the court of Valladolid was
overcrowded and all visitors had to appear before don Diego
de Ayala. As in modern day customs offices, the visitors had
to declare the nature of their business and the intended
length of stay (132 n1). The speaker's attitude toward the
inspection is quite clear: he finds the inspection absurdly
tedious and expresses his complaint with an exaggeration:
"*registrè luego desde el Bonete al Clavo de la Mula.*" He
complains that not only was he inspected from tip to toe, but
from the cap on his head to the hoof of the mule on which he
was riding. The implication is double-edged: first the visitor
is less than a gentleman since he rides a mule, and secondly,
Valladolid is so stuffed with gad-abouts at Court that even
his mule must be registered for proper equine lodging. The
allusion to the physical inspection of a pretentious bumpkin
and his mule is funny, but telling in that the Spanish Court
is so packed with bumpkins looking for favors that Don Diego
has had to take extreme measures to control overcrowding.

The second quatrain initiates a series of verbal oppositions
which expose the ugly realities of the Royal Court. For
example, the angry visitor denies that he was able to find the
illustrious Royal Court in the care of don Diego (de Ayala) or
even in the city of Valladolid. If the Court is in the city,

remarks the visitor-poet, it is undercover and disguised ("*O en la Ciudad no está, o se disimula*"). The play on words is calculated to induce readers to giggle and chortle at the speaker's observation. His witty remarks uncover the true state of the Court at Valladolid: instead of gluttony he witnessed restricted diets for lack of available foodstuffs.[23] Indeed, according to the disappointed speaker of the poem everything he witnessed denied his expectations of the court and exposed the "real nature of things." He found flattery and formality dressed in mourning (first tercet) since, because of overcrowded conditions at court, courtiers were refused entrance to Valladolid (Carreira 133 n4). The image painted for readers in this sonnet involves a topsy-turvy environment in which hordes of lamenting human vultures covet entrance to the King's court to abate their lust for a scrap of meager royal rations. Their lasciviousness displaced what might be taken for, in other circumstances, loyalty and honor to the King. There is nothing flashy about the poetic speaker or the others who, like him, waited for an opportunity to take part in the meager feast at the King's court.

The disillusioned speaker highlights the ugly and unexpected situation in the final summarizing tercet of the sonnet. A first reading seems to suggest, ironically, that nothing is lacking in this busy and overcrowded city. To paraphrase a superficial reading of the final tercet: as in a drugstore, you can find anything you want in this Babylon: large alembics and more jars than cans. Appearances deceive no one, however, since a straight reading makes no sense in terms of the other burlesque images in the sonnet. A closer reading that follows the established oxymoronic structure and persistent exaggeration of the sonnet is much more telling. "Babilonia" is a reference to the incessant traffic and confusion due to the overcrowded conditions in Valladolid (Carreira 133 n7). The referent of *grandes alambiques* is not large stills for abundant production of alcohol but instead, as Carreira suggests with an inversion of modification between the *alambiques* and *grandes*, is a reference to the *grandes* of the court who distill their favors from the King drop by drop (133 n10). The disillusioned speaker mocks the ugly situation of the Court with one final insult against the state in which he finds the Court at Valladolid. In his final verse he scoffs at the worthlessness of the titled nobility: "*y más en ella títulos*

que botes." The *double entendre* is unavoidable here: the Court
is little more than a common drugstore that offers bargain
titles of nobility for a price; titles have indeed lost their worth
since there are more *"títulos que botes."* *"Botes"* are not jars
but the blows of a lance executed in combat (Carreira 133
n10). There is more pretensiousness than brave deeds of the
true warrior. The speaker's mockery is clear: in this
overcrowded and wanton *Babilonian* Court titles are no
longer an appellation of earned distinction, but instead cheap
merchandise for common sale to inferior pretendants.

The burlesque mockery of the despicable state of the
Spanish Court (overcrowded conditions, low-class pretenders,
famine, lasciviousness and cut-rate sale of titles) is amusing
in spite (or perhaps because) of what might be labeled as
seriously dilapidated conditions. The amusement obtains
because the one who is displeased by the situation of the
Court in Valladolid is no better or different than the other
counterfeit patrons he admonishes in his complaint. In his
outcry he bemoans his own situation. He is one of the lucky
few who has made it to the Court to seek his fortune only to
find his outlandish expectations denied by a miserable
reality. Readers laugh because the speaker is a pretentious
low-life who has gone to Court seeking riches and honors who
finds, to his disappointment, hordes of others like himself
who are begging for a few table scraps from tables that are
already bare.

The potentially disturbing burlesque critique of the
dilapidated situation at Valladolid is harmless because,
ironically, the complainer is *not* a nobleman. Readers laugh
because the contrasting situation is grotesquely distorted and
hence absurd. Because the speaker of the poem is just one
more eager, bogus courtier, his anger must necessarily be
attributed to his inability to control or abate his own
lasciviousness. The complainer is a pretentious churl who is
frustrated at rampant social and moral decadence only
because of its implication for his personal social
advancement. The dilapidated situation at Valladolid does
not allow him much opportunity to maneuver for social
position or advantage. He is portrayed, hilariously, as a
frustrated social climber.

The burlesque critique of the Royal Court at Valladolid is
rendered harmless because his disgust cannot be taken

seriously by readers. He imitates, grotesquely, the disgust that a high-brow courtier would express upon seeing the social decadence at Court. Instead of feeling concerned about apparent social and moral decadence outlined in the sonnet, readers laugh at the fraud's blindness and incompetence: he is looking for social advancement where, given the rigid social caste system and the poverty of the Republic, there is none to be had. Contemporary readers, outside the sonnet, knew that there was no room for real social mobility in their life-time. The ubiquity of picaresque literature concerning the fraudulent attempts of common churls to advance themselves socially indicates that the aristocracy was indeed concerned with upstarts, their delusions of upward social mobility, and their excessive practices of scavenging and deception. Picaresque autobiographies are a case in point.

Fictional picaresque autobiographies became popular in Spain especially after the publication of Mateo Alemán's *Guzmán de Alfarache* in 1598 because they provided readers with funny, and often grotesque, stories about a rogue's troublesome past history told from the perspective of the reformed picaroon who was usually forced by society to accept his social station as low-born. The whole of the fictional picaresque autobiographies focused on the deceptive practices and common delusions of commoners who tried to advance themselves, failed hilariously, and pretentiously moralized *in writing* about their failures to improve their social lot *(medrar)*.[24] Fictional picaresque autobiographies are informative pieces of literature because the tales of "when I was young and foolish" include a register of roguish acts that spell out, albeit indirectly in fiction, many of the social ills of sixteenth and seventeenth century Spain. Some of the more intractable contemporary social problems are known: charity and poverty; wholesale and retail commerce; the ideological push for spirituality and morality; and marriage outside one's social caste. They are scanned and mockingly assessed as the foolish rogue attempts challenging traditional and hence, "respected" social barriers time and again. Nevertheless, the picaresque autobiography, despite social contents, is always funny and amusing to readers. The systematic social deviance of a foolishly pretentious rogue is much more entertaining than the systematic social compliance of a reformed trickster.[25]

There is quite a bit of coincidence between picaresque autobiographies which employ techniques used in burlesques and burlesque sonnets like Góngora's sonnet analyzed above. Certainly the burlesque sonnet also has a fictional autobiographical structure and deals hilariously and mockingly with difficult contemporary social problems. The language in this sonnet, like the language used by ex-picaros in their autobiographies, is not particularly difficult. The allusions are clear and gruff. Both picaresque narratives and burlesques appeal, disappealingly, to the senses. Both rely on acceptable literary conventions for the telling of their hilariously distasteful tales. And both employ implied direct dialogue with an often implied audience.

There is, however, one major distinction between picaresque narratives and the burlesque modes: there is no burlesque lens in the picaresque that temporarily misguides readers. In picaresque autobiographies the narrating ex-picaro never relinquishes the authority of perspective. Clearly, the ex-picaro knowingly mocks himself. Burlesques, on the other hand, always imply some sort of temporary ambiguity of authority. In the sonnet discussed above the poem requires that we read on two opposed levels to extract the sonnet's meaning: on the one hand there is outlandish and hyperbolic praise of the Court hub that seems to be such an attraction that there is no more room for anyone or anything; and on the other, there is a severe warning against the sort of stuff of which the hub is made. The admonition against the Spanish Court situation is one that certifies that the Court is a Babel, what Julio Caro Baroja has called, "*un saco donde cabe todo.*" The criticism of the observable reality of the Royal "*saco*" is deliberately ironic: the Court at Valladolid is a place where misery, immorality, and the ugly reign, or, the tale is the opposite of the teller's expectations. The burlesque perspective of the impertinent and toilworn impostor is amusing and not particularly critical. The perspective is that of a dissatisfied rogue who unknowingly becomes the butt of a larger joking framework that, ironically, he helps construct. The frustration and near repulsion that the common upstart feels is hilarious because the "earnest" complaints of social problems and preconceived notions about abundance at the glorious Spanish Royal Court are a travesty of the very "fictionalized" historical facts. Readers cannot accept the ludicrous pretentiousness of such a churl as serious. The burlesque mockery is ambiguous. If even a pretentious swindler's stomach can be turned by the grotesque conditions, the situation could be interpreted as a tragic one. However, the complainer's words (because of the foolish sort of person who utters them) are not taken seriously, and the complaint arouses laughter.

Laughter at situations and at pretentiousness is key for burlesque because it implies both reception and what goes with it: timing, context, place, speaker, performance, theatrics, etc. Readers are amused precisely because everything is exaggerated and out of proportion and at the same time, proper and in proportion. This contradiction needs further explanation: for a short moment, readers wear the distorted eyepiece of the disgruntled upstart and view Valladolid through a deformed perspective which seems to put the Court, ironically, in its proper perspective of Babel or chaos. At the same time the reader recognizes that, considering the source, this "proper perspective" is horribly out-of-proportion and unreliable. Even though the burlesque lens allows for a more detailed, experiential, sensorial and critical view of the Spanish Court at Valladolid, it is unacceptable and readers laugh in mockery at this foolish upstart who is an unworthy and unreliable judge. Burlesque laughter *misleadingly* mocks the *serious* and all the *seriousness* about it. Burlesque laughter subverts the perversion of ideals and creates "authentic" ambivalence toward serious concerns.

Burlesque Representation of Serious Issues in the Quevedesque Tradition

Francisco de Quevedo is well known as one of Spain's greatest writers of love poetry in the *amour courtois* tradition and of satirical-burlesque verse in a tradition that might best be labeled "the chamber pot". The following analysis will illustrate that satirical and burlesque poems like the one below--with all their scatological and sensualist imagery and theatricality--provide as telling a commentary on contemporary life as any *learned* poem written by Quevedo or others who imitated him.

In an oft-quoted sonnet attributed to Francisco de Quevedo, the relationship of burlesque laughter and serious issues is clear. *"Melancólica estás, putidoncella"* (first verse) was published with sonnet XVII under the title *Encarece los años de una vieja niña* (Praising the years of an old girl). The contemporary title given to the two sonnets by José Antonio González de Salas indicates that both poems were read within a burlesque vein by contemporary readers. Both are clear examples of burlesque parodies of the very popular Petrarchan sonnet which was often used to express courtly love. I have relied here on the Buendía and Luís Astrana Marín edition of the poem (*Obras completas* 179) although two versions exist. The Blecua edition, *Obra poética*, reads "*Melancólica estáis, putidoncella*," and is perhaps a more vehement burlesque than the Buendía edition that follows:

> *Melancólica estás, putidoncella,*
> *solapo de la paz, buen gusto grato,*
> *raída como empeine de zapato*
> *cuando de muy traído se desuella.*
>
> *¡Oh quién te viese abierta como armella,*
> *pasada con la broca de un mulato,*
> *y de tu carne haciendo franco plato!*
> *Mas lleve el diablo quien comiese de ella.*
>
> *Válgate Barrabás, ¿de qué te enfadas,*
> *impertinente virgen del putaco,*
> *atalaya que acechas carretillas?*
>
> *Pues que tu ama tiende sus frazadas,*
> *tiéndelas tú también marisobaco,*
> *que no son para menos tus faldillas.*

The structure of the sonnet is based on the common use of apostrophe, whereby the poet addresses the subject to which his poem is directed. The dissatisfied speaker in this sonnet does not hold back vulgarities nor does he cloak the graphic details of his experience. The fictitious situation of the sonnet is commonplace: the voice of an enraged client in a brothel addresses his sexual partner, calling her an impertinent fraud and a worn-out harlot who has billed herself as a fresh virgin. He condemns her and anyone who would lie with her, orders her to hide her toil-worn body ("*raída como empeine de zapato cuando muy traído se desuella*") and disgusting smell ("*marisobaco*") with her skirts. The grotesque images function as a disintegrating scheme which systematically deforms the commonplace situation of "business as usual" and renders the situation outrageously humorous.

The gross, vulgar and obscene images of the prostitute's body are constructed through the exaggerated deformation of the victim's material body which, according to the unhappy client, calls out invitingly (and perhaps teasingly) to passersby as a plate of irresistible food. Her impertinence is that as an experienced and hence overused prostitute she has procured the reconstitution of a false maidenhood with which she inveigles men: a common shish-kebob offered as a delicious plate.

The customer takes offense because, through experience he determined that his sexual partner was not firm, tender and smooth as a young virgin ought to be, but instead she was flabby, raw, and well-worn from being skewered once too often. Just as the fraudulent virginity button is rendered ridiculous and impertinent in an obviously experienced and aging prostitute, so is the conjugal act between them rendered worthless, loathsome and hilariously absurd. The act has lost its pleasurable, not to speak of its regenerative, functions. The "disillusioned" or "*desengañado*" stance of the angry client, however, holds little weight in this particular situation. His abusive words strike out vehemently at his sexual partner grotesquely hyperbolizing the reclined woman's lower stratum as he supposedly positions himself at her feet in contemplation of a union recently consummated.

The grotesque imagery suggests sensorial experience which elicits more comicality from the situation. The angry client has been hooked by the showy appearances of artificial allurements. The amusing portrait is not only of the virginal whore who is expected to ply her trade with appearances, but also of the customer who mirrors his own degradation in the object he ridicules. He is the fool who has been deceived by cheap "tastes."

Only readers are allowed to see through the haughty, cursing discourse of this indignant character's one-sided dialogue whose unfolding deceptions give readers a good look at the situation from an unusual perspective. The technique of apostrophe is a strategic ruse: the sonnet was certainly not intended to be read or heard by the fictitious female object of ridicule. The readers of this sonnet are not only expected to understand the impertinence of the initial ridicule of the fraudulent prostitute, but more importantly the foolishness of the speaker who catches the earnest jest of deceiving appearances just a bit late. There is something theatrical in all of this: readers *spectate* the laughable situation through the burlesque prism implied in the dramatic structure of the sonnet. They laugh at the situation of an angry client who is repulsed by the common prostitute's allurements and successful seduction because they see the client for what he *is*, a fool who seeks virgins in brothels, and not as the gallant seducer of a damsel that he might want others, and himself, to think he is.

The cursing client does not attack the age-old clandestine business of prostitution, but he complains that he cannot be sexually satisfied by an old and smelly whoring woman with a retread maidenhood. He is angered and moved to cursing because of his own deception and ideal illusions. With his complaint he vents his anger and warns other fools who, like himself, might be deceived by the practice used to inveigle ill-advised lusting men. He curses himself when he curses her because he has been guided by his own obsessive sexual needs, and aided by her ostentation, to seek and enter into a conjugal relationship with what he now finds to be an abhorred beast. The ridicule is displaced from the degraded female object to the disgusted client who, in turn, becomes the object of his own derision. He is, hilariously, the painter of his own grotesque portrait.

As in Cervantes's notorious case of the *baciyelmo* in *Don Quixote* (I: 21) the use of a perfectly articulated oxymoron, *putidoncella*, is the key to the staccato-like development of the burlesque in the four standard divisions of the sonnet into quartets and tercets. The mutual dependence of the two contraries, "whore" and "maiden," are in fact a mutual exclusion of the two.

Here the poet serves the poet, "conceptually," to distinguish for readers to what degree good appearances conceal ugly realities. One function of the burlesque, after all, is to provide a method for going beneath social appearances (like maidenhood, love, virtue, virginity, etc.) to the reality of social practices (like prostitution, sex, impurity, sin, etc.). Although the burlesque mode of exposure seems like any of Quevedo's *conceptista* endeavors, the use of the oxymoron *putidoncella* here anticipates the disparities that lie within it: the appearance conceals an opposite reality and hence its hypocrisy is exposed in the very act of being propagated as reality. The appearance is not convincing and, in a burlesque sense, not real: a *putidoncella* is what she appears to be, a real fraud, representing everything that is inauthentic in love or in love sonnets.

There is yet another displacement implied in the burlesque sonnet. Ridicule is displaced from the mocked customer who seeks virgins in a brothel to readers who inadvertently scoff first with the mocking customer and later at the fool who reveals his deception to everyone. Readers fall prey to the very mockery that bites the smugness of the client. If readers are turned off by the disgusting images of the sonnet, they, too, have fallen prey to mockery. They are no different than the angered client. What were readers expecting to find in a burlesque sonnet about an "old girl?" The sonneteer inveigles readers who have certain expectations concerning the sonnet: where readers might have expected to find a courtier's confession of virtuous love they are instead amused to find the confession of a pretentious but ordinary oaf who foolishly expects to find virgins in a brothel. The irony is that willingly or unwillingly readers are allied with the speaker through invective and laughter.

Although the displacement of derision is implied in the grammar of the sonnet, it is much more prominent in the poetic structure itself. The parody of form in the *amour courtois* and Petrarchan tradition depends on a reversal whereby the refined is substituted by vulgar content. Instead of representing a young courtier's confession of desire and aspiration to consummate a love that, given the woman's condition, would not be granted, here the speaker contrives "mental orgasms out of frustrated desire" (Olivares 7). The parodic version burlesques and degrades the basic elements of courtly love.

Here is a clear example of burlesque parody of the very popular Petrarchan sonnet. This sonnet to a *putavirgo*, that is, to a professional prostitute who puts on airs of purity, burlesques the serious sonnets to perfect ladies by imitating a series of situations and forms. A man addresses a woman in a bipartite division of two quatrains and two tercets. The rhyme scheme which emphasizes the ridiculous caricature by using a common rhyme in courtly love poetry (-ella and -ada) in the two quatrains, and contrasting the common rhyme pattern with vulgar rhyme patterns in the tercets (-illa and -aco). The imitation follows the standard of the client's "burden," "double problem," or "reflection" as well as a cry of indignation up to the sextet which redefines the problem grotesquely. The sublime of the love sonnet has been rendered absurd by a ridiculous exaggeration of the reversal of form and content.

The tables are turned on the client: the "beloved" or female object of male desire is not elevated to a place of physical and moral superiority above the anxious lover because, in this case, he is a client of a house of prostitution. Thus the refined female object is subordinated instead to little more than a receptacle of foolish desire. The ennobling force of love, as a standard of courtly tradition, turns into a constant reference to a cursing "lover" whose "frustrated desire" is now a rash drive to attain sexual satisfaction. Yet he is one who encounters the flames of his dangerous passions doused in disdain as he contemplates realistically, and not idealistically, his lady's physical "attributes."

The traditional courtly conception of love as an ever unsatisfied, ever increasing desire for an unrequited love is displaced by an ever decreasing desire for physical union with this grotesque portrait of the object of love. Desire turns to disgust. The melancholy tone and sweet-pain expressed by a "virtuous" lover in the courtly tradition is displaced by capriciousness, haughtiness and contempt. The declaration of the aging prostitute's revolting inferiority--as opposed to the admiration of the lady's perfections--is no secret, but a warning to others who, through deception of artificial lures might seek her services.

Seduction is part and parcel of the strategy of the burlesque parody here. The courtly tradition idealized the woman systematically "into a goddess vying with the sun's splendor and strategically amplified the beloved's beauty through the ordering of brilliant images" (Olivares 43). The plan was to cause the "lady" to virtually disappear as a flesh-and-blood reality, and to preserve instead only an abstract model of perfection. The female creation was to be "a harmonious composition and proportion of the bodily parts, together with appealing color and grace, which is a certain light that shines from the soul, and glows in the face and most of all in the eyes" (Olivares 43). The burlesque aspect of such traditional representations amplifies the image of physical ugliness and moral pretension through systematic grotesque deformations. While in the courtly tradition "beauty" can only be possessed by the "cognitive faculty, aided by windows through which the mind's eye strains to perceive a glimpse of the beloved's soul" (Olivares 43) in the obscene burlesque versions of the same tradition ugliness can only be perceived through the senses.

Readers are drawn into the lively vulgarities of sensualism through the external appearances of a love sonnet in the tradition of courtly love. In this sense, the seduction of readers parallels the seduction of the client. The foolish client sought lively *lovemaking* with *virgins* in a *brothel*. What do readers expect to find in a burlesque sonnet about a man who has been deceived by his own illusions and seduced by those of others? Surely they cannot expect innocence. The sonnet is relentless in recreating the repulsive sensorial experience of the client in a sort of reverse seduction of readers.

In the first two quatrains, for example, readers confront a repulsive visual image of a gaping orifice whose torn, rough flesh can only be perceived by tactile experience. A reference to "taste" is pursued in the second quatrain as well:

¡Oh quién te viese abierta como armella,
pasada con la broca de un mulato,
y de tu carne haciendo franco plato!
Mas lleve el diablo quien comiese de ella.

The female object of desirous simultaneously one of disgust: it has been skewered too often and is too "hot" to eat. The meat that she offers as a main dish is a "tasty" meal fit only for someone bound for the fires of hell. The angry client scolds the fraudulent prostitute for billing herself a virgin when only a retread. By extension he curses his own lot for being led by desire and insatiable lust to the house of prostitutes. Carnal copulation, ordinarily a good pleasurable whim ("*buen gusto grato*") and the release of erotic desire and the "natural seed" which, if "overlong kept (in some parties) it turns to poison", is in this case a bad habit of all sensualists who are carried away headlong with lustful pleasures to lose grace, glory, and good health (Burton 179).

The use of the word "*armella*" (a wreath-like object often placed on doors beckoning all to enter) suggests that the invitation for sexual satisfaction is open to all who desire to taste the sweet pleasure of "bursting the bubble" of a "*doncella*". The difficulty is that the retread on this woman is not at all convincing and the client's complaint is that he cannot be sexually excited or satisfied by an old, smelly, whoring woman sporting her retread maidenhood and recurring title of "*doncella*". Every bit of potential or anticipated pleasure is lost to inevitable disgust.

As a response to an implied situation between the "melancholy" woman (who seems sad because she is not going to receive her full salary this time) and deception, the enraged client deals out insults calling the fraudulent woman an impertinent whoremonger's virgin who is as good at bringing in the clients with propaganda and artificial allurements as she is good at acquiring social diseases. *Carretillas* refers to the horse-drawn coaches of "courtesans" that carried potential clients but also implies specifically, and absurdly, those "gentlemen" who rode in them carrying syphilis (Covarrubias).

The references to the offensiveness to sight and touch are topped by a reference to the offensiveness to olfactory perception. The disgusted customer commands his "lady" to use her skirts to cover her bad odor:

Pues que tu ama tiende sus frazadas,
tiéndelas tú también marisobaco,
que no son para menos tus faldillas.

The social world of prostitution represented in caricature is not a pretty or tasteful one. The disgruntled client makes a suggestion: he argues that the madame of the house hides her abused body with covers and enough wrappings to conceal the distasteful old hide underneath and his partner ought to do the same. The poem's final words mirror the sentiments spoken by Don Quixote after Sancho empties his bowels in fear. "*Peor es menearlo* (*Don Quixote* I:XX). Once the deed is done, it's better left alone.

The angered client's monologue implies a dialogue with a second person (tú), the present impertinent, "deflowered" whore. But the oaths, fury, and madness are unbecoming, odious, and absurd when hurled at a re-virginized prostitute by a fool who seeks the services of virgins in a brothel. The point is that the full impact of the burlesque depends on the distinction between the writer of the poem and the narrator. Even though the object of ridicule appears to be a grotesque, dissembled and angry woman, the poem is really about the immediacy of an emotional outburst experienced by the woman's client. The theme, then, is not the commonplace alienation or disillusionment of love sonnets, but instead these burlesque verses speak of desire and the inability of the rational faculty to suppress desire in its physical form. The consequences of this radical shift are that since the client is able to attack in others the weaknesses and temptations that are really within himself, he heartlessly, and distantly, converts every possible ambiguity about passion and reason into a positive rejection.

What characterizes love-making here is, then, the melancholia of a moral conflict between passion and reason. The derision of the fraudulent whorish-virgin and the indirect derision of the client are poetic manifestations of the poet's inner conflict--but all topsy-turvy. The angry client vacillates burlesquely between sexual desire and abhorrence, passion and reason, praise and abuse. As affirmed earlier, the burlesque is a rejection not only of the woman's pretensions but also of the would-be lover's blindness. The quarry without the perfect lady, through imperfection, becomes the quarry without the poet.

This amusing situation is not an excerpt of real-life dialogue but instead a singular exaggeration and hyperbolic burlesque deformation of a man's contempt for deceiving appearances stylized meticulously into a *High Style* sonnet. Laughter and grotesque rejection imply also distance: the distance between the zone of the author (his study, pen in hand) and the zone of the narrator (a client in a brothel caught with "his pants down," so to speak) cannot be disregarded. In fact, readers can be certain that the male writer considers himself far superior to this fictitious character who cannot see beyond his own discontent. The character of the client, as in all dramatic irony, gives away more weaknesses and vices than he intends, but perhaps not more than the writer intends. The character's assumed superior position toward the hypocritical prostitute is undermined by the poet's burlesque. The irony depends on the contrast of the woman who is both "prostitute" and "virgin" and the implied contrast between what the speaker claims is the situation and what readers must infer about his irrational experience as expressed in the sonnet.

And now it is time to reiterate the point missed by most modern critics who have refused to deal with, and thus marginalize, obscene burlesque verse: the *Low Style* is only low because it contains all the aspects of the *High Style*. One reacts on the other dialectically, otherwise it is not *burlesque*. It is well known that the burlesque is a rhetorical process of highlighting social realities by going behind the superficial appearance of social claims. The issue dramatized is that the outward appearance and essence of things do not coincide directly, except, of course, in rhetorical cover-ups. Thus, going behind superficial appearances in society is no simple task. The burlesque of this sonnet assumes that the *puti* that lies behind the *doncella* (or the representation of these social realities) is not simply there to be found. The social realities are found out when the burlesque laughs them out of their hiding place. This is why the *low* or *burlesque* style deals, necessarily, with the contents of the *serious* or *high* style.

The levels of mockery and derision are thus manifold. The grotesque portrait goes beyond the original target to mock the abusive client. The amusing burlesque representation of the deformed reality of *business as usual* moves to the moral conflict of passion and reason, *melancholia*, which causes the fraudulent woman to become distempered and disillusioned in the presence of her berating customer. The abuse is not restricted to baits or conditions of prostitutes and their clients, to old age, physiognomical signs of melancholy, men's delights with sexual recreation, sin, or false "virginity," but rather it becomes a somewhat hilarious burlesque on the inability to see beyond arrogance, superiority, and one's own self-deception. There is no reprieve from burlesque distortion.

The viewpiece through which readers *perceive* the extremes of passion and reason in the sonnet that is, the peculiar *mode* of narration, prescribes the ways in which the words of the burlesque sonnet's language must be articulated and connected to express critical thought about serious philosophical matters. Just as a serious sonnet might probe the processes governing everyday human thought and conduct the burlesque sonnet also investigates (in an amusing manner) the laws that regulate human behavior and gird reality. The particular idiom of burlesque is different than the idiom of serious speculation precisely because the characteristic but unusual patterns and techniques which make up the language of burlesque involve outlandish distortion of common, serious representations of preconceived and accepted statutes of behavior.

The burlesque, in its very act of mocking imitation, is entertaining but also a means to refer to another serious way of looking at realities. Because it is fundamentally a "mode," the burlesque does not have independent being: it has as its foundation that which is "other" than itself (e.g. the "serious" the "high" or "learned"). Thus, the consequence that can be derived from the Quevedo-like burlesque sonnet is crucial for the discussion of burlesque. If, in fact, the burlesque has as part of its operating mode something other than the low or frivolous, it is clear that, in order to be authentically a travesty as it truly pretends to be, it cannot be only one-sidedly burlesque. Ironically, then, the burlesque here is *not* only low or frivolous precisely because it *is* really burlesque; vice-versa, it is really burlesque because, referentially, it is simultaneously, other than *only* travesty. The burlesque is decidedly dialectical. And, in some instances, such as in the case of the *Quixote*, the dialectical manner of integrating mutually the serious and frivolous is carried to its logical end.

The Case of the Burlesque *Romance*
The Language of Burlesque in Góngora's *Fábula de Píramo y Tisbe*

Góngora's burlesque ballad or *romance*, *La fábula de Píramo y Tisbe* (1618), is considered to be, along with the more famous *Polifemo*, one of Góngora's master works. As opposed to the more serious *Polifemo* Góngora's burlesque ballad makes a laughingstock of the Ovidian myth of two star-crossed lovers and their tragic suicides. A common, vulgar, and pretentious storyteller offers his audience a hilarious new representation of the mythical tragedy by exposing the *true* and *absurd* nature of the midnight encounter between Pyramus and Thisbe. In dressing the myth for modern times, the cunning storyteller refuses to accept as heroes the two young fools who, against their parents' prudent wishes, sneak out to frolic and indulge in illicit sexual activity, miss each other, and commit double suicide. According to the tell-all (but not know-it-all) storyteller of the modern, burlesque version, the two young and foolish "lovers" made all the wrong decisions for all the wrong reasons. The doomed protagonists were not beautiful but coarse youths, not virtuous but lewd, not obedient but rebellious, not smart but foolish. Thus, in the burlesque interpretation of a previously serious legend, lovers were not worthy of the valiant and tragic deaths that others may have ascribed to them. Góngora's burlesque *romance* makes a mockery of making heroes out of dunces. In other words, the burlesque here seems to unmask what has been a cover-up of an absurd outcome.

From the first few verses readers are aware of the comic nature of the burlesque version of a tragic story, the absurdity is especially evident in the storyteller's coarse representation of factual and historical evidence or, perhaps even more appropriately, rumor. He declares that the city of Babylon is famous not for her walls but rather for her unfortunate children, two lovers who, dead and skewered on a sword, have traveled the world like a shish-kebob.

> La ciudad de Balilonia,
> famosa, no por sus muros
> (fuesen de tierra cocidos
> o fuesen de tierra crudos),
> sino por los dos amantes,
> desdichados hijos suyos
> que muertos, y en un estoque,
> han peregrinado el mundo,(1-8).[26]

The story pattern highlights, in an exemplary and archetypal fashion, the case of two attractive but doomed lovers. The rude storyteller's vulgarity in employing the notion of skewered ("*en un estoque*") coupled with the virtually insignificant and impertinent query concerning the construction materials of the Babilonian walls (*cooked* or *raw* earth; that is, brick or adobe) initiates the burlesque framework for the rest of the poem. The attitude of the storyteller is playfully indecorous and thus the subject matter of youthful "romantic" love is treated in bad taste. In fact, the poem's audience is given every indication that the *fábula* will be an unmerciful *roast* of other more tragic and heroic versions of the Ovidian legend. Readers do not doubt, from the initial verses, that this irreverent version of the *fábula* is an *hazmereir*, whereby the "classic" lovers themselves are mocked less than the tragic version about them.

While the cultural or literary dialogue is assumed to be with Ovid's version of Pyramus and Thisbe the storyteller implies a dialogue with his listening audience. In a mockery of learned literary tradition, he solicits the aid of a Muse in an apostrofe and requests that she lend a hand in entertaining his *ordinary* listener.

> *citarista, dulce hija*
> *del Archipoeta rubio,*
> *si al brazo de mi instrumento*
> *le solicitas el pulso,*
> *digno sujeto será*
> *de las orejas del vulgo (9-15).*

The storyteller quickly identifies the caliber of his audience, subject matter, and his intention. His audience is not a reading audience, but rather an ordinary listening audience ("*de las orejas del vulgo*") who only hears, perhaps, what is said on the surface (note the use of *orejas* and not *oídos*). The intended subject matter fits the listener: what the storyteller plans to tell is fit for the average non-reader and not for another audience that is *culto*. The emphasis on entertainment of the *vulgo* may be, ever so subtly, a mockery of Lope de Vega and his poetics for theatre, the *Arte nuevo de hacer comedias.*[27] Góngora could be making a mockery of the contemporary polemics concerning entertainment and art.

The storyteller spells out that this ballad is proper entertainment for commoners and not for those who might expect to find a serious imitation of the Pyramus and Thisbe story. He specifies that he wants popular acclaim in spite of his audience's *low brow* reputation: "*popular aplauso quiero,/perdónenme sus tributos*" (15-16). All things considered, the storyteller announces that he is about to tell an inelegant tale and he wants an audience that can be amused by its *burlesque language*.

The *language* of burlesque does not depend only on rude, irreverent, or obscene words. Language implies structure, grammar, meter, expression, thoughts and feelings and meanings. Burlesque's *language* is made up of techniques and patterns which involve travesty, imitation, caricature, parody, irony, and lampooning, etc., but more importantly, the *language* of burlesque implies a keenly crafted framework of meaningful (and entertaining) interchanges of thoughts. The isolable techniques and patterns of burlesque in a particular text can be analyzed, but the *language of burlesque*, like any language, determines and is determined by the accepted meaning or interpretation of that particular text.

Now then, what is the relationship between the burlesque mode of representation here and the Ovidian myth of Pyramus and Thisbe? The storyteller employs grotesque caricature and exaggeration to characterize the fictional world of Pyramus and Thisbe. Parody also plays a role. The general outline of the story of doomed lovers was usually secure as given: details might vary but in choosing variants, poets made plots. It is the *given* materials of Pyramus and Thisbe that provide the category of "legend." In Góngora's *Píramo y Tisbe* the making of the myth of the doomed lovers is ridiculed. The storyteller here begins by snubbing one of the propagators of the myth, Ovid: he perverts his family name "Naso" with the pejorative nickname "Nasón," makes an indelicate matter of the length or pug of his nose, and more importantly, labels him a fool for mistaking, as writer or poet, the shameful blush of the fruits of the white mulberry tree to purple for a respectful and honorable tribute (18-28). The accusation is clear: Ovid misinterpreted the data by privileging honorable innocence and virtue over shameful guilt and offense. The storyteller rectifies the story: the mulberry tree was so ashamed for housing the remains of the two disreputable would-be lovers that its fruits could not bear the dishonor. Driven by a sense of shame, it blushed in horror.

The burlesque rectification of Ovid's mistaken opinion about, and idealized representation of the white mulberry tree initiates within the burlesque framework a series of *corrective* anecdotes about the "true" history of Pyramus,

Thisbe, the wall between their homes, the moonlight, the fierce lion, and the deaths of the youths. All of these corrective anecdotes are amusing because they deform and exaggerate to the point of making ridiculous and ugly, the sacred and accepted (but under-investigated and unsubstantiated) beliefs about the myth. In this mock-ballad the storyteller intends to right the misrepresentations of Ovid's myth by scratching out the basic flaws in the original representation. Here again, as with the sonnet attributed to Quevedo, the burlesque is both itself and something else more serious. The chicken-scratch description (*"los mal formados rasguños de los pinceles de un ganso"*) of Pyramus and Thisbe leaves little idealism of the tragic myth represented by Ovid (42-43). In fact, the rough sketch of the disgruntled storyteller demonstrates that neither Pyramus nor Thisbe nor their *amorous* situation are worthy of tragic or idealized emulation. In his own rough fashion the narrator mockingly scratches out the earthy details of their *true, rightful and legitimate* legend.

The use of grotesque caricature is unparalleled in the burlesque accout. Thisbe had fused eyebrows, a ruddy complexion, and a smudge of almond paste for a nose. She squeaked a bit, had the breast (*"pechugas"*) of a phoenix and had a physique which would have insulted even the hairy and knock-kneed gods (Palas and Juno respectively). The comparison of Thisbe's breasts and the breast-bone of the phoenix (a mythical Egyptian bird) is the catalyst for calling Thisbe a Figpecker (*"papahigo"*) later on. The storyteller insults Thisbe's image by arguing that she is the envy of both sexes, *"Creció deidad, creció invidia / de un sexo y otro"* but immediately qualifies his ironic praise by saying: *"¿qué mucho que la fe erigiese aras a quien la emulación culto?"* (85-88). In layman terms the storyteller informs readers that they will just have to *take his word* for what he tells as *truth* even though his representation is a travesty.

The caricature of Pyramus has much less to do with his physique than with his coming of sexual age. The account tells that he was neither effeminate nor ferocious, but he was a fashionable young boy. He encased his ears in locks of hair like a page-boy, and sported a pasty forehead and a fluffy crest of hair. His cheeks were rather drawn and his chin was nearly bare of facial hair. His eyebrows, however, were two black thrusts that stood on end in a very sweet fashion so that even two strong thrusts with a sword would have only bent them (110-120). Pyramus's claim to fame was the love-dart that Cupid sent him. This then, explains the storyteller, was the neighbor, lover, and ruffian of the virginal turtledove who, hilariously, groaned like a widow bird.

> *Este, pues, era el vecino,*
> *el amante y aun el cuyo*
> *de la tórtola doncella,*
> *gemidora a lo viudo. (125-9).*

When Thisbe whined like a bereaved widow who had been separated from her husband, Pyramus served her as paramour and pimp (*"amante y aun el cuyo"*). The storyteller leaves no doubt that the two doomed youths are adolescents interested in satisfying the desires of newly acquired sexual instincts.

The introduction of the adolescents' exaggerated physical attributes, and Pyramus's lewd intentions is in line with the *rhetoric* of burlesque. The grotesque caricatures of Pyramus and Thisbe run in direct contradiction to the *ideal* caricature offered by Ovid. They are not anything like the idealized versions of Ovid's tale. In fact, the not-so impressive Pyramus and Thisbe are upstaged by the *heroic*, but imperfect, wall that lies between their houses (a wall that weakens and cracks on the behalf of the youngsters years after being subjected to the loud screams of young Pyramus and Thisbe),

> *Oyólos, y aquellos días*
> *tan bien la audiencia le supo*
> *que año después se hizo*
> *rajas en servicio suyo. (37-40).*

The inference seems to be that the wall was trying to get back at Pyramus and Thisbe for their incessant cries. The two lovers are also upstaged by a smelly and sweaty go-between from the Congo. The detailed description of the go-between (the woman Pyramus chooses to turn Thisbe from a fearful innocent to a willing victim) is amusing because it is full of absurdly grotesque sensuality:

The storyteller uses an apostrophe (*"los críticos me perdonen"*) to remind his audience mockingly of their role in the spectacle. He begs the critics' pardon for employing a learned word for delicious small grapes, *ligustros*, in what is otherwise a grotesque description that offends the senses and all good taste.

Calificarle sus pasas
a fuer de Aurora propuso:
los críticos me perdonen
si dijere con ligustros.
Abrazólo sobarcada,
y no de clavos malucos,
en nombre de la azucena
desmentidora del tufo,
siendo aforismo aguileño
que matar basta a un difunto
cualquier olor de costado,
o sea morcillo o rucio. (145-156).

The grotesque caricature of the paid go-between is the embodiment of evil. She may be the dawn, but she is the dawn of darkness. She is not the embodiment of mysteriousness but rather the illicit means to a dastardly end. She is the unsightly and repulsive instrument who takes on and carries contraband as a ship carries its cargo. Pyramus's foul and loathsome design for deception and sexual gratification is transported to Thisbe. The go-between is propelled by unspeakable thoughts ("*que la mulata se gira / a los pensamientos mudos*") (165-66). And, metaphorically speaking, she smells no worse than Pyramus's intentions. One whiff from the side would be enough to kill a dead man ("*que matar basta a un difunto / cualquier olor de costado*") (154-55).

The bizarre and grotesque caricatures of Pyramus, Thisbe and the go-between are earthy and ribald, but they are funny and not particularly repulsive in spite of the distasteful sensorial experience the storyteller offers through indiscreet description. The mocking descriptions are neither superfluous nor dispensable. Burlesque language employs caricature and exaggeration to blow things out of proportion, on the one hand, and to put important dark realities in perspective, on the other. The overall function of burlesque distortion is to bring, laughingly, to the ugly surface the *absurd* nature of things. Pyramus's intentions are hilariously abominable: he wants to seduce a young innocent for the purpose of satisfying his sexual needs. Similarly, Thisbe's virtue is questionable since, after suffering a nightmare concerning her own misfortune, she stupidly ignores her own intuition. She recognized that Pyramus was the incarnation of ill will when, according to the legend, she lamented that the crack in the wall would be her downfall:

> *Había la noche antes*
> *soñado sus infortunios,*
> *y viendo el requicio entonces,*
> *Esta es, dijo, no dudo,*
> *esta, Píramo, es la herida*
> *que en aquel sueño importuno*
> *abrió dos veces el mío*
> *cuando una el pecho tuyo. (177-184).*

Thisbe suspects the fissure in the wall to be her perdition. What she draws attention to is the symbolic relationship between the fissure and the breaking down of her will. She laments her situation and draws a parallel between it and the betrayal and invasion at Troy:

> *Mas ¡ay!, que taladró niño*
> *lo que dilatará astuto,*
> *que no poco daño a Troya*
> *breve portillo introdujo. (201-204).*

Thisbe summarizes the danger of the situation: if you give a young boy an inch he will take a yard. Thisbe's worries that Pyramus will simply gnaw away at the crack until it is a large hole are sincere, but they are quickly transformed by her agreement to meet Pyramus at midnight of the same day. The poem's audience cannot be surprised by the quick turnabout since they have already been prepared for the meeting by some knowledge of the renowned myth. More importantly, however, they are not surprised since all along the storyteller subverts mockingly false pretensions through the systematic use of rough and raw vocabulary and allusions. With precision he ruthlessly reduced the idealized lovers of Ovid's tale to common scatterbrains ("*casquilucios*") who were interested in little more than satisfying nascent sexual urges.

The focus on earthy, ignoble and unashamed human activities is paramount to undercutting the sublime, noble and heroic intentions attributed to Pyramus and Thisbe in Ovid's myth. The ribald and irreverent nature of the rough caricatures of the two scatterbrains lends itself as a basic staple of the idiom of burlesque. The unrestrained and blatantly crass descriptions have a startling effect on the poem's audience: they laugh because it seems uncustomary and unnatural to find such lewd allusions and raw language in a stylized and eloquent ballad. The implication of the raucous burlesque is clear: the storyteller is unconvinced that the intentions of Pyramus and Thisbe were other than sexual ones. He makes a mockery of applying tragic and heroic intentions to common lasciviousness. We have two ironies: first, the ideal is burlesqued; and next, the burlesque is graced by eloquent verse, usually reserved for ideals.

The visual imagery of the burlesque ballad borders on the obscene, its impact on the audience is heightened by lofty descriptions of a common crime. Pyramus's overt obsession with sex is highlighted cleverly. His words are lewd and suggestive. He praises the cracked wall because its mere existence makes the conquest so much more desirable for both parties.

> *"Barco ya de vista, dijo,*
> *angosto no, sino augusto,*
> *que, velas hecho tu lastre,*
> *nadas más cuando más surto:*
> *poco espacio me concedes,*
> *mas basta, que a Palinuro*
> *mucho mar le dejó ver*
> *el primero breve surco. (233-240).*

Pyramus's wishful thinking is obscene: he refers to his desired sexual encounter with Thisbe and spells out graphically, and in nautical terms, how he experiences the union in his mind. He sees her writhing when she is filled up ("*nadas más cuando más surto*"), and although she may not give him much *leeway*, he will take what he wants from her. Pyramus desires fervently what he does not have and what has been kept from him. And, he surmises, he has to start somewhere: Palinuro only saw the first wake as his boat pushed out to sea.

Pyramus is explicit in his obsession: he wants some "skin" (*"conducidor de la conquista o del hurto de una piel"*). His words to the wall highlight his erotic desire for Thisbe: *"Tus bordes beso, piloto, / ya que no tu quilla buzo"* (249-250). Pyramus's words are lewd because they conceal his actions which are obscene. Like a marionette he jabs his fist into the hole in the wall only to remove it empty.

> ¡Cuántas veces impaciente
> metió el brazo, que no cupo,
> el garzón, y lo atentado
> le revolcaron por nulo! (297:261-4)

Pyramus's jabbings into the fractured wall are more than obscene. They seem ludicrous and mechanical. The suggestion is that Pyramus and Thisbe are marionettes who respond only to libido. Thereby, the storyteller negates that there was anything more than sexual instinct at work here. No one is misled to believe that there might have been a serious relationship between sexual desire or erotic passion and virtuous love. In fact, virtuous love, somwhat akin to the events in the earlier *Celestina*, is sytematically discounted by allusions to sexual frustration:

> ¡Cuántas el impedimento
> acusaron de consuno
> al pozo que es de por medio,
> si no se besan los cubos! (265-8).

Pyramus and Thisbe just wanted to dip into a little lovemaking activity. The "buckets" (*"cubos"*) are the young "lovers'" mouths that kiss the wall and drool against its borders but stay empty of "well water" that might cure them of their sexual frustration. Since their "buckets" remain on opposite ends of the "well" and never pass and meet on their way through the metaphorical well's shaft, to kiss the hole leading from one side of the wall to the other was to incite both the wrath of frustration and the erotic excitement of increased desire.

The storyteller insists that it was illicit sexual love and not sanctioned marital love that occasioned the tragic encounter between young Pyramus and Thisbe. Foolish Thisbe (*"la boba"*) gave in, and chose to meet with her unlawful lover:

Amor, que los asistía
el vergonzoso capullo
desnudó a la virgen rosa
que desprecia el tirio jugo;
abrió su esplendor la boba
y a seguillo se dispuso:
¡trágica resolución,
digna de mayor coturno! (273-281).

The tragic decision was fit for a worthier person (*"digna de mayor coturno"*) than a foolish tart who was willing to meet her young lover at midnight out on the edge of town. Thisbe's decision to offer herself up as willing and easy prey to Pyramus, a predator of innocence and purity, is labeled in the verse narrative, ironically, as the only tragedy of the whole affair. The mock-tragedy was Thisbe's whimsical decision to forego good behavior for bad and not the unforseen misfortunes that led to the deaths of the two incompetent lovers.

In Góngora's burlesque version of the legend many of the major elements of Ovid's Latin elaborations are topsy-turvy.[28] What is important is that the names and labels provided in the Ovid model version have not been changed to protect the innocent. In fact, in the burlesque version no one is innocent or virtuous. The storyteller does not emulate the unparalleled attributes of a handsome and courageous Pyramus or the peerless Thisbe, but instead provides a bombastic, gauche and ironic account of a series of blunders and flops that lead up to union in death.

y en letras de oro: "Aquí yacen
individuamente juntos,
a pesar del Amor, dos,
a pesar del número, uno. (505-8).

In the final verses the storyteller provides the serio-comic touch: his burlesque version is a hilarious parody of the legend of doomed lovers. The irony of their separate togetherness condenses and reiterates succinctly the profusion of contradictory images and allusions that give abundant evidence to "successful failure" in the final 124 verses of the *romance*.

Thisbe's bodeful journey leaves her dogged and she arrives at her destination all worn out and teary-eyed. In fact Thisbe's state of health resembles the state in which she finds their nuptial bed:

> *Olmo, que en jóvenes hojas*
> *disimula años adultos,*
> *de su vid florida entonces*
> *en los más lascivos nudos,*
> *un rayo, sin escuderos*
> *o de luz o de tumulto,*
> *le desvaneció la pompa*
> *y el tálamo descompuso.* (303-8).

The withered nuptial bed at the foot of the elm tree whose ruined splendor is wrapped lasciviously in the vines knotted around its trunk is not only a bad omen but also an explicit forecast of the unsuccessful attempt at physical union. The storyteller's commentary on the bad omen is hilarious. He argues in a *frivolously* practical manner that the mountain of ashy remains will make a good hundred bleachings. The commentary is hilarious but telling since, through extension, it implies that the double suicide of Pyramus and Thisbe will also have the practical purpose of washing out dirty realities.

Thisbe is not the only one who successfully fails time and again. Pyramus is the champion of successful failure. The caricature describes him as a late-comer (*"tardón"*) who, because of his indecisiveness, does not even get to "first base" with Thisbe.

> *En esto llegó el tardón,*
> *que la ronda lo detuvo*
> *sobre quitalle el que fue,*
> *aun envainado, verdugo.* (354-7).

The object of his indecision is suggestive of sexual potency: he cannot determine whether he wants to come armed and fully dressed or unarmed and *naked* to his first sexual encounter with Thisbe. He shows up armed and carries his sword sheathed.

> *Llegó, pisando cenizas*
> *del lastimoso trasunto*

de sus bodas, a la fuente,
al término constituto,
* y no hallando la moza,*
entre ronco y tartamudo,
se enjaguó con sus palabras,
regulador de minutos. (357-364).

Pyramus's continued inefficacy is due to his anti-heroic qualities. Pyramus is a burlesque of heroism in every aspect. He is neither prompt nor patient. He is foul-mouthed and anxious. His impatience drives him to examine empty and coarse cavities of tree trunks (improper hiding places for his *fine* Thisbe). Pyramus is also painted a coward. Upon seeing the false signs of deception (Thisbe's bloodied veil and the growling lion) and drawing a misinformed conclusion, Pyramus becomes statuesque. He does not unsheathe his sword to take vengeance, but instead freezes like a horse with his weight balanced on one foot.

* Viólos, y al reconocellos,*
mármol obediente al duro
sincel de Lisipo tanto
no ya desmintió lo esculto
* como Píramo lo vivo,*
pendiente en un pie a lo grullo, (393-98).

Through burlesque exaggeration this tragedy remains a bad decision for two unsupervised youths, not the deaths of heroic individuals.

One of the three Fates, seeing such a poor excuse for a hero, occasioned the fearful Pyramus to skewer himself on his own sword. Any potential serious feeling for the young man's foolish suicide is denied when the storyteller adds a series of insults to Pyramus's fatal injury in a cruel apostrophe:

¿Tan mal te olía la vida?
¡Oh bien, hideputa, puto,
el que sobre tu cabeza
pusiera un cuerno de juro! (303:433-6)

In these four verses the storyteller accuses Pyramus for his irreverence for life (433), his foolish lack of respect for virtue (434), and his flippant irreverence for Natural Law (436).

Within Góngora's burlesque context the legendary situation can be paraphrased as follows: The two lovers "come up against a brick wall, they lose the day, they succumb" to sexual instinct instead of defending virtue and honor, Pyramus does not have "a leg to stand on", Thisbe "trips up", their nuptial bed is "struck down" by lightning, Thisbe does not even "slip through" Pyramus's "fingers", they "cut one another's throats", and have "two strikes against each other". The mutual dependence of an idea and its opposite in this burlesque ballad is fundamental to the critical burlesque reading of the tragic legend--encouraged throughout the travesty. Readers are quite sure that the storyteller wants to admonish Pyramus and Thisbe's successful failure to consummate a sexual relationship. Through mockery the storyteller condemns their attempt to mock social virtue (a Law of Nature established and accepted by Spanish society) by arranging a clandestine encounter to satisfy sexual instinct (a Law of Nature not accepted either by Spanish readers or the claims of the traditional story-pattern). Moreover, the lengthy and highly stylized *romance* seems to be an ironic exemplary eulogy to their run of bad luck.

The burlesque here depends on the disparity and similarity of ideal virtue and this hilariously bogus burlesque representation of improbity. The banality of the social world in which Góngora's characters "live and breathe" moves this burlesque version into the realm of the mock-heroic. The social world of the Gongorean Pyramus and Thisbe does not resemble in the least bit the idealized society in Ovid's myth where the memory of the tragic lovers is commemorated with the purple blush of the mulberry tree. The storyteller depends on the contours of the story but, parodically, is not committed to straight imitation of Ovid's myth. He is committed to demonstrating that the original Ovidian version is an idealizing and hence misleading gloss on the ugly imperfections of illicit sensuality. Anticipating artists like Goya and Valle-Inclán, Góngora and Cervantes show that idealism itself *is* a distortion. The burlesque mode of representation is almost always the catalyst for such an exposé. The storyteller lays bare the grittiness of the real everyday world, the fraudulent and deceiving intentions and motives within the glorification of true love, and the ugly but hilarious end results of trying to sell immorality as morality or sensualism as virtuous love. This continues to be a key argument about the burlesque mode and its study. The storyteller suggests that Ovid's version was idealistic, false, and misleading. The Ovidian myth made a rose out of a dung heap and shrouded unacceptable immorality and promiscuity in a veil of virtue and true love. In this sense, Góngora's *Pyramus and Thisbe* version must be read closely in terms of his *Polephemus and Galatea.*

Góngora's *Fábula de Píramo y Tisbe* sets a trap for the fraudulence of myth, the artifice of idealism and the connivance of artistic creation. The *"fábula"* blows the cover of deceiving appearances and gritty reality by blatantly pointing out that for generations and generations many have been put over by the cunning idealization of ordinary sensualism. The intention of the burlesque mode in this *"fábula"* is to to strip illusion and to show sensualism, myth and illusion for what they are.

Góngora accomplishes the strip-tease of illusion by thwarting expectations. The so-called *high style* language identified with his elite poetry is not replaced by *low style* language, but instead there is a very uncomfortable and paradoxical (and therefore often hilarious) coexistence between "high" and "low." Or, to put it another way: the *low* and the *popular* are as highly stylized in serious poetry. Góngora's burlesque does not deny eloquence, the extraordinary nature of *romance*, or the essence of *culteranismo* or *gongorismo*, nor does it merely show their reverses (dissuasive illogicality, commonness, and a half-learned poetic structure). The burlesque *Fábula de Píramo y Tisbe* like the serious *Fábula de Polifemo*, is imbued with learned and popular elements that amuse and entertain because of their contradictions. Góngora's eloquently banal portrait of an inherited ideal of *true love* (which denied sensualism through absence) is, in fact, an artistic portrait of imperfection. The two sexually potent youngsters simply are not up to the ideal or tragic script of doomed love. Indeed, this is imperfection at its best as the tragic course of two doomed lovers is reduced to the hilarious spectacle played out by absurd youths. In this respect, Góngora's burlesque romance is no less a model of poetic achievement than his acclaimed masterpiece *Polifemo y Galatea.*

Góngora's specific use of the burlesque mode in a major poetic work can help review the basic thesis that burlesque imitations integrate, dialectically, two opposite paths of discourse --the low/high or popular/elite or farcical/tragic. Pyramus and Thisbe not treated directly as ridiculous nincompoops or scatterbrains, but rather as nincompoops which stand for a shift from the legend's elegantly tragic youths. The surplus of burlesque mishaps are grotesquely funny only because they coexist with the waste of excellence that characterizes tragedy. Thus, in order to see what the one extreme of farcical love is, readers must at the same time know what the opposite, tragic love, is--which farce is burlesquing, negating, deconstructing and subverting. This is, then, the function of the burlesque mode: within Góngora's burlesque ballad there seems to be a unity of high tragedy and low burlesque only because, in terms of common sense, there can be no such unity. It would be a fraudulent unity. The burlesque mode contends that what is articulated as ideal love in fiction is silly sexuality in history. When one reads seriously articulated burlesque through the prism of writers like Juan Ruiz, Cervantes, Góngora, Quevedo, Goya and Valle-Inclán, they might see, as illustrated clearly through *Píramo y Tisbe*, that the burlesque mode subverts official idealism only to defend common sense and sensuality--but without deploring the dangers of *common* sense and vulgar sensuality. In short, future studies might do well to examine rigorously the social and materialist foundations of the burlesque mode in literary texts.

The Constants of Burlesque
The above analyses of burlesque verse provide a useful, albeit somewhat perplexing, set of patterns and techniques that seems to be a constant in diverse burlesque texts of the Golden Age. A review of the diverse elements of burlesque present in three poetic texts might serve as a draft for the blueprint of burlesque which can then be applied to Cervantes's theatrical interlude, *El Retablo de las Maravillas* and to Salas Barbadillo's *El descasamentero*. There is, for example, an element of dialogue (with implied readers) present in all three burlesque poems. The speaker seems to be somewhat preoccupied with distinguishing himself to fame and seeks to enhance his reputation and excellence by

recounting a detailed burlesque version of everyday Spanish life to an audience. None of the speakers/storytellers in the poems live up to the standards of their authors or readers. Therefore readers consider the speakers inferior and their complaints laughable and ridiculous. The burlesque appearance is a harmless critique of that which is represented through *burlas*. Readers see through the unreliability of the speaker and his bogus complaints about his perception of the situation, and they laugh.

Readers recognize the fictionalized situation for what it is: a hilarious *staged* event for their amusement. The staged event includes a convincing fraud who imitates the ethos of virtue and, wittingly or unwittingly, mocks the deceiving appearances of Spain's idealized notions concerning true love, morality, mortality, honor, distinguished personages, fidelity or truth. The fraud assumes a particularly magnanimous stance of superiority and handles the materials of his story/complaint with reputable skill. He offers an audience a peculiarly detailed and artistically respectable account of unseemly and rather seedy realities. Ironically, the burlesque *show* is best explained by the suspected reality or "*veras*" that becomes manifest through the mocking portrait. In other words, understanding the burlesque mode of representation consists in going beneath the appearance (of, say, the social situation between the client and the prostitute in *Melancólica estás, putidoncella* or the upstart and meager prospects for social mobility at Court) to the reality underlying it (the false values of courtly love and their inappropriateness in terms of the struggle between sensualism and morality or, in the case of the upstart, the unrealistic expectations of many upstarts who--through deception--want to get ahead).

The humorous disposition is also a constant of these burlesque poems. These poems are laughing matters. The surface burlesque is often lively, attractive, convincing, and, in a sense, real. The portrait of the court's visitor being searched from the tip of his hat to the hoof of his mule, as though they were one in the same, is funny. The report of the tactile experience that the client has with his sexual partner who is "*raída como empeine de zapato / que de muy traído se desuella*" paints an amusing, although disgusting, portrait. In the same fashion, the ridiculously obscene antics of Pyramus are entertaining. The mode of representation is inherently fraudulent. Thus, the amusement and ensuing laughter is first at the silly situation and then as a response to the uneasy awareness that readers too have just been tricked into considering the "*veras*" that holds the silly situation together. Laughing *matters* and, in this sense, the effect of amusement is *real.*

The hoax or jest is the classic illustration of the distinction and connection between burlesque and seriousness. Burlesque obtains when readers realize that the self-baptized hero (a not so convincing imposter) is mocked and ridiculed. The ironic dimension of the poems suggests that the burlesque appearance is also misleading since readers exploit the common fraud by laughing at the social madness that led to the upstart's burlesque imitation of ideals. In this sonnet the disappointed visitor to Valladolid is only one of many pretentious thugs who had been deceived by appearances that were given lip-service outside the gates of the city. In *Melancólica estás. . . .* the situation of the angry client in a common brothel chides man's lot for being susceptible to artificial allurements that cover up the ugly realities of the physical world. His complaint is offered as a warning to others who, like himself, will be easily taken in. In *Píramo y Tisbe* the storyteller rights Ovid's wrong by informing his audience that they have been duped by a glorified, fictional and idealized account of what is little more than common sensualism. Thus, the burlesque appearance is inseparable from the seriousness of the overall hoax that tricks readers into thinking about critical issues through laughter.

The Social Issues in Burlesque: *El descasamentero*
The analysis of burlesque mockery effected through the absurd distortion of certain beliefs about critical issues is crucial to understanding how contemporary Spaniards were handling the confusing issues of their time. These issues have to do with foreign policy, infidelity, abuse of local authority, corruption, social deviance, madness, marriage and idealism, for example. The resulting laughter from recognized mockery is an awareness of absurd oppositions between structures of perceived reality. Commonly accepted beliefs about specific issues like fairness, independence and authority are no longer acceptable or common to the observer of burlesque, but

instead funny and uncanny. Thus the optional and often ambiguous set of beliefs offered from the text's humorous perspective becomes temporarily an acceptable but absurdly laughable alternative. In real social terms, burlesque does not effect change but simply a social awareness of attitudinal divergence and changeability in social transformation. *Fiestas de la boda de la incasable mal casada* is a representative example of how burlesque representation distorts preconceptions about courtship, marriage, social responsibility, frivolity and even madness to enable readers to perceive their idealistic beliefs about these common matters and laugh at them.

Salas Barbadillo (1581-1635) was the contemporary of Lope de Vega, Cervantes, Quevedo and Góngora. His major works are *La hija de Celestina* (1612), *La ingeniosa Elena* (1614), *Corrección de vicios* (1615), *El caballero puntual* I (1614) and II (1619), *La estafeta del dios Momo* (1627) and *El curioso y sabio Alejandro, fiscal y juez de vidas ajenas* (1634). *Fiestas de la boda de la incasable mal casada* (1621) is one of Salas Barbadillo's works that has been significantly overlooked by most scholars who have dedicated time to the study of Salas's literary production. They may have shied away from *Fiestas* because it is a book full of rather diverse entertaining and didactic texts held together loosely by an exemplary tale about a frustrated courtship and a bad marriage.

Fiestas is an unusual text in that it cannot be categorized neatly into any genre or category because it is loosely held together by the framing exemplary tale about one bad marriage, and enhanced by a variety of poems, tales, theatrical interludes and stories that are meant to convince Dorotea, the female protagonist of the framing tale, to amend her behavior. These interludes, stories and poems are provided in their entirety. To clarify, the reader is presented with an unusual reading situation: readers read the *script* of the theatrical interludes while Dorotea and her guests are viewing the performance. While many seventeenth century texts relied on the interpolation of other genres, I cannot recall any seventeenth century text with a prose narrative frame that requires readers to read a *script* of a play or interlude while textual spectators are *viewing* what readers are imagining in the theatre of their minds.

Fiestas has been identified as a burlesque book by Scherer, Peyton and Place although it is not a burlesque except in the broadest sense--that is, in terms of the relationship of burlesque to its etymological origin, *burla* and its tripart equivalents mockery, illusion and deception. In spite of the unusually incongrous but intriguing title *Fiestas de la boda de la incasable mal casada*, the framing tale does not employ burlesque representation as its primary means of representing critical issues, but instead a satirical representation of issues with a didactic and corrective purpose. In the introduction to the "*vulgo*" the author warns: "*que puede tanto la fuerça de una perversa costumbre, que al estado del casamiento, que se avia de solenizar con lágrimas, escandalizamos con agoreras alegrías, siendo aquel gozo violento y breve presagio de su tormento eterno*" (F1, my emphasis).

The declared intention is to scandalize with omnious merriment. In *Fiestas* the entertainment is a ploy whose intention is to shame and mock Dorotea, the unmarriageable marrying woman, and other women like her, into making different choices (to marry well in social termas and to treat others with respect) and to recognize her foolishness for making bad choices. In spite of her beauty, virtue, social standing, and intelligence Dorotea's social behavior leads readers to believe she is little more than a social dunce and a historical fool.

In constrast, Cervantes demonstrates that individual intentions like Dorotea's in *Fiestas* can be judged as noble or virtuous ideologically if they are taken from their social context and viewed in isolation. In *Don Quixote* the mad hidalgo's discussion of arms and letters or Marcela's declaration of freedom and freedom of choice are examples of speeches that seem just and ordinary until read in context. However, once placed in their social context where individual intentions and declarations must be judged and tested, individual desires like those of Dorotea, the mad hidalgo or Marcela often constitute social deviance. The relationship between social deviance and its gravity or frivolity depends on how deviance and the deviant as well as the ultimate consequences of deviant behavior are represented. The mode of representation determines the relationship between burlesque, farcical or satirical laughter and serious issues.

In *Don Quixote* Marcela did not lose her virtuousness with her declaration of freedom although she was indirectly critiqued for refusing to participate in an accepted social institution and directly critiqued and mocked for refusing all suitors. Salas Barbadillo does not allow any ambiguity for Dorotea. Dorotea is stripped of any noble behavior or just cause by the narrator's cynical sententiousness. She is described as a bad daughter (*desobediente, revoltosa, rebelde, maliciosa*), a bad person (*vana, desafiante, consentida, pretensiosa y tonta*) and a bad wife because she marries a deformed and unworthy man for all the wrong reasons based on the wrong decisions. The narrator draws her as a foolish character because, as he suggests, she knows what she should do and does the opposite only to be able to rule in her own home. In order to *take* control she lets herself get *out of control.*

The weakness of Dorotea's character in terms of the overall narrative is that she does not inspire disgust, hate, sympathy, or admiration. She is bland and readers are indifferent toward her. Neither comicality nor tragedy functions with indifference. Likewise, her suitors, Don Fernando and Don Luis, are no better off in terms of the narrator or readers for, in spite of their genteel attibutes, they are also considered fools, although not victims, for spending time and money on a worthless, silly woman especially when the pertinent wedding festivities which are orchestrated by them to set Dorotea straight are wasted on her. Thus, Salas Barbadillo's declared intention of scandalizing by entertaining means does not function within the text nor does the framing exemplary tale serve its didactic function very well outside the text for readers. When scandals breed indifference the ensuing reaction can be neither raucus laughter nor pitiful sorrow.

Overall in *Fiestas* social commentary outweighs Salas Barbadillo's commitment to entertainment. In spite of the already documented influence by Cervantes, Quevedo and Góngora, Salas Barbadillo was either unwilling or unable, for the most part, to write a good burlesque. In the frame novel his characters are insignificant and evoke indifference. His timing is poor. He bores readers with lengthy warnings and diatribes against bad marriages, disobedient daughters, foolish suitors, wasteful celebrations, and ostentation rather than building entertaining suspense with word play, burlesque repetitions, or narrative jokes and hoaxes. The result is that he does not show how funny people and situations are but rather how stupid and foolish they are. The labels *"agoreras alegrías"* and the *"gozo violento y breve presagio"* of his introduction are far more accurate than any scholar's attempt to categorize *Fiestas* a burlesque book.

Unlike the cynical and bland world of the unidimensional characters in the frame exemplary tale, however, the short poems, tales, and theatrical interludes set up by Dorotea's scorned suitor and cousin, Don Luis, to enlighten Dorotea and her guests are hilariously funny. These ludicrous scandals of bad marriages which are used to entertain and teach are functional for readers or listeners outside the text because they employ burlesque representation as the means of digging up distorted versions of common issues for entertainment. A good number of theatrical interludes are interpolated for the guests' viewing pleasure during the wedding festivities.

The variety of wedding entertainments includes *El descasamentero*, a domestic comedy and a burlesque seventeenth century representation of Divorce Court. It is the most remarkable of these interpolated scandles, and I have chosen the *Descasamentero* for brief analysis in terms of the burlesque representation of serious issues. *El Remendón de la Naturaleza* (Nature's mender) involves a quack who makes fools of people who want to change nature. *El cocinero del Amor* is a burlesque ballad which euphemizes recipes for sexual gratification with recipes for food. *Las aventuras de la corte* is a dark farcical interlude which relies on a father's ludicrous pride in his two whoring and swindling daughters. The comedy *El Malcontentadizo* makes a mockery of a man who never gets what he wants and feels victimized about his impotence. And in a final tale comicality turns to tragedy in the story *la Mayor acción del hombre*.

El Descasamentero is a hilarious burlesque theatrical interlude. Given the state of courtship and marriage in the early seventeenth century it is no wonder that Salas Barbadillo made a mockery of bad marriages and their disolution in a fictional interlude such as *El Descasamentero*. If fictional representations of deceptive courtship and bad marriages by Salas Barbadillo, Francisco de Quevedo, and

Cervantes (to name a few), and the historical representation about the outrageous expense of these affairs in the memorials by the *arbitrista* Sancho de Moncada are any indication of how ludicrous and out-of-hand the entire marriage process had become, then readers today can assume that the burlesque representations of courtship and marriage serve to identify how some Spaniards perceived the imperfections and ridiculousness of this process.

The *Descasamentero* anulls or divorces couples held captive by the bonds of matrimony. The judge argues that since: "*los más de los casados desean salir a la libertad,*" he demands "*[que] vengan ante mí, presenten su querella, que yo seré el rompedor de su cautiverio*"(F44). The function of mocking marriage burlesquely through absurdly exaggerated cases of bad marriages and their dissolution or retention is to make fun of the social, economic, legal, and political factors involved in making and breaking up marriages. The religious or sacramental aspects of Catholic marriages are never brought to the foreground since a matchmaker, not a priest, is responsible for all the bad unions. A review of the cases brought to the divorce court is warranted for discussion of how these marriages are represented in a burlesque mode. The *Descasamentero* is an interlude which we read and view in our minds while the fictional wedding guests of *Fiestas* see the short play. The implication is that the burlesque one-act play serves a social function on at least two levels: the wedding guests are witnesses to the burlesque, readers are witnesses to the burlesque as a part of a more didactic and serious tale.

The characters of the interlude are simple, stereotypical, complaining, undereducated and ridiculous. They are socially inferior to the characters in the frame story. The setting, the language, gestures and topics are exaggerated and toil worn. Rumor, caricature, gossip and stereotype rule in the court where illogical reasoning is set forth to justify the unreasonable requests of many. The judge, for example, requests that all women litigants be gagged since all they do is scream and start scandals. His secretary explains that gags cannot be used on those who ask for justice. All the divorce cases deal with women who, one way or another, deceive their husbands and thereby make a mockery of their marriage. The first petitioner is Dorotea, who portrays herself

ironically as "*una muger más dorada en los pensamientos, que
en los cabellos, en la carne cristalina, en el talle dispuesta, y al
fin en el alma tan aliñada, y crespa que rompe galas de
agudezas, y elegancias...*". Dorotea's situation is simple: her
husband married her for her money and seeing her orphaned
without an inheritance after a ten year marriage, he becomes
a tyrant. She pleads with the judge for an annulment. When
her husband, Mauricio, agrees that an annulment is in order
because he fears being beaten and cuckholded by his wife
("*ser coronado por mi esposa*") (51) the judge rules in her favor.
Roles are reversed and exaggerated. The husband is proved a
weakling and Dorotea the tyrant at a time when women were
considered saleable goods. Here expected codes for behavior
are ridiculed as they are played exactly the opposite of what
is expected.

Fabio, the next litigant has only been married a month
but he arrives flogging himself as he enters the chambers. He
reports that after losing a dog his wife falls ill and barks at
him like a dog. In response Fabio beats her and the "*faldera
esquadra de perros*" begins to bark in her defense. Even after
leaving his home the dogs continued to mock him with their
barking. When his wife, Angélica, is brought in for the
defense she is such a sight with her barking dogs that the
judge immediately grants an annulment and wishes many
dogs on her so that they might devour her.

The third case introduces Claudio who fell in love, spent
money courting Filida with old-fashioned and nonsensical
pastoral ballads, and who was betrayed by an evil
matchmaker who convinced the lovely Filida to marry a
previous suitor. Claudio wants his bride back--a case which is
out of the judge's jurisdiction, of course, since what Claudio
wants is marriage and not divorce. Claudio is offered and
ungratefully receives part of the matchmaker's estate but is
unsatisfied since he was marrying for money in any case.
Here a case of "true love" is mocked burlesquely when money,
not love, becomes the overiding factor for the suit.

The fourth case belongs the the lame tailor Ardenio who
is ridiculed by the court for his physical deformity and for his
inability to handle his familial situation. His peg-leg makes
for a mocking situation. When Ardenio falls against the court
door the judge argues that had Ardenio played the wise

incompetent when the marriage was arranged he would not be asking now for an annulment.

Mi: *Aquí viene un hombre coxo.*

Lu: *Triste del, y que lástima le tengo, pues si viene a descasarse no (h)abrá llegado con toda la diligencia que (h)abrá menester. Quien viene a pedir justicia con pies de palo pereçosa resolución espera, porque la solicitada diligencia es la puerta de todas las negociaciones.*

Mi: *Una cayda grande dio a nuestra puerta.*

Germ: *Si otro tal como ella hubiera dado en la cuenta, quando le pedían que se casasse, no tuviera necesidad ahora de querellarse en nuestro tribunal...*

Ardenio "doesn't have a leg to stand on" but the judge agrees to let him out of a four year marriage which has produced five births and two live children. His wife is happy to give him his freedom in exchange for her dowry, and the judge agrees to the annulment.

The next case has to do with a woman who mocks her husband, Conrado, by dressing "*de entremés,*" and falling into wine vats when drunk. The case of Conrado and his drunken wife is by far the funniest because when he tells how much he has suffered the members of the court decide that no man could live through such mockery and shame. The judge explains what attitude should be adopted in this case:

"*Doblen por él todas las campanas, porque es justo que hagan sentimiento los bajados, por quien fue tantos años tan grande majadero. Védesele el hazer testamento, porque no es justo que tenga última voluntad en la muerte quien nunca la supo tener en vida,...*" (My emphasis).

The judge degrades Conrado's lack of courage and will to leave a bad marriage earlier by refusing to listen to a request from a dead man. The court members then recite poetic epitaphs which serve to commemorate the death of a numpskull. (*octosílabas*)

Germano:	*Lucino:*
Conrado está aquí, la espada	*Un mártir del maridaje,*
Mortal redimia sus daños	*Duerme en esta losa fría*

Hombre que sufrió veinte
   años
A una mujer afeitada.
Huesped con voz lastimosa
Llora por este afligido

Pues murió de ser marido,
Que es la muerte más rabiosa.
(69v,70)

Talque aun viviendo,
   dormía
Sugeto a perpetuo ultraje.
En sus trabajos mostró
Grandeconstancia, y
   firmeça,
No le dolió la cabeça,
Aunque mucho le pesó.
(v69)

The mocking and insulting poems get the judge and the secretary started on a competition of epitaphs. Conrado, who waits impatiently finally interrupts the competition by telling the court that he is not dead, but alive, and by asking the court to return to order, to give up such jests and annul his marriage. The judge mockingly replies that Conrado makes an inopportune request since death has already annulled his marriage. As death and foolishness are considered one, the competition continues and Conrado joins in the game with some of his own self-deriding epitaphs. On the basis of his final two quartets (below) the judge offers him his freedom.

> *Aquí está quien por costumbre*
>   *Necia, y bárbaros engaños,*
>   *Cautivo vivió veynte años,*
>   *En maridal servidumbre.*
> *Murió, y halló feliz suerte*
>   *En estado tan mortal,*
>   *Que de cautiverio tal*
>   *Solo redime la muerte.* (73v,74).

Only death can put an end to such foolishness.

The concluding case concerns a woman poet who makes fun of her illiterate husband. The husband requests the annulment which is quickly granted when the absent ex-wife sends a hilarious sonnet to the judge praising him for excusing numbskulls from bad marriages and returning, in most cases, women their freedom:

> *Piadoso Monseñor, feliz Germano,*
>   *Que exercitando liberalidades*
>   *Excusas mil casadas necedades*
>   *Quando descasas con prudente mano.*
> *El mísero mortal género humano,*

Que tanto padeció en otras edades,
Respire con tan francas libertades
Devidas a tu pecho cortesano.
Yo porque me has librado de un marido
Tan descortés, glotón, rudo, y grossero,
Eternas cantaré tus alabanzas
Maestro de dançar el más lucido
Eres, pues sabes grato y lisongero
Hasta en el casamiento hazer mudanças. (81v)

In a world which seems beset with bad marriages, tyranical women and impotent men, the poem eulogizes the work of the annulment judge who is willing to make changes in those marriages. The resulting laughter from the mockery of bad marriages which could have been prevented with a little foresight builds an awareness of absurd oppositions between what should be and what is. Commonly accepted beliefs about the specific issues of courtship and marriage which depend almost exclusively on inheritance, dowries, pretentiousness, and beauty are no longer acceptable or common to the observer of burlesque, but funny and uncanny. Thus the optional and ambiguous set of beliefs offered from the text's humorous perspective becomes temporarily an acceptable but an absurdly laughable alternative in fiction with implications for history.

Burlesque Entertainment and Social Consequence: *Retablo de las Maravillas*[29]

Cervantes's *Retablo de las maravillas* exposes the discursive mechanics of burlesque through the play-within-a-play or joke-within-a-joke structure. In the *Retablo* Cervantes dramatizes the controversial problem of showy appearances and ugly realities in such a way that historical readers (or spectators) outside the *Retablo* might understand how some fictional Spaniards were responding to social issues including entertainment, honor, authority, and pedigree. The result is that the burlesque representation of honor and family bloodline illustrates how *funny* some fictional Spaniards are when they try to be those they are not.

The *Retablo de las maravillas* is a fifteen minute play that involves both a staged puppet show and a performance with human puppets. The puppet show is held on a make-shift stage, its curtain is no more than a threadbare cloth, its stage managers, two swindlers, and a young waif who serves them as their sound man. The human puppets are a bunch of local country bumpkins who attempt to show off their finery, knowledge and even their artistic abilities only to demonstrate that they are clearly the bumpkins that the swindlers Chanfalla and Chirinos take them for. No matter how presumptuous, the town's men are cowardly, stupid and gullible, and the town's women are coarse and oversexed.

According to Asensio, the interlude aspired to little more than lively entertainment; its characters were *"personas socialmente humildes,"* and he specifies what sort of *unassuming* characters were involved: *"campesinos, gente del hampa, chusma callejera, modesta burguesía y algunos profesionales. . . médicos, abogados"* (7). Although the social state of the characters may be *unassuming* there is very little else that is unassuming about these stock characters. None of the characters in the *Retablo act* unassumingly. In fact, all the characters, except the quartermaster, Chirinos, Chanfalla and Rabellín, act the part of social frauds in order to protect their social reputation. Chirinos, Chanfalla and Rabellín, of course, also play the part of frauds but then they do so for money as *actors* and not in order to protect their *good* names. None of the characters in the interlude appears to be virtuous or honest. Yet, because of the joking situation readers suspect that they are honest people--gullible country folk-- who have been duped by a social mania concerning Spain's heritage.[30] Readers (and spectators) of the *Retablo* are prepared to view the funny antics of gullible and uneducated folk because the theatrical category *entremés* required a specific caliber of stock character as its medium for expression and laughter as its intended result. No one expects to find virtuous or noble characters in the confines of an *entremés*. As E. Asensio highlighted in the introduction to Cervantes's *Entremeses*, the *entremés "es un género humilde, sin humos nobiliarios ni pretensiones de haber sido legislado por Aristóteles"* (7). The expectations for interludes were different than those reserved for the *comedia*. The interlude did not aspire to more than *"un pasatiempo popular, esparcimiento breve entre dos emociones nobles"* (Asensio 7). Asensio suggested that the interlude was simple comic relief set between noble emotions. A logical extension is that the short burlesque play served as a go-between, straddling, as it were, the realms of *low culture* and *high* culture, or serious themes and farcical potential. The set of expectations for an interlude was then, necessarily, *low*, and thus different than those of the more *noble* plays which sandwiched them into fifteen minutes or so.

The *low* expectations for interludes could probably be gauged by the refusal on the part of dramaturgs to sign their name to them. Most of the interludes were anonymous and, as Asensio explains, during the ten years between 1611 and 1621 "*no hay un único poeta, famoso u oscuro, que se digne firmar con su nombre los que a veces acompañan las colecciones de comedias*" (7). Most maintained their anonymity, except, of course, for Cervantes who published his unrepresented comedies and interludes together. The general expectations surrounding the interlude placed it in a category of dramatic entertainment that created laughter at the expense of notions of fraud, sensuality, immorality, pretentiousness and comicality. Perhaps playwrights did not want their names associated with performances that *in name* appealed to and were primarily directed toward the *vulgo*.

The basic stuff of the interludes was not, in general, politically, morally or socially *dangerous* although the humorous victimization in any mocking treatment of commonly accepted social ideals was contagious. Somehow neither the writers nor the readers of burlesque works, or of humorous works in general (and obscene or pornographic texts in particular), ever *keep their hands* completely *clean*. The creation, representation, and even perhaps the study of what has been termed for centuries "low style" literature has contaminated writers, readers and producers with the common stigma and expectations associated with the *género chico* and all works of a humorous nature--what has often been called an "adolescent" or "wise-guy" way of jesting with serious issues. What critics often forget is that the *género chico* of theater, the "Low Style" drama, is only *low* because it contains, through the burlesque mode, all the aspects of the "High Style" drama. The *entremés* was not necessarily a poorer quality product. In fact, because the intention of the interlude was to entertain an audience by imitating the ethos of the main attraction it accompanied, the interlude was necessarily a very fine burlesque imitation of style, theme, character and content.

In general, the *entremés* was more than anything else a hilarious distortion of rather serious issues concerning unhappy marriages, dishonor, and impure blood, for example, for the purpose of making readers or spectators outside the *entremés* aware of how certain things can get out of hand and, at the same time, how funny extreme behavior can be. The uproarious laughter occasioned by the slapstick, stereotyped *rough* characters, word plays, social blunders, vulgarities, off-color sexual allusions, clichés, popular refrains, lewd dances, insults, and curses (in short, "low humor") is all part and parcel of the aims of the burlesque. The laughable situations served to off-set the serious tone of the main theatrical attractions and to cure imbalanced dispositions. In other words, laughter was thought to have balanced the spectators' disposition after viewing the serious problems of the full length play.

The staged event of the *entremés* usually employed a setting which was urban. The urban setting offered a broad range of social types who, when imitated burlesquely in a variety of fictionalized social situations, made for a lot of theatrical fun. The Spanish countryside, by the early 1600's, had been idealized by the celebrated playwright Lope de Vega and rural living, for all of its backwardness, was thought well of. The unusual rural setting for the *Retablo de las Maravillas* is pertinent because "*el panorama de vida rural o aldeana sirve de contraposición burlesca a la imagen idealizada del campo que nos proporciona, por ejemplo, Lope de Vega en sus principales comedias de la primera década del XVII*" (Spadaccini *Entremeses* 17). Lope's idealization of countryfolk is laid open to public inspection in the *Retablo de las Maravillas*.

More important than the *dialogue* with Lope de Vega's idealized comedies, perhaps, is the reality of the staged joke situation. The fact is that Chanfalla's hoax works particularly well in a rural setting where supposedly unassuming types are, in spite of their rusticity, virtuous Old Christians who have been contaminated by urban fears, and, more specifically, bitten by the bug of (il)legitimacy of birth and (im)pure bloodline. The Spanish hysteria concerning *limpieza de sangre* and, to a lesser extent, *limpieza de oficio* was in the consciousness of every Spaniard, rural or urban. While rural townsfolk were quite certain of their own ancestry and that of their neighbors as well, they could be taken in by the rampant hysteria concerning New and Old Christians. Chanfalla and Chirinos play on the rural townsfolks' foolish adoption of urban hysteria in order to dupe them and swindle some petty cash.

In the introduction to Cevantes's *Entremeses* Spadaccini points out quite correctly that the adoption of an urban hysteria quite unrelated to the everyday existence of the townspeople has serious ramifications: "*La grotesca reinvindicación del linaje por parte de los villanos ricos del* Retablo *rige la estructura del entremés. Esa obsesión por la legitimidad tiene obvias ramificaciones socio-económicas y ético-morales*" (63). The burlesque hysteria concerning bloodline may have obvious social and economic ramifications or moral and ethical consequences. All these ramifications and consequences must be interpreted through burlesque, however, because the hysteria over social honor in this small town is a sham.

The townsfolk in the *Retablo* do not simply imitate their urban counterparts, professing high rank, magnanimity and respectability, but they also imitate the ethos of city folk. Their imitation follows the stereotype of what they perceive city folk to be: learned, artistic, refined, reputable, skillful, arrogant, and pompous. They fall prey to Chanfalla's hoax only because they are preoccupied with distinguishing themselves as ideal citizens of Spanish society. Chanfalla orchestrates a mockery of the local town councilmen and their ladies with rules for spectating the famous *Retablo de las Maravillas*:

> Por las maravillosas cosas que en él se enseñan y muestran, viene a ser llamado Retablo de las Maravillas; el cual fabricó y compuso el sabio Tontonelo debajo de tales paralelos, rumbos, astros y estrellas, con tales puntos, caracteres y observaciones, que ninguno puede ver las cosas que en él se muestran, que tenga alguna raza de confeso, o no sea habido y procreado de sus padres de legítimo matrimonio; y el que fuere contagiado destas dos tan usadas enfermedades, despídase de ver las cosas, jamás vistas ni oídas, de mi retablo.[31]

Chanfalla credits the wise fooler "*el sabio Tontonelo*" with the creation of the *Retablo*. Tontonelo is fabricated to make the Spanish audience laugh, but the internal spectators who also hear the name *Tontonelo* do not suspect the sham. Chanfalla stipulates that anyone who does not visualize the *Retablo* is tainted with an impure bloodline (*"raza de confeso"*) or is illegitimate (*"no...procreado de sus padres de legítimo matrimonio"*). Anyone who cannot *see* the spectacle is an impostor of social honor. Indeed, the rules for spectating fraudulently proposed weeding out anyone who had contracted one of these two *common* social illnesses (*"el que fuere contagiado destas dos tan usadas enfermedades"*).

Chanfalla's rules for viewing seem to have to do with morality, honor, fidelity and truth, but the truth of his verifiable wit lies in the last line of his introduction to the *spectacle of miracles.* Chanfalla uses common rhetoric for the fantastic and tells his spectators that they should prepare to see and hear things they have never seen or heard before (*"las cosas, jamás vistas ni oídas"*). Because the contingency for proper viewing depends on legitimacy of birth and purity of blood, both a racial and religious question, those who see nothing of the spectacle must consider themselves bastards, tainted with *converso* blood. The swindlers Chanfalla and Chirinos are able to swindle them because the rural officials are trapped by ideological notions of legitimate origin which have nothing to do with them. They are Old Christians and they know who their ancestors are, yet they, like urban Spaniards, are suspicious of gossips and prefer to accept lies as truth. Ironically, then, they know who their ancestors are but they are not sure *who* they are--herein obtains the burlesque. Appearance is more important than the reality of reputation and, hence, fictionalized versions of events are more important than actual events. The burlesque mode highlights that pure old Spaniards have a difficult time acting out before others who they really are. The burlesque proves to be a hilarious situation and a devastating subversion of the ideology of *limpieza.*

Chanfalla's trick is infallible in a Spanish society that is haunted by the proposed idealism of purity. While the swindler's trick is to make money by pulling off a good hoax at the expense of ignoramuses, the overall function of the burlesque is, ironically, to preserve local townsfolk from the attacks of impractical and impertinent adoptions of urban issues and from attacks of idealism. Mockery of their gullibility based on accepted and self-imposed cultural ideologies sets a humorous example for the gross impracticality of subscribing to legitimate but unrelated ideologies. The targets of the burlesque here are not the country bumpkins themselves (which would make them the *end* of the burlesque). The rural characters are the means to a broader awareness of the contagiousness of extreme and absurd interpretations of social honor and legitimacy.

For all practical purposes, then, the *Retablo* might be considered an exemplary document that, like an original *retablo* (a wooden altar piece that told a religious or historical story, or a box used to represent fictional accounts of history with puppets), tells the story of how and why Spaniards prefer to accept lies as truth, especially when they know they are lies. The jest has made their interpretation of appearances (and, indirectly, that of all Spaniards) more important than reality.

The comicality relies on the human puppets who, driven by their own pretensions and caught in an ideological trap, go to extreme lengths to perpetuate the myth of pure blood and legitimacy orchestrated by the opportunist Chanfalla. Indeed, the credulous appear to be marionettes moved by the strings of contemporary ideology. They appear ridiculous in their gesticulations, jumps and dances. Even the governor and mayor gesticulate with the clumsy actions of poor bumbling comics. The staged result is pure slapstick. The locals try to keep up illusions by mindlessly imitating what they feel are appropriate acts, given the unusual circumstances.

The local townsfolk appear ridiculous as they are victimized by their own *unfounded* doubts. They feel the need to put on airs when Chanfalla assumes the belabored language and defiant stance of a magician and beguiles them with what they must see as sophistication from the city and they want to follow suit. The country spectators are delighted with the possibility of a little entertainment and they welcome Chanfalla who says he is a professional actor. Chanfalla explains that he is on his way to a local religious brotherhood to take charge of theatrical shows, and claims arrogantly: "*Hanme enviado a llamar de la corte los señores cofrades de los hospitales, porque no hay autor de comedias en ella, y perecen los hospitales,...*" (219). The local officials trust that Chanfalla will provide the necessary illusion, but they never suspect that the rogue's trick consists of the conversion of spectators into the authors of their own illusions.

More importantly, *successful* participation in the now "prestigious" entertainment is determined by Chanfalla's stipulation for viewing his show. If the spectators are unwilling to transform reality to see the illusion they will label themselves illegitimate or New Christians. Chanfalla tricks the internal spectators into private doubts. By obliging them to accept fictionalized urban suspicions as the ideology that governs public interpretation of events the locals publicly deny their own perception of reality. Just as Don Quixote's madness based on fictional chivalric heroism makes him appear a public fool, the adopted social obsession concerning bloodline and legitimacy makes the local officials and their families behave in a manner that can only be viewed as crazy and foolish by outsiders: "*¿Está loca esta gente?*" (235). The local townsfolk willingly or unwillingly participate *actively* in the theatrics because to do otherwise would be socially damning.

Entertainment for the sake of maintaining *false appearances* is never without serious consequence, however. In the *Retablo* there is a hefty price to pay for fraud. Benito Repollo, the most stubborn and skeptical of the local townsfolk, makes a fool of himself in order to keep his *good name* reputable. Like all the other spectators he sees none of the extravagant activities that Chanfalla and Chirinos, and the others who follow suit, say are occurring. He *hears* words but does not *see* what the words suggest: an illusion of legendary realities. He too, for the sake of honor and perhaps even amusement, humors himself and the others by playing out on a make-do stage marvelous illusions of unheard-of events. The local mayor is intrigued by the lewd dance pantomimed by his nephew and the imaginary Herodías. He sees his nephew dancing lewdly with no one yet Benito Repollo incites *them* to dance. He is willing to bend the rules of reality in order to enjoy the creations of his imagination. Illogical rules are taken to their logical end: Repollo and his companions end up in battle when they openly opt to apply the rules of Chanfalla's fictional world to the reality that surrounds them.

Unlike the mad hidalgo who, at a critical moment, could not distinguish between Maese Pedro's fictional representation of mock-heroism in a puppet show and the reality of that presentation by Maese Pedro and his puppets, (*Don Quixote* II: 26) these human puppets choose to erase the distinction between fiction and reality. When the army's quartermaster appears and, in the name of the historical Spanish Republic, interrupts the dancing, gleeful screaming and general hoopla, Benito tries to turn the intruder's reality into the collective illusion just as they have turned illusion into a sort of historical reality. Repollo insists that the real arrival of the authentic army is one more illusion created by the wise Tontonelo in order to test the local citizens' identity. In other words, the intruder is like the rest of the entertaining *retablo*, a test. Notice that no matter how often the concerned puppet-master assures him that the quartermaster is not part of the entertainment, Repollo chooses to follow the rules of the collective illusion and mental artifice instead of those prescribed by the senses and physical reality:

BENITO. *Yo apostaré que los envía Tontonelo* (233).

Benito refers to the soldiers as though they were part of Chanfalla's make-believe world that is both test and entertainment. Benito refuses to suspend his disbelief and chooses to maintain the *illusion* of *reality*. Chanfalla assures him of the *reality* of the *illusion*.

CHANFALLA. *No hay tal; que ésta es una compañía de caballos que estaba alojada dos leguas de aquí* (233).

Ironically, Benito makes threats against Chanfalla and the magician Tontonelo when it seems that efforts to avoid unpleasant realities are fruitless .

BENITO. *Ahora yo conozco bien a Tontonelo, y sé que vos y él sois unos grandísimos bellacos, no perdonando al músico; y mirá que os mando que mandéis a Tontonelo no tenga atrevimiento de enviar estos hombres de armas, que le haré dar docientos azotes en las espaldas, que se vean unos a otros.*
CHANFALLA. *¡Digo, señor alcalde, que no los envía Tontonelo!* (233-34).

Benito and Chanfalla volly the illusion of historical reality and historical realities of illusion until Benito strikes the key to the burlesque:

> BENITO. *Digo que los envía Tontonelo, como ha enviado las otras sabandijas que yo he visto* (234, my emphasis).

Benito adamant refusal to distinguish between social realities and the play-world is hilarious because he has, in effect, *seen* absolutely nothing. When it appears that the quartermaster is not an illusion Benito Repollo becomes angry and threatens Chanfalla for having created an unpleasant illusion that is not at all amusing. No one wants an unpleasant imposition by Spanish troops. Repollo only wants to be entertained. He does not want any harsh reality to play a part in his amusement. The quartermaster's return leads to violence. His flippant remarks concerning the arrival of soldiers and their horses infuriate Benito because now he feels they have all been trapped by the fabrications of *Tontonelo* and the historical unpleasantries of housing soldiers.

The Governor, unlike Benito Repollo, had earlier admitted to himself (in an aside) that he failed Chanfalla's test of identity and that he planned to lie to protect his honor:

> GOBERNADOR. [Aparte.] *Basta; que todos ven lo que yo no veo; pero al fin habré de decir que lo veo, por la negra honrilla* (229, my emphasis).

The cover-up to protect his *negra honrilla* is amusing because, ironically, when the Governor covers up what he assumes is his individual disrepute he simultaneously uncovers for readers and viewers the collective obsession concerning honor (and identity) and the townsfolk's collective dishonor. By exposing what is *not* there to be *seen*, he and the others act out like wooden puppets (and in front of their neighbors!) the collective disgrace of those who foolishly adhere to the mania of *negra honrilla*. When the Governor makes an attempt to distinguish between appearances and reality:

GOBERNADOR. *Yo para mí tengo que* <u>*verdaderamente*</u> *estos hombres de armas* <u>*no deben ser de burlas*</u> (234, my emphasis).

the hilarious juxtaposition of "truly" (reality) and "should not be" (appearances) establishes the now *ambiguous* identity of the illusion of historical realities and reality of historical illusions. The Governor's attempt to *get serious* is laughed at by the quartermaster.

FURRIER. *¿De burlas habían de ser, señor Gobernador?* *¿Está en su seso?* (234).

The quartermaster's question, "*¿Está en su seso?*", recalls the over-serious eclesiastic's question to the Duke and Duchess who were enjoying the madness of Don Quixote (II:31). It is, once again, as if Cervantes, through the burlesque, were addressing all Spaniards and their apparent obsession with ideals and miserable realities. Here Cervantes echoes what the *arbitrista*, Gonzalo de Cellorigo, wrote of Spaniards in his *Memorial* of 1600 recalled by P. Vilar and others more recently: Spaniards seem to act "*fuera del orden natural.*"[32] The proof that all rational and proper behaviors have been set aside is evident in Juan's petition, "*que haga salir otra vez a la doncella Herodías*".

JUAN. *Bien pudieran ser atontoneleados; como esas cosas habemos visto aquí. Por vida del Autor, que haga salir otra vez a la doncella Herodías, porque vea este señor lo que nunca ha visto; quizá con esto le cohecharemos para que se vaya presto del lugar* (234).

Ironically, Juan refers to the voices they have heard and not seen. The hilarious opposition between seen/unseen is the paradox that frames Juan's bribe. Juan conjures up the virgin Jewess, Herodías, so that he can do openly and without fear what he would not even dare to do in private: if the quartermaster were to see him dancing publically--and in a lewd manner--with a Jewess, what the quartermaster saw (were it to happen in reality) would be interpreted as a public scandal. Juan assumes that they might bribe the quartermaster with what is now called a "peep show" or "exotic dancing." The intention of the bribe is to either pay the quartermaster off with the illusion of a "peep show" or horrify him with what, in reality, would scandalize him.

The local townsfolk jump at the chance to make good on an illusion. They are not happy to be the recipients of the troops. Just as they readily joined as private individuals to perpetuate the illusions suggested to them by Chanfalla and Chirinos, they band together against the quartermaster in public denial of reality. Their serious concern with *negra honrilla* and social identity is made a laughing matter as the local bumpkins make every effort to ward off the arrival of the soldiers by promoting the illusion of indecency.

> CHANFALLA. *Eso en buen hora, y véisla aquí do vuelve, y hace de señas a su bailador a que de nuevo la ayude.*
> SOBRINO. *Por mí no quedará, por cierto.*
> BENITO. *¡Eso sí, sobrino, cánsala, cánsala; vueltas y más vueltas; ¡vive Dios, que es un azogue la muchacha!¡Al hoyo, al hoyo! ¡A ello, a ello!* (235).

The revelry with obscene activities is quite a hilarious spectacle. The nephew is dancing wildly with *no one* and the mayor is urging him on with the equivalent of the modern catcall. The overly serious quartermaster, who is just doing his job, is caught hilariously in the burlesque test of social identity when Capacho fakes surprise at his inability to see the dancing Jewess.

> CAPACHO. *¿Luego no vee la doncella herodiana el señor Furrier?*
> FURRIER. *¿Qué diablos de doncella tengo de ver?*
> CAPACHO. *Basta: de ex il [l] is es.* (235).

Capacho quickly catches the quartermaster in the jest by labeling him a Jew. The accusation against the quartermaster causes a burlesque riotous situation, starting with a sword fight. The point is that, while the country bumpkins would, in private, gladly have fought against another imposition by the government's soldiers, they never would have done so openly because it was dishonorable. Yet, under the pretense of illusion the bumpkins lead a riot against the quartermaster and the army.

Triumphantly, Chanfalla and Chirinos herald their own success only after Chirinos remarks that, in a sense, they were *saved by the bell* since there was no better ending to their hoax than general chaos.

> CHIRINOS. *El diablo ha sido la trompeta y la venida de los hombres de armas; parece que los llamaron con campanilla.*
> CHANFALLA. *El suceso ha sido extraordinario; la virtud del Retablo se queda en su punto, y mañana lo podemos mostrar al pueblo; y nosotros mismos podemos cantar el triunfo desta batalla, diciendo: ¡Vivan Chirinos y Chanfalla!* (236).

Even Chanfalla is surprised at the extraordinary turn of events. Chanfalla and Chirinos, successful in their hoax, are anxious to try the experiment of social identity on more local townsfolk the following day. Their success was determined by their ability to capitalize on the local officials' unwarranted suspicions and their desire or need to keep up appearances without angering them. The locals do not see themselves as gullible nor do they feel victimized by an unreasonable hoax that makes them behave like fools in public. They want others to believe they are being entertained.

Cervantes's fictional locals are driven to eccentric behavior by the Spanish ideology of purity, an irrational suspicion concerning their own heritage. The irrational suspicion is rooted in their pretentious attempt to cover up their common heritage, education and background from the initial meeting between the tricksters and the local officials. Nevertheless, the *Retablo de las Maravillas* by Cervantes is not merely a simple hoax, although Chanfalla's "*retablo*" played out within the play before a "double" audience might be. The *Retablo*, like the sacred story told on a wooden *retablo*, is a document of human gullibility and willingness to play the game of make-believe when to do so is convenient, profitable or amusing.

The local townsfolks' induced or willing gullibility and their clumsy application of ideals concerning honor and *limpieza* on their own behavior are laughable. Like the mad hidalgo, Don Quixote, they choose fiction over reality, and, like Sancho

Panza they choose feigned gullibility when it is to their advantage to do so. For these bumpkins, the realities of truth and fiction are determined both by perception (the social madness that led to the imitation of what they considered classy--that is, urban snobbism--and by experience of exploitation by the government's armed personnel.

These bumbling comics of the *Retablo* are hilarious because they are wooden characters that are manipulated by the mechanical strings of ideological discourse and social pressure. As human beings who act out populist myths, they would be extremely dangerous. The *Retablo* and its fictional characters are not dangerous, however. From the point that Chanfalla establishes the rules for viewing the show, all that is said and done is in the name of entertainment. The *Retablo* is an amusing *exemplar* of how funny and foolish people look when they put on airs for the sake of appearance and make mockery of themselves and the ideological notions they live by.

In the *Retablo*, what is burlesqued (and hence, travestied, criticized and laughed at) is what has already, by itself, become an absurd version of legendary truth. The burlesque imitation of Old Christian values contingent on *blind* faith is a logical result of inscribing illogical codes for the interpretation of historical events. In the *Retablo* it is the function of the burlesque to point out, at all turns of the dramatic episodes, that the opposition of Old Christians and New Christians, truth and fraud, illusions and concrete reality, serious aims and comic results, does have significance.

In summary, Cervantes means his burlesque interlude to highlight the foolish performance of "pure blooded" Spaniards, especially the sort of ignoramuses that act out fully (and hence blindly) the ideology of *limpieza*. A set of behavioral features are dramatized which, even through the burlesque, form a framework of travesty that can be applied to any concrete historical situation. The perspective employed in the *Retablo* is a well-known burlesque play: it is the play-within-the-play, or in other words, the theoretical mechanics that allow the situation of the *Retablo* to refer to and reproduce itself. The show-within-the-show plays burlesquely on the way in which the fabricated rural Spaniards in ordinary entertaining situations present themselves and their honor to others, the ways in which they guide the impression others form of them, and the kinds of exaggerated behavior they may or may not act out (like wanting to see again the *empty nothingness* they have been *seeing* all along) while sustaining their historical performance before the magical--albeit fictional--performance of the puppeteer's human puppets. Cervantes never makes light of the potential gravity of his burlesque: the puppet-show presents things that are make-believe and always under the control of Chanfalla. The historical show of the rural spectators presents things that are, by contrast, real and hence spontaneous, and unrehearsed.

The popular *entremés* lends itself to the burlesque mode of representation by providing short entertainment and thus relief from seriousness. However, the ability of burlesques throughout history to subvert official culture by imitating it absurdly cannot be ignored. The burlesque acted as a go-between, straddling, as it were, the realms of low and high culture, or of serious themes and their farcical potential. Bakhtin's discussion of laughter and seriousness in *Rabelais and His World* is a model for the social function of the burlesque mode in Cervantes's theatrical interlude: to preserve the serious without the canker of sentimentality one had to make it frivolous and then provide relief through laughter.

The *Retablo* might also be a divisive imitation, not of historical Spaniards, but of the fictional stereotyped old Christians excessively idealized on the Spanish stage by Lope de Vega and others. Like all good burlesques it succeeds in exaggerating the type of *dramatic performance* that might have appeared in the regular production of a "rural" *comedia*-- that is, of course, had Cervantes's *entremés* been produced on stage. The *Retablo* is broader in burlesque tone and style than parody and can serve as a test case and blueprint of what the burlesque mode really is, its many techniques, functions and problems. The reason for this claim is that Cervantes succeeds in plugging the burlesque into the dramatic technique that best captures the theme of appearance and reality: the play within a play. Because the burlesque situation created for and by legitimate (albeit fictional) Spaniards forces readers (or potential spectators) to distinguish between the reality of the public of the *Retablo* outside the *entremés*, in history, and the reality of the spectators of the *Retablo*, inside the *entremés*, in fiction. Readers or spectators must question to what degree Chanfalla's puppet-world is a social reality akin to the play-world of Cervantes's *entremés*? The distinction points out, burlesquely, the potential and actual convergence of *"burlas"* and *"veras."* The hilarious conclusion at the end of the play is that there is no way out of the dilemma of social blindness; it is built into Spanish society.

Burlesque and Scholarly Inquiry

No one, to my knowledge, has ever denied the fact that the burlesque permeates the representative texts studied here. No one has denied that the burlesque is pervasive, explicit, inhering in most details, phrases, images, proverbs, characters and action. Yet, despite global agreement of the burlesque presence and dominance, most of the work on the burlesque in terms of such burlesque texts is only suggestive and intuitive, indicating therein, possibilities, but offering no definitive explanations. The question of various readings or diverse and often contradictory interpretations as well as the provocatively ambiguous historiography of the period are often relevant to one and only one factor: the mode of burlesque in Cervantes's *Don Quixote*. What is the position of the burlesque mode within the literature of the Golden Age?

Burlesque parody, no matter how frivolously amusing, is one of the most calculated and analytic literary techniques. The scatological representations of the love sonnets of Quevedo, the devastating travesty of Góngora's popular legend of doomed yet no-so-tragic young lovers Pyramus and Thisbe, Salas Barbadillo's mockery of practical judgement, and Cervantes's hilarious yet very purposeful burlesque of cherished national myths in the *Retablo de las Maravillas* illustrate the social function of the burlesque. In each case the burlesque is a means for searching out, by way of subversive mimicry, any weakness, pretension or lack of self-awareness of its model. All distinctive and artful uses of "official" or "established" communications are susceptible to burlesque imitation. Yet it has been hard to discuss a major work like *Don Quixote* whose entire narrative mode depends on one burlesque mimicry after another while the meanings of

Cervantes's burlesques have been subject to sweeping verdicts, confusing interpretations and repetitive debates.

One can no longer take basic information or knowledge for granted. This is why it may be a good idea to to put forth--as a conclusion to this chapter and as an introduction to the following analysis of burlesque laughter and serious concern in *Don Quixote*--a concrete example that illustrates both the burlesque mode in general and its serious function in the *Quixote*. The burlesque often deals in deflationary impersonation. In *Don Quixote* the common hidalgo's heroic or chivalric claims, for instance, are represented as burlesques by reason of their conflict with the established norms of chivalric heroism. Romances of chivalry deal "sympathetically" with heroism while the burlesque representation of romances deals distantly or "unsympathetically" with chivalric heroism. The impersonation of heroism is narrated as a travesty yet modern readers (at least during the past 180 years) are often made to feel that his burlesque impersonation--that is, the funny mimicry of the chivalric romances--or the hidalgo's madness--is a madness often dignified by rationality and by nobility of purpose and style.

The imagery of the characters' *ill-fitting* clothes play the role in giving to this burlesque a sense of anachronism, of being out-of-step in modern times. The hidalgo's chivalric attire, as *ill-fitting*, is burlesque, and often, as it is in the Sierra Morena episode, is quite grotesque: the heroic clothes here "caricature" mockingly yet amusingly, the hidalgo's impersonation. The act of highlighting the burlesque ingredient of heroic anachronisms, however, might suggest that the weight of burlesque mockery at the expense of impersonations in chivalric romances could be stronger than at the expense of the impersonator, the mad hidalgo. The ambiguous distinction between the madman and his madness--both very funny and with serious consequences--is the key function of the burlesque mode in *Don Quixote*. The madman's thoughts are noble and heroic but, like his ill-fitting clothes, his thoughts are a mockery of Spain's claims to a heroic destiny. The burlesque mode is both highly comic and highly critical. What follows is a reappraisal of the *Quixote* in terms of the burlesque. The reappraisal highlights the *Quixote* as a paradigm of what burlesque is and what its

diverse functions might be. What readers are to understand
by burlesque (and its related modes) is explained and
illustrated throughout *Don Quixote* with remarkable clarity.

CHAPTER FOUR:
DON QUIXOTE AND BURLESQUE
REPRESENTATION

"*Don Quixote* is a satire which uses the techniques of burlesque. Its author is an accomplished ironist. He was to remain an inspiration to European novelists until the time of Flaubert. The novelistic formula that he invented includes a sophisticated narrative manner known by antomasia as Cervantine, and is based on the opposition between an illusion-haunted hero and prosaic social reality; it is used to mock the one and panoramically scan the other, and has a certain roundness in the conception of character. All this is common knowledge, yet very little of the significant criticism written over the last hundred years has concerned itself with Cervantes as a comic artist--satirist, ironist, parodist, or whatever--and much of it since 1925 leaves the uninitiated reader without even an inkling that Cervantes was any of these things" (Close 1-2).

Don Quixote: Burlesque book

The categorization of *Don Quixote* as a burlesque book is less an eighteenth, nineteenth and twentieth century notion than a seventeenth century one. Anthony Close's provocative argument regarding the *Romantic approach* or the *over-serious* interpretations of Cervantes's *Don Quixote* targets what several hundred years of criticism have either taken for granted or overlooked: that Cervantes's *Don Quixote* is, when all interpretations are done, a burlesque book. Following a lengthy study of diverse critical trends in *Quixote* criticism, Close suggests that modern readers have been misled to believe that Cervantes's narrative is perhaps a study of lost ideals and, through them, lost illusions. He questions readings that reveal that *Don Quixote* is more a tragedy than a *funny book* about a failing hidalgo who rides out as a chivalric hero. Close defines the *Quixote* as a burlesque parody whose very narrative manner is burlesque. Nevertheless, his substitute categorization of this loose and seemingly a-generic narrative is not absolutely clear. He calls *Don Quixote* a satire, a burlesque novel, satiric burlesque, and a confusion of high burlesque with parody, yet his intuitions concerning satire and burlesque seem to be a good place to begin the discussion of *Don Quixote* as part and parcel of seventeenth century burlesque literature in Spain.

Because modern readers have often reacted *sympathetically* to the heroic attempts of the crazy hidalgo and the witty reactions of the gullible peasant, the reading of Cervantes's *Don Quixote*, perhaps more than any other single instance of critical evaluation, has become a test case of what modern receptions or critiques of *classic* works are, of their many polemics and ambiguities. Even though the controversy has gone very far in sophistication, the importance of the debates has been reduced ultimately to one and only one issue: whether the relentless burlesque mode of the narrative should be a primary concern or not. If *it is a purely burlesque work* according to some, others deny the predominance or even importance of the burlesque in the *Quixote*. The phenomenon of the burlesque mode of representation in *Don Quixote* (with all the necessary ramifications which range from parody to travesty to laughter and to amusement) is quite indisputable. Yet the analysis and interpretation of *Don Quixote's* comicality--and even more specifically, the burlesque mode--in the cultural histories of the last two centuries have raised confusions and countless difficulties for readers and critics.

Close certainly is not alone in asserting the comical quality of *Don Quixote*, nor is he the first to suggest that it be read as a funny book. The 1614 apocryphal sequel by Avellaneda to *Don Quixote* Part One is an important indication of how contemporary readers read at least the first part of Cervantes's *Don Quixote* (1605). Contemporary productions that imitated Cervantes's creation in addition to Avellaneda's *Quijote*, such as Guillén de Castro's *Don Quijote de la Mancha* or Salas Barbadillo's *El caballero puntual* and a long list of theatrical imitations catalogued by García Martín, provide others. Clemencín's eighteenth century notes and edition to *Don Quixote* provide another gauge (Bradford). In his 1969 study P.E. Russell argued convincingly that Cervantes's contemporaries read *Don Quixote* as a funny book, and that no matter how influenced modern readers have been by naturalism and the trends of *Romantic* criticism about the serious endurements of the *Quixote*, above all, they still laugh at the madman and his *squire*. In the more recent book, *Cervantes*, Russell explained that Cervantes was careful to maintain a systematic mode of narrating comicality. He insisted that "Gaiety, more than disillusion, is despite what some have suggested, still the prevailing impression it communicates to the open minded reader, specially if the latter can read the book in Spanish" (55).

Russell and Close suggest that the overly serious trends focused on the hidalgo and his representation of ideals. Therefore certain textual problems, such as the hidalgo's madness, became stumbling blocks to a *converse* reading of the *Quixote* as critics tried to make a hero of an antihero. Russell and Close represent the attitude that the mad hidalgo is an unconvincing counterfeit hero whose madness, especially if read in the Spanish original, is at the crux of the text's comicality.

Russell points out that the basis of counterfeit heroism throughout the narrative relies on the disparity between the claims of the hidalgo and those of the narrator:

> Fenced off as he is from the real world by his delusions, Don Quixote is a supreme egotist. We must not be misled by his constant talk of succoring the weak and combating evil; only one thing really drives him--his search for chivalric fame that will earn him a romance devoted to his achievements. Even his total devotion to the imaginary Dulcinea is altogether egocentric. But the fame he achieves in Part I is not what he seeks (*Cervantes* 46).

Thus the hidalgo's madness becomes the mediating factor between outlandish and utopian idealism and harsh social realities. The implication is that the narrative's comicality is never sacrificed for the sake of the hidalgo's idealism. Yet critics such as Avalle-Arce's *Don Quijote como forma de vida*, Castro's *Cervantes y los casticismos españoles*, Lopez González's *La actualidad político-social de España en el Quijote*, S. Madariaga's studies on madness and psychology in *Guia del lector, ensayo psicológico*, Martínez Val's *El sentido jurídico en el Quijote*, Ortega y Gasset's *Meditaciones del Quijote*, and Unamuno's *Vida de Don Quijote y Sancho* have argued, often persuasively, that Cervantes's book seems to be anything but, and *much more than, funny*. Yet there is little doubt that Cervantes thought his book was funny and lauded it for its ability to *divertir* or *desocupar*.[33]

Close and Russell are only two of many who have attempted to explain away the *over-serious* readings. The most serious challenge to nationalistic, patriotic, romantic or perspectivist trends is surely Anthony Close's study, for he attempts to chart the historical shifts in readings only to discover that the *Quixote* is best understood as a burlesque parody. No one has questioned that Cervantes billed his book as an invective against chivalric romances, and that in his mockery of them, the most effective technique of such invective is *burlesque imitation*.

The interpretation of invective and the *burlesque* mode and their literary or social function have created numerous difficulties and confusions. Russell insists that even the invective has been interpreted too seriously precisely because part of the burlesque is determined by Cervantes's writing an invective against the romances of chivalry when such an endeavor was like "flogging a horse that was anyway near dead" (*Cervantes* 25). Russell explains that by 1600 chivalric romances were already out of fashion: "In Spain, though not elsewhere, the vogue of the chivalry books had been in a fast decline since at least the 1580s. The last new chivalric romance had already fallen out of fashion. Thus, Cervantes's harsh mockery of the old-fashioned chivalric romances served at least two purposes: to save the virtues of chivalric ideals from the canker of sentimentality and to bring into clearer perspective the wacky idealism of anachronistic illusions.

Cervantes's declared invective against chivalric romances can best be understood as part of a burlesque which neither completely destroys nor offers the slightest inclination to spare chivalric romances. Certainly by stripping away layers of ideological notions concerning ideal and heroic behavior Cervantes attends to both the aesthetic and moral aims of much of this sort of fiction, but not without bringing to the fore the effect of such an endeavor on readers. It seems that the initial objective of lampooning chivalric romances is readily upstaged by something to which the rules of intentionality do not apply: the reader's amusement and *admiratio* or amazement.

The humorous disposition of Cervantes's book and its readers is inscribed in the prologue to Book I: "*Procurad también que, leyendo vuestra historia, el <u>melancólico</u> se mueva a risa, el <u>risueño</u> la acreciente, el <u>simple</u> no se enfade, el <u>discreto</u> se admire de la invención, el <u>grave</u> no la desprecie, ni el <u>prudente</u> deje de alabarla*" (my emphasis).[34] The friend of the prologue identifies at least six types of readers and their expected reactions to the "funny" book. Most readers will laugh but none will be outraged. In one of the most notorious cases of "self-referentiality" Sancho Panza succinctly confirms what contemporary readers thought of the *true* history of the mad hidalgo's misadventures. Indeed everyone seems to be talking about Don Quixote and his crazy antics:

> --*Pues lo primero que digo--dijo,-- es que el <u>vulgo</u> tiene a vuestra merced por grandísimo loco, y a mí por no menos mentecato. Los <u>hidalgos</u> dicen que no conteniéndose vuestra merced en los límites de la hidalguia, se ha puesto don y se ha arremetido a caballero con cuatro cepas y dos yugadas de tierra y con un trapo atrás y otro adelante. Dicen los <u>caballeros</u> que no querrían que los hidalgos se opusiesen a ellos, especialmente aquellos <u>hidalgos</u> <u>escuderiles</u> que dan humo a los zapatos y toman los puntos de las medias negras con seda verde* (II:2 56, my emphasis).

Here Sancho highlights the fact that no one--not the *vulgo*, the *hidalgos* or the *caballeros*--takes the madman seriously. The adventures of the mad hidalgo are funny in the overall context of Book I because they are extravagant, out of the ordinary, and off the beaten track. They are the antics of a madman. The hidalgo misses the point that those who do not consider him mad consider him an upstart. He hilariously counters Sancho's report of readers' interpretation of *his* extravagant dress and impertinent sallies as knight errant with an explanation of his unusual and somewhat shoddy appearance:

> *--Eso--dijo don Quijote--no tiene que ver conmigo, pues ando siempre bien vestido, y jamás remendado; roto, bien podría ser; y el roto, más de las armas que del tiempo.* (II: 2 56).

The hidalgo points out that he dresses the part of the hero just fine and that if his appearance looks shabby, the shabbiness is due to battles (a hilarious reference to ruthless beatings--*armas/roto*) rather than time or being old-fashioned.

Sancho proclaims the essence of hearsay concerning the hidalgo's imitation of knights errant and their virtues:

> *En lo que toca--prosiguió Sancho--a la valentía, cortesía, hazañas y asumpto de vuestra merced, hay diferentes opiniones: unos dicen: "Loco, pero gracioso": otros, "valiente, pero desgraciado"; otros, "Cortés, pero impertinente"; y por aquí van discurriendo en tantas cosas, que ni a vuestra merced ni a mi nos dejan hueso sano* (II: 2 56).

According to Sancho's report there is no doubt that the written history (Book One) of the mad knight amused contemporary readers with serio-comic oppositions (*loco, pero gracioso. . . valiente, pero desgraciado*). To back up his claims, Sancho has also overheard rumors about the laughable written history of the adventures with his master, Don Quixote, and its success amongst contemporary readers.

Sancho reports that children, youths, adults and older people find the true history of the adventures of the pretentious hidalgo and the gullible squire Sancho Panza to be the *"más gustoso y menos perjudicial entretenimiento que hasta agora se haya visto."*(II: 3 64) If Sancho's account of contemporary readers is accurate, there are two sets of symptoms that must be attended to: readers laugh and there is something that makes them laugh. Cervantes records in

the second part that *Don Quixote* Part One is a funny book
for readers of all ages.

Avellaneda's 1614 sequel to Cervantes's 1605 *Don Quixote*
is ready evidence for establishing contemporary readings. In
his *"Prólogo"* the author of the apocryphal account calls the
history of Don Quixote *"casi de comedia"* (*Prólogo* 51). He
highlights the 1605 book's humorous disposition as the
fundamental difference in the nature of the approach of these
two authors of the history of the mad hidalgo. He suggests
that their intention to *"desterrar la perniciosa lección de los
vanos libros de caballerías, tan ordinaria en gente rústica y
ociosa"* is the same (*"Prólogo"* 51). According to Avellaneda
both he and Cervantes intended to purge readers of the self-
serving books that ordinary and lazy Spaniards were reading.
He also pointed out that the means by which they carried out
their intention was different.

The author of the apocryphal account writes that he has
*"tomado por medio entremesar la presente comedia con las
simplicidades de Sancho Panza"* (51, my emphasis).
Avellaneda means his sequel to be an extravagant
accompaniment to Cervantes's *comedia* of *Don Quixote.*
Avellaneda employs the dramatic category of the *entremés* to
describe the nature of his business: he recognizes that his
apocryphal *Quixote* is a go-between that bridges Cervantes's
Don Quixote, Part One, and Cervantes's promised Part Two
which, ironically, is published shortly after Avellaneda's
apocryphal history. The 1614 apocryphal version is meant to
be a burlesque imitation of Cervantes's 1605 *Don Quixote.*

Avellaneda's intention to delight and entertain readers
with a burlesque interlude of the hidalgo's madness and
Sancho's gullibility promises to be an inoffensive gloss on a
story well begun. The focus of the burlesque imitation is
different: Sancho, along with his wife María Gutiérrez are
appointed the subjects of the sequel. Avellaneda's mocking
version is vindictive. Sancho is an angry, vulgar and
unforgiving Sancho. He is a salaried Sancho. The author of
the apocryphal second part confirms what readers of both
versions learn: *"En algo diferencia esta parte de la primera
suya; porque tengo opuesto humor también al suyo"* (*"Prólogo"*
54, my emphasis). Avellaneda argues that a writer's
disposition and the imbalance of humors affects narrative
behavior: Avellaneda's *opuesto humor*, which could be

described as vengeful and rancorous, determines the ill-humored nature of his narrative.

Both versions deal with a madman by the name of Don Quixote, Sancho Panza, numerous jokes and diverse cures and ugly social realities, but Avellaneda's burlesque sequel tells of a vengeful madman whose crazy acts have seemingly little rhyme or reason and whose cure is imprisonment. Both narratives are marked by a different disposition and perspective toward the characters. Avellaneda's Sancho and Don Quixote depend on but are not like Cervantes's characters. Unlike Cervantes's entertaining tale of a mad hidalgo and amusing excuse for a squire, Avellaneda's story gives an account of terrorizing social deviants who are laughable *and* dangerous. Avellaneda's mocking imitation of Cervantes's *Don Quixote* uses elements of burlesque, but in the prologue to Book Two, Cervantes made it well known that the grotesque distortion of the humorous disposition into a dark imitation and serious lampoon against his own characters were hardly received as a laughable matter.

No matter what the reaction of Cervantes, the point is that the comments in Avellaneda's *"Prólogo"* highlight Cervantes's satirical or burlesque disposition. Avellaneda's comments on the humorous disposition of Cervantes's narrative are echoed in other contemporary accounts. The wide-spread influence of Cervantes's *Don Quixote* can be witnessed in theatrical imitations and a variety of glosses throughout the seventeenth century. (See García-Martín) These recorded readings are convincing indications that for nearly 100 years after its writing, *Don Quixote* was considered a funny book. There is no doubt that Clemencín's notes in the Bradford edition, *Indice de notas*, indicate that *Don Quixote* was persistently read as a book of burlesque and ridicule: *"Es cierto que Cervantes tiró á ridiculizar cierta clase de hidalgos de la Mancha"* (66). The implications are clear: *hidalgos* appear ridiculous because their imitations of bookish heroes are burlesque pretensions.

Early seventeenth century readers did not seem to question Cervantes's mockery and ridicule. They were simply amused by the hero's burlesque antics in *Don Quixote.* Yet the reception of the *Quixote's* mockery and ridicule has not always fared so well historically because the cultural baggage necessary to appreciate comicality is not always transhistorical. Clemencín called attention to the difficulty of reading comicality in the *Quixote*. In particular he cited Capmany's preoccupation with readers who are unfamiliar with the seventeenth century system of conceptual patterns needed to appreciate the book's humor. Don Antonio Capmany implicates readers of translations and foreign readers, and uninitiated readers as potential misreaders of the *Quixote*:

> *En efecto (dice): ¿cómo penetrarán debidamente el talento exquisito de este autor, cuando ameniza y engalana su locución con <u>frases burlescas,</u> dichos festivos y voces graciosas; cuando sazona el lenguaje de Sancho con plausibles refranes y naturales alusiones; cuando Don Quijote imita los idiotismos caballerescos y los términos antecuados; cuando adorna el diálogo de los demás interlocutores con todos los donaires y delicados equívocos de la expresión castellana, si entre los mismos españoles no es el vulgo quien siente toda su fuerza, sino las personas que poseen perfectamente la lengua?*[35] (My emphasis).

Capmany highlights the humorous composition and significantly burlesque style of Cervantes's text: burlesque sentences, festive sayings, witty words, popular proverbs, vulgarities, imitation of chivalric nonsense, archaisms, and word play. The challenge was and is to interpret the *Quixote*'s burlesque mode of representation.

P.E. Russell argued that some of the *Quixote*'s burlesque allusions are unavailable to modern readers. He believes the comic impact was stronger for Cervantes's contemporaries than it is now for modern readers because contemporary readers were "still familiar enough with these works at first-hand for them to respond to the burlesquing of their contents with an instant discernment that, in the absence of markers, may well elude the modern reader" (*Cervantes* 25). The implication is that Cervantes's narrative is laden with burlesque patterns, techniques and markers which challenge readers to learn to appreciate ridicule and understand the function of the book's amusing humor. Francisco Ayala adds another serious difficulty concerning modern readers and the comic sense of the narrative:

> *Al lector actual, formado en el Naturalismo, y para quien*
> *la demencia no pasa de ser, o es ante todo, una enfermedad*
> *objeto de estudio y una desgracia digna de compasión, la*
> *burla del héroe loco tiene que repugnarle; se sentirá obligado*
> *a apartar de sí cualquier tentación burlesca; y, desde luego,*
> *no percibirá tampoco ese escalofriante titilar del espíritu a*
> *través de las brumas de conciencia perturbada, que diera al*
> *demente su prestigio antiquísimo, convirtiéndolo en un ser*
> *sagrado y sometiéndolo al trato ambivalente que a lo*
> *sagrado se aplica siempre* (Haley *El Quijote* 178-79).

Ayala pinpoints the historical error of judging the *Quixote* by modern standards and categories. The effect has been that in spite of the overwhelming textual evidence that comicality is central to the narrative, the majority of studies of *Don Quixote* either take humorous aspects for granted, make mention of them in passing, or simply disregard them altogether. There is a large body of critical literature dealing with *Don Quixote* in terms of a wide variety of serious cultural aspects including contemporary folklore and folk culture, mythology, classical and contemporary literatures, genre distinctions, rural and urban manners and customs, contemporary medicine, polemic political factors of the day and of a glorious yesteryear, social and moral concerns of Spain's consciousness of political, social, economic and moral decadence, elitist and popular notions about religion and ethics, serious philosophical difficulties concerned with idealism and lost illusions, psychological studies of madness and its relation to society, and popular and learned lexical and semantic curiosities.

There are few books which contain as many utterances which intimate historical correspondences with contemporary society as does *Don Quixote* with the contemporary Spanish society in which Cervantes lived, and wrote. In an effort to establish historical relations between the text and Spanish society many cultural aspects have been analyzed and appraised. Certainly the breadth and diversity of critical investigations of this overwhelmingly multifaceted text provide some of the necessary historiographical and cultural groundwork against which any discussion of burlesque must be tested. These studies by some of the most celebrated scholars of nearly four centuries and countless countries provide clues to a deeper understanding of the workings of the overall jest of *Don Quixote*. No matter how *serious* or in earnest these apparently historical utterances in the *Quixote* might seem on their own, and no matter how closely they seem to represent contemporary society, they are embedded in a burlesque narrative which reminds readers that it is possible and often even necessary to have *fun* with all that appears to be grave or moral or historical.

Cervantes breaks down the legendary perception of past and contemporary events that haunted Spaniards during his lifetime by slating burlesque's irreverence against chivalric sentiments and ideal love, thereby exposing through laughable images "false seriousness and false historic pathos" (Bakhtin 1968, 439). The perception of crisis--be it moral, economic or political--breeds concern for transition and change. Burlesque is thus both effect and cause for building a critical awareness of how others might confront puzzling situations and difficult issues. Cervantes effects the burlesque mode by interpreting tragic and comic events through the distorted eyepiece of the burlesque. The result is that readers see a caricature of a Spain that foolishly believes in and lives by official *myths*. The strip-tease of the showy caricature of common Spaniards reveals that the mad hidalgo is not the only one dressed in *ill-fitting* clothing. The mockery of pretentiousness and the strip-tease of Spain's ill-fitting clothing lead to the authentic emotion of *laughter*. The counterfeit representations rely on the contradiction between the intimate and less than glorious setting of La Mancha and a common hidalgo who is less than a tragic hero and ideal conceptions of them. The result for readers is that the burlesque does not permit them the comfort of believing blindly in what was being said or imagined about Spain, its past or present. For this reason, interpretations should not avoid the burlesque, but rather highlight the strategic spots where the burlesque functions ambiguously as both *funny* and serious.

Surely most investigations of the *Quixote* point to a somewhat ambiguous but pertinent relationships between contraries such as history and fiction, reality and illusion, sanity and madness, or seriousness and playfulness. Cervantes's 1605 and 1615 narratives critique the established traditional borderlines between these historical, cultural conventions. It follows, then, that an argument can be made for a discussion of the seriousness of the jest. Cultural historians have argued that the history of madness is also the history of sanity and that any history of irrationality must rely on, quid pro quo, the history of reason.[36] There is much to be gained on this from close inspection of the functions of the burlesque mode. An objective of this study has been to demonstrate how serious cultural aspects of society are enmeshed with and within burlesque discourses. Another concern has to do with the nature and function of the burlesque mode itself. Because the burlesque mode of discourse highlights through mockery the artifices that hold a cultural society, and any representation of it, loosely and precariously, together, *Don Quixote*'s burlesque mode, along with its predominant comicality, must be analyzed critically rather than simply taken for granted.

Recently, critics have been called to seek historical correspondences through the narrative's jesting and apparently burlesque and parodic nature. Both cultural historians (such as Vilar and Maravall) and literary critics (such as Close, Russell, Auerbach, McCallum, and Creel) look to analysis of burlesque patterns as a means to identify correspondences between the fictional text and the social reality in which Cervantes produced the *Quixote*. Their findings are of particular interest to this investigation because they open up new avenues and channels for approaching the problems of comicality and burlesque.

In Creel's study concerning *Don Quixote* as a humorous representation of a culture in crisis, he calls *Don Quixote* a broad satire and stresses the "broad humor of the work's mock-epic style, including the parody of heroic dignity and situations where comical ineffectiveness of Don Quixote's attempts at physical action becomes glaringly apparent (21). Creel points out that *Don Quixote* is a humorous representation of a culture in crisis. His reading labels the *Quixote* as a social satire which, no matter what the social comment, rests on madness, the times and the ideological implications of the chivalric code. Creel, however, by concentrating on the historical correspondences that are often right on the mark, can at most only suggest how the historical references for Cervantes's fiction might relate to the pervasive comicality of the burlesque narrative.

McCallum's historical approach to an interpretation of the protagonists madness in *Don Quixote* stresses that analysis of mockery and ridicule somehow provides the key to reading through Spanish ideologies of 1605 and 1615. McCallum calls attention to the relations between what Maravall has called *Utopía y contrautopía* and its implications for analysis of comicality in *Don Quixote*. McCallum argues that "This disparity between an ideal or utopian performance and a ridiculous performer happens to be the key to Cervantes's art of parody; the clue to the connection between the hidalgo's madness and Spanish ideologies; and, finally, it is this disparity that relates effectively the fictional narrative to its age" (13).

The interests of McCallum, like those of Creel, can lead to investigations that seek out historical dimensions beyond or within satire and parody. Though different in approach, what these studies provide are valuable clues to the "imaginary social relations" between the madman and a society that perceived itself to be in crisis.[37] In an earlier attempt, the historian Pierre Vilar provided an explanation of the role of comicality in *Don Quixote* and its ideological connections to Spanish society. Vilar appraised the historical significance of Cervantes and his novel:

> Spiritual grandeur and nobility carried to an extreme, an inexhaustible fount of popular wisdom, a decaying fabric in an expanding world--these contrasts take on life in Quixote-Sancho, ideal and reality, individual and society. Since Cervantes possesses a genius for comedy, this makes us laugh, but as he has a gift for nuance, these contrasts are in effect complementary. As he has also a sense of the universal, the story becomes philosophical; but it remains also national and valid for its time. Don Quixote seeks medieval solutions to a modern world: crusade, adventure, the mystique of a world fashioned by the sword and embellished by the pen. Madness, it is true, but only because of the implicit anachronism. A symbol of Philip II, and of a Spain ineffective because ill-adapted, the armour of Don Quixote presents the same challenge to the bourgeois as Chaplin's jacket does to the worker: these are historical turning points and at the same time eternal works of art. Cervantes is the earliest and the subtlest of the *arbitristas*, those analysts of "decadence"; he lies at the heart of his nation's history. (*Spain* 43).

According to Vilar, then, *Don Quixote* is a funny book with serious implications for its time. It is an index to the Spanish crisis and an indication of transition and change. *Don Quixote*'s mockery of anachronism challenges and tests the social function of the ideologies represented by the ill-fitting clothes worn by the common fifty-year old hidalgo from La Mancha. Vilar also confirms that while Cervantes used an entertaining medium for *arbitrismo* and building social consciousness, he was able to make valid comments on the perplexing problems of his time.

There can little doubt now that these studies by social and cultural historians of the relationship between *Don Quixote* and the perceived crisis of Spanish imperial decadence are, in a sense, springboards for the study on the ideology of mockery in the literature that accompanied, step by step, the national perception of *decadence*. Cervantes's approach to *arbitrismo* is different than that of Sancho de Moncada or González de Cellorigo and the effect is necessarily different as well. Vilar understands that the subtle playfulness of the narrative's humorous disposition, historically speaking, does not lead to any violation of social and cultural conceptual patterns which, if advocated, might conjure up negative feelings or anger. By way of the burlesque mode Cervantes makes challenging statements about social, moral and economic decadence in an apparently harmless and non-threatening manner. The underlying premise is that through the subtle playfulness of the burlesque mode of representation there is no violation of social and cultural concepts. If Cervantes had approached the difficult questions of his time in another way the not-so-ambiguous discussions of women and marriage (in terms of Marcela, Dorotea or even Camila), honor and nobility (in terms of Alonso Quijano el bueno, Fernando, the Duke and Duchess) and hard times (in terms of the the unpaid innkeeper, the unsalaried Sancho or the young Andrés), for example, might have conjured up negative feelings or anger.

Theoretical approaches to the phenomenon of amusement are similarly indispensable for understanding the role of comicality and especially of burlesque and the relationship between an amusing text such as the *Quixote* and its particular historical age. *Don Quixote* is filled with seemingly harmless or purely entertaining jokes, tricks of thought and speech, illogicalities, and paradoxes which present unusual events which often seem uncanny, strange or even shocking. Sancho, for example, is made the governor of the "island" Barataria for the entertainment of the Duke and Duchess. Sancho relies on his own common sense to get by as governor and, surprisingly, his judgments seem sound. He provides reasonable judgments in unreasonable situations and readers laugh. Sancho's governorship is a hoax, otherwise his pretensions would have to be judged as those of a bogus impostor. The narrative provides readers with subtle or obvious clues that indicate that words and actions need not be taken seriously. Readers are reminded that much of the narrative is suspect of burlesquing since the narrator's words, for example, are not much more reliable than the mad hidalgo's. Narrative clues consistently remind readers that they are confronting a fictive representation of entertaining situations and amusing objects and not the situations or objects themselves. There is the connection between the burlesque mode of representation and ideology. A systematic study of most joke situations and motifs in the narrative would indicate that jokes are not directed satirically against the various characters, but rather, burlesquely, towards the attitudes, values and beliefs they represent through words and actions.

There is no better test for the function of burlesque than an investigation of the one constant target of many jests. The mad hidalgo is persistent in resisting attacks against his chivalric persona and in defending his heroic ideals. In his deluded state of mind he maintains his loyalty to the pursuit of reestablishing the Golden Age in spite of the constant jeering, joking, and mockery occasioned by the public exposure of his curious and *strange* madness. The mad hidalgo is steadfast in his imitation, but his perseverance is not only pertinent to the burlesque, it is an indispensable element of the burlesque. His persistence in explaining away failures or criticism with unreasonable reasoning based on chivalric discourse, and his easy and quick recovery from beatings time and time again are part and parcel of the narrative technique which only allows certain pains and gains to last as long as the narrator needs them to increase amusement. The mockery does not end here with the hidalgo. Amusement is not the only effect of burlesque mockery.

Ironically, modern criticism has somehow assumed that readers feel compassion and sympathy for the mad hidalgo and his apprentice-squire. Thus, they fail to accept the constant jesting as harmless, and instead deal with hilarious situations as serious matters for psychological, moral and philosophical speculation. When the distance between readers and literary characters is lessened, as it is through burlesque mockery, readings not only gain seriousness, but also a sense of "realness". Throughout the *Quixote* the narrator(s) tease readers by asking them to judge the words and actions in the episodes as if their role as readers influenced impending episodes and further interpretations of the text. The tease cautions readers against minimizing the distance between *reality* and *art*, *history* and *fiction*, or play and the ordinary world and at the same time gives them the freedom to enjoy the stripping of layers of fraudulence without feeling outraged.

In *Don Quixote*, the jesting is a means to a desired end: Cervantes means to expose a *consciousness* of fraud, self-deception, false pretension and anachronism--precisely the weaknesses of his age. There is no doubt that the *Quixote* can be considered a sort of treatise on jokes, a manual for jokesters, a social history of joke butts, and a register of seventeenth century comic techniques. But it is much more than this. The question that confronts readers is, how is it possible for so much *historical* evidence and cultural analysis to enter a seemingly frivolous and funny book? What is the connection between the burlesque mode of representation and meaningful content? Roger Scruton's four propositions concerning amusement as a kind of *aesthetic interest* can be helpful in determining the historical foundations of fictive burlesque: since the amusing discourse of *Don Quixote* requires distance and the hoaxes *a mode of reflective attention*, since the *Quixote* does not concern itself with the acquisition of new beliefs or the verification of old ones, and since the burlesque narrative is not a motive to action and is not felt for some *ulterior reason*, burlesque relies a great deal on abstract thinking and transcends both practical and immediate historical considerations.[38]

The effect is that through the burlesque mode of representation Cervantes is able to make readers consider *as a laughing matter* the historical implications of *fictional* explorations into the social, moral, political and economic crises that everyone was talking about and at least imagined they were suffering on an everyday basis. The analysis of a relation of conflict between what Spaniards perceived, remembered, or imagined the crisis to be, and the conceptual patterns of the amusing Cervantine narrative and their attendant expectations provides a litmus test for puzzlement and the ability to handle uncomfortable situations adequately while relying on previous historical experiences and preconceived cultural notions. Thus, an *anatomy* of amusing narrative behavior in the *Quixote* becomes an accurate tool for the interpretation of the burlesque mode of representing critical issues.

The Basis for Mockery

As scornful derision of persons and their acts, *mockery* is a paradox. It acts as an indirect go-between for Don Quixote's madness based on chivalric romances and the *historical* situations in which he attempts to act out, madly or anachronistically, his utopian projects. Mockery also functions as a mediator between Cervantes's fictional account of a supposedly *real* hidalgo gone mad in an everyday (but off-kilter) Manchegan reality of the early 1600's, and the ideas of contemporary readers familiar with concepts for how behavior and thought should be, what they seem to be and how they are. Ridicule through the burlesque mode has to do with uncanny defects, vulgar distortions, and grotesque deformities in fictionalized *everyday* living. As Aristotle argued, ridicule or any malicious belittling of persons usually belongs to the genre of the ugly.

In *Don Quixote*, ridicule has to do with caricature and the grotesque. Don Quixote's archaic, crude armaments physically deform his slight figure and make him sluggish and heavy. His armor weighs him down and makes his physical movements exaggerated and slow. The distortion of normal human movement is funny. The armor is amusing because it is archaic and theatrical even by contemporary seventeenth century standards, and perhaps even more so for what the rickety metallic equipment covers up. Underneath the exaggerated and dramatic exhibition of metal and ribbons there is an old, scraggy hidalgo who pontificates about proper (but fictive) chivalric behavior at every turn.

Willy-nilly, the archaic armor becomes an offensive and defensive physical mediator between the supposedly sane society and the mad hidalgo. Similarly, Don Quixote's madness becomes the means for arbitration between fiction and reality. The mad hidalgo bills himself a heroic knight errant, but he comes off to readers, outside the text, and spectators, inside, as a hilarious unconvincing counterfeit. Don Quixote's imitation is, by nature, a mockery while his "ill-fitting' chivalric clothes caricature burlesquely the hidalgo and his pretensions.

There is a symbolic link between the mocking label *triste figura* and false presumptions of Spain's past glories, now dusty, impoverished, and a sham deserving of mockery. There is no doubt that the mad hidalgo asserts that he rides out to right wrongs, save damsels in distress, and to serve his lady, Dulcinea, in a time when justice is effected through different means--through the efforts of the local authorities called the Santa Hermandad, for example--, when *doncellas* are more often than not *semidoncellas* who do not desire or need his help, and when serving a lady was an economic fiasco more than an experiment in virtue (I:43 526).[39] The apparently harmless parody of those chivalric romances which were already out of fashion is not unlike the physical and *ill-fitting* exaggeration in the hidalgo's armor. It is much more than parody. It is the mockery common to burlesque.

The role of parody cannot be disregarded. The hidalgo's imitation of fictive heroes is guided by the rigors of bookish knight-errantry (enchantments, unrequited love, battles, etc.). He imagines first, and then verbally and physically vindicates in what is depicted as contemporary Spanish society, the social function of a fictional heroic knight. The hidalgo's mad portrayal is a grotesque deformation of the fictive chivalric model. The burlesque representation, like the clumsy, armored hidalgo, is strange, unsightly, ugly, and always funny. The incongruous meshing of the "ill-fitting" armor (and all it represents), and the bony mad hidalgo with all his verbalized foolish delusions of an ideal (albeit fictional) yesteryear is an amusing mockery of a bookish knight's utopian "good intentions."

The madman's venture to reinstate *utopia* in what Maravall labeled *counterutopia* is, through the mechanism of burlesque, stripped of dignity. Those who meet him or read about him scoff at his continuous self-presentation as knight-errant. The value of the hilarious counterfeit for the overall burlesque is that humility and self-glorification which work together for the chivalric hero, work against each other and the mad hidalgo.

Close explains the apparent dichotomy of Cervantes's narrative that is at the same time the fundamental grounding for almost all burlesque mockery:

> There is throughout the novel a double viewpoint on events and on the hero's part in them: the deluded attitude of the hero himself, and the realistic attitude of any sane, sensible observer (a category which normally excludes the simpleton Sancho). The fact that we look at events from both standpoints enables Cervantes simultaneously to manipulate both "high" and "low" burlesque with all their variants. This is because, when judged by the realistic criterion, what Don Quixote says anddoes as self-supposed knight-errant represents "high burlesque" (though it occasionally slips into the low form), and what other characters say and do, when measured against the assumptions of the deluded viewpoint, represents "low burlesque" (though often it mimics that viewpoint and passes into the high form). Thus, so far from being an unusual burlesque because it quickly denies its nature, *Don Quixote* is unusual because it so perfectly and comprehensively fulfills it (Close 20).

Close highlights the function of the "double viewpoint" to explain how Cervantes makes possible both high and low burlesque. What Close calls the "double viewpoint" needs further exploration. The crux of the mockery in *Don Quixote* rests in that *space* between two conventionally distinct but mutually dependant realms of existence: that of social experience (the mad hidalgo's experience with everyday Spaniards in everyday life) and chivalric or literary discourse (the mad hidalgo's experience with extraordinary fictive adventure books which he, in his elevated discourse, believes is also an admissible and necessary alternative reality). Indeed, *baciyelmo* is a paradigm of how the conflict is illustrated: what is real in one realm of existence may or may not be real in the other (I:21). In fact, an analysis of the paradox *baciyelmo* does not really yield new meaning; instead the amalgamation falls apart into the two opposed realities.

The madman, in confusing a historical reality with a more ideal one, or labeling one thing as its opposite, does not adhere to preconceived patterns of logical thought or what might be considered normal or sane perceptions of the everyday world. He mistakes prostitutes for courtly ladies and address them, perhaps during their business hours, as though they were damsels of noble blood. He addresses the women according to his chivalric script, but his actions, interpreted against the established norms of social relations, are playful and theatrical, even insulting. The burlesque frame relies on the disparity between the rather outlandish discourse of love and the particular social situation of prostitutes for hire: the women expect sexual hire and the madman, a potential customer, answers with woebegone conventions of courtly love.

The amalgamation of the hidalgo's perception of who he is and what he represents, and the narrator's portrayal of the mad hidalgo's identity and what he represents for these everyday Spaniards--prostitutes at an inn--is meant to amuse readers. The readers' reflective attention is focused on the uncanny relation of conflict between what they are forced to imagine on the one hand, and well established conceptual patterns concerning real experience on the other. Amusement has less to do with deviance from normative behavior than one might expect and much more to do with an attempt to test the relative validity of assumptions and preconceptions concerning these two opposing realities which, for a split second, seem to be uncompromisingly fused.

Readers must consider the importance of social, behavioral and literary deviance: one cannot appreciate the incongruous conceptual conflicts drawn through burlesque imitation without recognizing the diverse cultural and historical categories and the set of established behavioral codes which determine what is considered to be normal and proper conduct in terms of those categories. The mad hidalgo is burlesqued precisely when he ventures out to reinstate an unreal, utopian world plucked from books of fictional and utopian chivalry. The narrative focuses on his crazy efforts as he promotes archaic ideologies which were still given lip-service among contemporary Spaniards even though most (with the notorious exception of the mad hidalgo) recognized their obsolescence for contemporary times. What is amusing about the hidalgo's high-blown utterances and his ludicrous antics relies on the readers' ability to compare ideals with inappropriate and funny material representations of them and to perceive common oppositions as hilarious conceptual possibilities.

The hidalgo, when mad, reconciles the incongruous split of heroic ideas and unheroic practice by propagating, as Blanco Aguinaga and McCallum have argued, the traditional ideology of *spirit* over *matter*. In this sense, the madman as the fool of tradition is labeled a social deviant by those perceived to be *sane*, yet he is the only one who acts in accordance with the official, although archaic, code which functioned as a means to protect the attitudes toward a glorious imperial past. Here the burlesque mode is coextensive with historical conditions. The madman imitates the bookish activities of chivalric heroes of the legendary heroic *Golden Age* and acts out these values, ideals and conventions accepted readily as part of the common consciousness in a Spain at the throes of a material crisis. His bookish portraiture of the archaic official codes is nothing more than a representation, although a deliberately burlesque one, of such a value system. Although these values and conventions might have been commonly accepted in principle, in practice they proved to be archaic, worn out, and certainly ridiculous when repeated in the words and mimicked in the antics of the madman and his apprentice Sancho Panza. The target of the burlesque here is the gamut of contemporary dominant ideologies.

One example is a crude burlesque of what contemporary Spaniards thought of the hidalgo's ridiculous portrayal of a bookish knight errant. The innkeeper, a believer in the truth of chivalry, succinctly states his different position from that of the mad hidalgo: "*Eso no -respondió el ventero-; que no seré yo tan loco que me haga caballero andante; que bien veo que ahora no se usa lo que se usaba en aquel tiempo, cuando se dice que andaban por el mundo estos famosos caballeros*" (I:33 398). The listeners Cardenio and the priest, like the readers, are amused at the diverse yet interconnected forces in the innkeeper's explanation of why he does not mimic knights errant like Don Quixote. The informed spectators of the narrative and readers outside the text recognize that the innkeeper is off base because they know, unlike the innkeeper, that chivalric fiction is fiction. Readers appreciate the innkeeper's misjudgment since his perception of chivalric books and their place *in* and *as* history is based on *secular* readings of chivalric romances, and is buttressed by those ideological notions concerning Spanish heroism and glorious adventure encouraged by dominant sectors of contemporary Spanish society. The innkeeper's misjudgment is laughable to the listeners and readers outside the narrative, but his argument is not entirely alien from those assumptions and values which must have been part of the common consciousness of many Spaniards.

The essence of the final version of Cide Hamete's history is this: a contemporary hidalgo, one of many like him, imitates fabulous fiction and is mocked routinely with everyday jokes and some fantastic, out-of-the-ordinary jokes by everyday Spaniards from all walks of life. These jokes and impractical hoaxes humorously recreate and reproduce an air of the fabulous and fantastic common to the outlandish romances of chivalry. Readers are not fooled by the theatrics. So, the amusement is heightened when all sorts of historical character types (innkeepers, merchants, prostitutes, noblemen, etc.) consistently debunk the penchant of putting outlandish and woebegone ideals into practice. The amusement is particularly spirited when the fellow who is putting fictive chivalric ideals into practice is an everyday Spanish hidalgo, Alonso Quijano *el bueno*, gone mad and outfitted ludicrously to prove his fictive anachronism. Moreover, comicality is enhanced when the mouthed and enacted ideological notions are not mocked or labeled obsolete, but hailed as sound by the hidalgo's contemporary, the innkeeper. Neither the visions projected by the chivalric romances of yesteryear, nor the hidalgo's rather unsightly representation of them, nor *Don Quixote* in its entirety, can be understood outside the burlesque mode of discourse within which acts, words, and expressions are situated as part of contemporary ideological discourse and social intercourse. The burlesque constantly tests the scope and direction of Spanish society.

Mockery and Reason

Burlesque mockery attends to the experience and awareness of the populace by creating an artificial perspective which distorts and distances familiar social notions about ideals and historical reality. In Cervantes's book the mad hidalgo tests the endorsement of commonly accepted attitudes concerning heroism and an idealized, glorious Spain by trying them out in an everyday, not-so-glorious or bookish setting. As in his madness, idea and materiality are forced to coexist as a possible, although paradoxical, unit for readers. The opposing realms of existence (or the opposition of *appearance* and *reality*) raise philosophical questions pertaining to the "reality of the conceptual world and about intellectual creativity," to discourse, or the manner in which any reality might be represented, and to the dichotomy of "experience and concepts" (Colie 13). The mad hidalgo, in order to live out his charge, must bend social rules. Don Quixote's madness forces him to operate at the limits of what for others are restricted categorical boundaries, but for him are boundaries which always seem to be shifting with the help of imagined or imposed enchanters and enchantments. Don Quixote, for example, chooses to attribute the contradiction between his own conception of lady Dulcinea (the epitome of perfection), and Sancho's burlesque representation of Dulcinea as a *wholesome* crass country wench to enchantment. Amusement here relies on the burlesque paradox of accepting the reality of a hoax as the unreality of enchantment.

The burlesque imitation operates within two realms of existence at once, each realm involving its own set of codes and values. The hidalgo's life as a knight-errant is both an authentic representation and a counterfeit of bookish heroism. Spectators and readers can be *misled* to read for only the social reality surrounding the hidalgo or only the fictional reality that the hidalgo imitates through madness. They can read for both only through the burlesque. The consistency of the burlesque mockery of mistaking illusion for reality throughout the narrative, and not just in terms of the mad hidalgo's activities and words, can be demonstrated with an example of the authenticity of the written history about the mad hidalgo's adventures.

At several points in the narrative, readers are teasingly encouraged to make their own decisions about the authenticity of the stories they are told. In mockery of Cide Hamete Benengeli's authority as the original author of Don

Quixote's adventures, for example, readers are asked to interpret the words, actions and sentiments of both the author of the history, Cide Hamete, and the teller of the tale of Montesinos's Cave, Don Quixote. In II: 24 readers are *reminded* by the translator and *told* by Cide Hamete, the *original* author of the mad hidalgo's adventures, that they must interpret the hidalgo's story on their own because Cide Hamete Benengeli does not consider himself an authority on the matter. In fact, Benengeli argues that he cannot be held responsible for what does not appear to be possible, authentic or real:

> *No me puedo dar a entender, ni me puedo persuadir, que al valeroso don Quijote le pasase puntualmente todo lo que en el antecedente capítulo queda escrito: la razón es que todas las aventuras hasta aquí sucedidas han sido contingibles y verisímiles; pero ésta desta cueva no le hallo entrada alguna para tenerla por verdadera, por ir tan fuera de los términos razonables* (II: 24 223, my emphasis).

Cide Hamete explains that he finds no *reasonable* way of accounting for the tale of extraordinary experiences that the hidalgo tells Sancho and the licenciate. He argues that neither the real *hidalgo* nor the imaginary noble *knight* that the hidalgo represents through his madness could lie:

> *Pues pensar yo que don Quijote mintiese, siendo el más verdadero hidalgo y el más noble caballero de sus tiempos, no es posible; que no dijera él una mentira si le asaetearan* (II:24 223, my emphasis).

Cide Hamete distinguishes between the integrity of the mad hidalgo (the reality of the illusion) and the virtues of the bookish knight that the hidalgo imitates burlesquely (the illusion of reality). In mockery of his own role in the artistic process of providing an historical account, Benengeli, ironically, refuses to take responsibility for reporting illusion as reality or reality as illusion. Benengeli interprets the tale without taking into account the mediating factor of burlesque representation: the outrageous tale is perfectly acceptable within the parameters of the mad hidalgo's burlesque imitation of bookish chivalric adventures and the hidalgo's

set of real experiences with the Spaniards he encounters on a
daily basis. When Benengeli begs readers to judge the
hidalgo's tale themselves he makes a laughing matter of his
own historical authenticity as the original author and also
creates the illusion that readers have some historical
relationship with the story as it is being told:

> *Por otra parte, considero que él la contó y la dijo con*
> *todas las circunstancias dichas, y que no pudo fabricar en*
> *tan breve espacio tan gran máquina de disparates; y si esta*
> *aventura parece apócrifa, yo no tengo la culpa; y así, sin*
> *afirmarla por falsa o verdadera, la escribo. Tú, lector, pues*
> *eres prudente, juzga lo que te pareciere, que yo no debo ni*
> *puedo más* (II: 24 223, my emphasis).

The irony is that Benengeli requests that the judgment of
authenticity be made by readers outside the text. What
readers outside the text understand about the burlesque
framework within which Benengeli's original story of the mad
hidalgo's tale, is, of course, much more than Benengeli is
supposed to understand. The very mechanics of writing
history, authenticity and originality, are burlesquely mocked
when Benengeli turns to the implied reader to distinguish
between the false appearance of the reality of his reporting
and the true reality of his absurd illusions about writing
histories.

The shifting or stretching of the boundaries between
appearances and reality or truth and fiction can be explained
through a brief analysis of the hidalgo's madness. If readers
look closely at what the enigma of the hidalgo Don Quixote is,
they recognize at least two matrices or modes of thought
where both rational and irrational discourses are at play.
Don Quixote's apologies, like the narrative in which they are
projected, are a clear example of paradox and of the exercise
of ingenuity designed to entertain and capture the critical
attention of audiences who are sufficiently acquainted with
the nature of the traditional arguments and the curious
nature of the hidalgo's madness to understand and
appreciate the hilarious situation. The hidalgo's apology on
arms over letters (I:37-38), for example, was perhaps a
worthy and defensible subject matter for bookish knight-
errants, and even perhaps for the yesteryear armed cavalry of

the reconquest of the Iberian peninsula and conquest of the
Indies, but when arms and letters are evaluated and arms
are favored over letters by the mad hidalgo, the subject
matter becomes contaminated by the ridiculously unsuitable
and unconvincing defender. Ironically, his discourse about the
superiority of arms through his superiority in letters is
convincing, and for this reason the burlesque mode of
representation has historical implications.

The narrator reminds readers that Don Quixote is as out
of order here as he was when he discoursed knowingly in
front of the ignorant goatherds:

> "*dejando de comer don Quijote, movido de otro
> semejante espíritu que el que le movió a hablar tanto como
> habló cuando cenó con los cabreros, comenzó a decir:
> Verdaderamente, si bien se considera, señores míos, grandes
> e inauditas cosas ven los que profesan la orden de la
> andante caballería*" (I:37).

What is intimated in the comparison is that the mad
hidalgo has, hilariously, wasted another excellent speech.
What is laughable about the serious discourse delivered by
the hidalgo is that he shows off his rhetorical skills and
incites the admiration of onlookers, yet he instills only
admiratio or amazement in an audience who finds his
pompous rhetoric or outlandish babbling, perplexing, and
inappropriate to the situation. The encomium, delivered
during a presumably noisy meal--Sancho, readers are
reminded, asks his master to sit down and be quiet several
times--receives little attention because the goatherds are a
less initiated audience and also because they are much more
concerned with eating than listening to the high-blown words
of the strangely dressed hidalgo. The heroic words are
doomed to mockery.

When the mad hidalgo discourses about the good old days
he refers to a utopia when "*todo era paz entonces, todo
amistad, todo concordia*" and to a harmonious world where
the ground was fertile and productive, where honesty
outweighed the need to be ostentatious and when a work
ethic was in effect, when spirituality ruled materiality, and
when there was no fraud or artifice, unlike "*nuestros
detestables siglos*" (I:11 156-7). All this praise of a utopian
yesteryear cannot be taken seriously because the pronouncer

is ridiculous, the pronouncement is utopian, and because it is senseless babble to Don Quixote's immediate spectators who, "*sin responderle palabra, embobados y suspensos, le estuvieron escuchando*" (I:11 157). Readers are familiar with the conventions of the mad hidalgo's discourse as well as the nature of its deliverer: in each case the reading audience is amused, but only because they handle the two conflicting realms of Don Quixote's imaginary adventures and his everyday misadventures as well as the attitudes, feelings and experiences normally associated with them, and the accepted codes governing them.

Don Quixote is a madman who reasons unreasonably or who unreasons reasonably. There is little doubt that the mad hidalgo's apology concerning arms and letters acquires a marked appearance of logical discourse which, taken out of its burlesque context, *seems* serious. The truth beyond the apology is that the madman's arguments might playfully persuade that he is in the right about favoring the Golden Age and deploring the decadence of the current age, and furthermore, that he is in his right mind, when, however, there is no doubt in the reader's mind that he in not. The apology spoken to the goatherds, however, in spite of its logic and particular attention to contemporary decadence is completely unreasonable because of the manner in which it is given. The inherent mockery points toward the perception of contemporary historical decadence, although never without setting this decadence against the pitfalls of emulating a woebegone fictional idealization.

The relationship between historical realities and the burlesque mode of representing them needs further illustration. In the above situation, the appearance of a logical argument concerning apparently pressing problems of contemporary Spain is tacked onto the façade of a true history of a valorous knight errant. Readers, too, are often persuaded by the convincing arguments; a review of critical studies concerning the apologies indicates that this is so. What is often missed is that readers are offered only the appearance that Don Quixote is on the mark, but owing to an overwhelming opposing contradiction (madness, costume, situation) the narrative never allows that anyone declare the mad hidalgo lucid or right, except perhaps, on that single mode of logically articulating an argument. The narrative persuades readers continually that there is always a compromise between logical indiscretion and indiscreet logicality based on his *idée fixe*. On this point P.E. Russell is representative of critical attitudes: "Cervantes is careful, by some trick of language, style, or situation, to remind us that, even in his lucid moments, we have to deal with a madman" (*Cervantes* 75). Readers are never allowed to forget that, even in the most serious discourses, they are reading a burlesque narrative.

Both Russell and Close point out that the romantic critics found madness and the burlesque nature to be obstacles to considering the narrative a study of an idealistic hero and his lost illusions in an indifferent society. Now it is clear that whenever the paradox and the jest are being read and accepted on their own contradictory terms, the paradox can easily become *orthodox*, and what is a burlesque book issues forth a potential discussion of national identity. There is no lack of studies on serious moral issues, social, political, economic and religious issues, popular-traditional and conventional literary issues that have sprung from analysis of the *Quixote*. The burlesque mode does not contradict nor is it contradicted by the value of these explanations. These studies provide the necessary historical correspondences to which the narrative burlesquely points. Yet the narrative is consistent and persistent in directing readers' attention to the *ingenio* (the equipment that makes up the burlesque mode of representation) to solve the intellectual incompatibilities (both perceptual and conceptual) and puzzling anomalies. The burlesque mode teasingly strips away layers of contradictions and exposes uncomfortable and hilarious associations concerning appearance and reality, history and fiction, morality and immorality, rationality and irrationality.

Cervantes illustrates that to deal with ideal significances of opposing and exclusive categories concerning intellectual, moral, and spiritual life in an apparently unintellectual, immoral and physical fashion is to play with human understanding in a most amusing, delightful and harmless, but often perplexing way. The implications of burlesque as a mode of representation raise the following difficulty: If burlesque is the totalizing element of the narrative within which all other interpretations must be discussed: is humor serious and is entertainment meaningful? This is a question about the results of a long burlesque narrative which need to be dealt with later. For now it is enough to indicate that burlesque creates a reaction of *admiratio* and laughter in its audience, it forces recognition of absurdities, it surveys absolute attitudes and preconceived notions concerning very serious issues and because of its jocular nature, it entertains and amuses.

Entertainment, Amusement and the Burlesque Narrative

Anthony Close poses another aspect of the problem of amusement: did frivolous, festive literature encourage contemporary Spanish readers to think seriously about topics explored in a burlesque manner? He argues through some wordplay that:

> Cervantes enchanted his contemporaries by his comic fantasy (*'regocijado ingenio'*), his inventiveness as narrator ('invención'), his intelligent good sense (*'discreción'*), and his *decoro and decencia*. Whether they grasped the finer nuance of his novel, such as the subtlety of his characterisation, or the general view of life that it conveys, we shall never know. It probably would not have occurred to them to think very seriously about such topics when considering a work of fiction (10).

There is little doubt that Cervantes was aware of the important role of entertainment for his contemporaries. In his introduction to Cervantes's *Entremeses*, N. Spadaccini suggests that Cervantes was well aware of the impact that public entertainment had on spectators and specifically, the difference between private reading and public performance. The *Quixote* does provide notions of the social function of entertaining artistic texts. For instance, the local priest from Don Quixote's hometown discussed the function of artistic productions with the canon from Toledo who met up with the caravan that was taking the caged hidalgo back home. In the verbal diatribe the priest reveals the decadence of the contemporary public theater, offers the canon his own opinion of bad plays, and moreover, tells what sort of function the play ought to have for spectators:

> *de haber oído la comedia artificiosa y bien ordenada,*
> *saldría el oyente <u>alegre</u> con las burlas, <u>enseñado</u> con las*
> *veras, <u>admirado</u> de los sucesos, <u>discreto</u> con las razones,*
> *<u>advertido</u> con los embustes, <u>sagaz</u> con los ejemplos, <u>airado</u>*
> *contra el vicio y <u>enamorado</u> de la virtud; que todos estos*
> *afectos han de despertar la buena comedia en el ánimo del*
> *que la escuchare, por rústico y torpe que sea, y de toda*
> *imposibilidad es imposible dejar de <u>alegrar</u> y <u>entretener,</u>*
> *<u>satisfacer</u> y <u>contentar</u>* (I:48 570-1, my emphasis).

The priest calls attention to the similarity in social function of theatrical and literary productions. What stands out in his reasons for eulogizing entertainments and diversions is that he identifies the role of many elements in a well orchestrated production: jokes make spectators giddy and light-hearted, the seriousness or truths (*veras*) teach a lesson, the events and outcomes amaze the audience as they become aware of the reasons and motives for the actions and tricks. The jesting *examples* of behavior viewed on stage or read in texts make audiences more astute and also respectful of virtue while, at the same time, and provide comic relief for common vices. He suggests that these representations "*para entretener la comunidad con alguna honesta recreación, y divertirla a veces de los malos humores que suele engendrar la ociosidad*" are socially necessary as safety valve (I:48, 571). He also bills books and theater entertainment as a cultural and social staple since all people need relief from physical and emotional stress (*el arco armado*):

> "*para honesto pasatiempo, no solamente de los ociosos,*
> *sino de los más ocupados; pues no es posible que esté*
> *continuo el arco armado, ni la condición y flaqueza humana*
> *se pueda sustentar sin alguna lícita recreación*" (I:48 572).

According to the priest, theatrical and literary productions have the social function of being an "*espejo de la vida humana, ejemplo de las costumbres y imagen de la verdad*" which serves to instruct and entertain (I:48 569). That is, amusing texts can entertain meaningfully.

These priest's statements concerning the social function of entertainment bring up three matters for discussion here. The first has to do with the contemporary regard for dramatic and literary representations as a means for depicting, however fictionally, reality and truth. Plays and poetry provide two of the most immediate means of addressing current issues. Plays are a valuable tool for the representation of urgent social messages because dramatic representation involves interpretation of sometimes sketchy or rudimentary scripts through everyday actors' actions and words. They also require direct and indirect communication with spectators who have certain expectations. Poetry, is also a valuable means of attending to social ills because of its economical means of production and distribution. Verbal jokes, in particular, have a similar social function since, by nature, they are often short, memorable, apparently harmless, and easily spread by word of mouth. Verbal jokes, thus, are also a handy means of dealing with urgent social issues.

The second matter of concern is, of course, the social function of amusement as a cure for social ills. Renaissance lay medical studies indicate what modern psychologists are just now beginning to understand scientifically: laughter is a means to keep healthy. An extravagant and burlesque representation of someone's obsessive perception of an apparently serious issue--war, hunger, poverty, social deviance, work or lack of it, a bad marriage, jealousy, melancholia, loneliness, and death--elicits laughter, and through laughter, a cleansing of the respiratory system, an increased level of adrenaline and blood flow.[40] It is well known now, as many suspected in the seventeenth century and even earlier, that laughter increases the oxygen level in the system and relaxes the human body by relieving tense muscles. The employment of amusement, diversion, and entertainment is used throughout the *Quixote* as a means for characters to handle difficult situations. The physiological response to relieve stress in emotionally trying times is also a function of amusement. Sancho and the Quijano household's gaming activities at the moment when the hidalgo lies on his deathbed and breathes his last is an indication that Cervantes was well aware of the *restoring* powers of laughter (II:74 591).

The therapeutic value of laughter and amusement elicited by teasing is brought to the fore time and again in *Don Quixote*. The teasing begins with the book's title and teasing address to the *desocupado lector* in the prologue, and from there on, the entertainments at the inns, Sancho's popular storytelling, the puppet show and the prophesying ape, the public ridicule of the mad hidalgo in the streets of Barcelona, the tricks of the traveling theater troupe, the private jokes (and especially the talking head of Don Antonio Moreno), and the expensive theatrical hoaxes perpetrated by the idle wealthy, and so on. The therapeutic value of social entertainment in *Don Quixote* is targeted by those who desire to cure the mad hidalgo while others, like Don Antonio Moreno or the Duke and Duchess use the excuse of social entertainment to perpetuate the hoaxes that keep them and their friends laughing.

A more general argument for the social value of entertainment and the defense of chivalric romances in particular, is made by the priest at the inn :

> *Ya os he dicho, amigo -replicó el cura-, que esto se hace para entretenernuestros ociosos pensamientos; y así como se consiente en las repúblicas bien concertadas que hay juegos de ajedrez, de pelota y de trucos, para entretener a algunos que ni tienen, ni deben, ni pueden trabajar, así se consiente imprimir y que haya tales libros creyendo, como es verdad, que no ha de haber alguno tan ignorante que tenga por historia verdadera ninguno destos libros* (I:32 397).

The priest highlights the relationship between reading entertaining fiction and playing games. For those who need or desire to be entertained, reading chivalric romances is just as fine an entertainment as chess, ball games, or tricks. Moreover, he points out who the participants, audience, and spectators need be: those *privileged* folk who, according to their state, need not work due to their economic condition, shouldn't work due to their social condition, or are incapable of it due to their physical condition. Reading is, of course, a mental activity which exercises the rational faculty and is good for everyone.

The priest accepts the social value traditionally attributed to entertainment. Entertainment might be the result of participation in a game, hearing a joke, viewing a play, or reading an amusing book. In most situations in *Don Quixote*, it is one of the most serious community members, the priest, who values and salvages entertainment for the good and health of the community. To entertain the mind is to promote mind over matter, the spirit over the physical body. In an earlier chapter the priest saved *Tirante el Blanco* from the fire for its merit as an entertaining book. The excited priest highlights, although somewhat indirectly, how mental entertainment must keep him from overt sensualism:

> ¡Válgame Dios! -dijo el cura, dando una gran voz-. ¡Que aquí esté Tirante el Blanco! Dádmele acá, compadre; que hago cuenta que he hallado en él un tesoro decontento y una mina de pasatiempos. Aquí está don Quierieleisón de Montalbán, valeroso caballero, y su hermano Tomás de Montalbán, y el caballero Fonseca, con la batalla que el valiente de Tirante hizo con el alano, y las agudezas de la doncella Placerdemivida, con los amores y embustes de la viuda Reposada, y la señora Emperatriz, enamorada de Hipólito, su escudero. Dígoos verdad, señor compadre, que por su estilo, es éste el mejor libro del mundo: aquí comen los caballeros, y duermen y mueren en sus camas, y hacen testamento antesde su muerte, con estas cosas todo eso, os digo que merecía el que lo compuso, pues no hizo tantas necedades de industria, que le echaran a galeras por todos los días de su vida. Llevadle a casa y leedle, y veréis que es verdad cuanto dél os he dicho (I:6 117).

The priest, the supposed paragon of virtue, legitimizes frivolous literature ("*un tesoro de contento y una mina de pasatiempos*") and saves the bawdy intrigues of characters like the virgin "My-life's-Pleasure" for himself and the barber. The priest's advice to the barber to take the book home and read it is all the more hilarious because the priest's commendation reveals an ambiguity in the word *necedades*: The chaste priest's eulogy appears less serious than truly praising since his approval of comicality and verisimilitude in *Tirante el Blanco* revolves around the libidinous aspects of the chivalric romance (Murillo 117 n27). The priest's legitimation of *Tirante el Blanco* marks the not-so-surprising (but not always commented) connection throughout the *Quixote* between entertaining literature, sexuality, censorship, and morality.

Burlesque as a Literary Category:
Cervantes' Working Definition of Burlesque Mockery
 There is no shortage of comments inside the burlesque narrative on the entertaining nature of the "history of the

valorous knight Don Quixote." To paraphrase L. Hutcheon's recent theories about *Parody* (very apropos to the study of burlesque), the unending "mirroring process" of the narrative is due to the constant presence within itself of many discourses on its own validating principles of burlesque and entertainment. Sancho's telling comments on Don Quixote or the book about him have been mentioned above. The *second author* of the "funny story", as the first reader of the history of the mad hidalgo's misadventures, qualifies the nature of unfinished portions of the "historical adventures" that he sought out for their more entertaining qualities. The tease is that without the hidalgo's crazy perseverance and meddling: "*el mundo quedará falto y sin el pasatiempo y gusto que bien casi dos horas podrá tener el que con atención la leyere*" (I: 9 142). (The two hour time limit is of course a jest). Moreover, the burlesque mode relies on the teasing representation of the hidalgo's misadventures and the storyteller's perseverance in telling readers that he is occasionally meddling in the way things are told.

Besides the teasing references to self-referentiality and the writing process itself, Don Quixote provides other insights as to how the burlesque mode transforms how things are treated. Chapter 22 of Book II provides some general perspectives concerning the category of festive literature, writers and their readers. The burlesque mode is indirectly, subtly suggested in the statements of the *cousin* who accompanied Don Quixote and Sancho to the Cave of Montesinos. The cousin declared himself a humanist who wrote books that were meant to entertain:

> *para dar a la estampa, todos de gran provecho y no menos entretenimiento para la república. . . de donde podían sacar y tomar las [libreas] que quisiesen en tiempo de fiestas y regocijos los caballeros cortesanos, sin andarlas mendigando de nadie, ni lambicando, como dicen, el cerbelo, por sacarlas conformes a sus deseos e intenciones* (II:22 205-6).

The cousin explains that he provides court gentlemen with entertaining tidbits that they otherwise would have to scurry about to get. This is a burlesque of what some people will do to get their hands on some lewd materials and also of distribution practices in general. But it is more than that because here, as elsewhere, a character's observation about culture and amusement is one more way for the *Don Quixote* text to "turn inward" in order to reflect upon its own burlesque mode and entertaining constitution.

The cousin's ensuing description of his entertaining works provides, moreover, some fundamental insights on contemporary readership. The cousin maps out the target audience for his books as a bunch of marginals who would be better off diverting their attention from their own problems: *"Porque doy al celoso, al desdeñado, al olvidado y al ausente las que les convienen, que les vendrán más justas que pecadoras"* (II:22 206). The list of marginals suggests that those who most benefit from the festive literature are these preoccupied marginals who need diversion from their personal plight. A jealous husband, an unfortunate fool, or those who consider themselves forgotten and abandoned are prime subjects for mockery, yet they are targeted as those who would most benefit from this sort of diversion built on mocking imitation.

It is of pertinence to the burlesque mode in and out of *Don Quixote* that the cousin's entertaining book imitates Ovid in a burlesque fashion.:

> *a quien he de llamar Metamorfoseos, o Ovidio español, de invención nueva y rara; porque en él, <u>imitando a Ovidio a lo burlesco</u>, pinto quién fue la Giralda de Sevilla y el Angel de la Madalena, quién el Caño de Vecinguerra, de Córdoba, quiénes los Toros de Guisando, la Sierra Morena, las fuentes de Leganitos y Lavapiés, en Madrid, no olvidándome de la del Piojo, de la del Caño Dorado y de la Priora; y esto, con sus alegorías, metáforas y translaciones, <u>de modo que alegran, suspenden y enseñan</u> a un mismo punto.* (II:22 206, my emphasis).

He argues how his book explains, in a joking fashion, an entire pseudo-history based on bits and pieces of *true* history that any contemporary Spaniard must recognize. As Murillo highlights in a footnote to his edition of the *Quixote*, the mention of *"el Angel de la Madalena"* on the tower of the Madalena church is a mockery since contemporary readers would recall that the angel's body was not something to be praised as a work of art for its body was deformed (206 n9). There is a great number of such contemporary burlesques

that, with the lapse of time, most modern readers might miss
entirely. The particulars of the nature of the burlesque mode
can be appreciated by modern readers as well as they were
appreciated by Cervantes's contemporaries. The cousin
highlights the nature of burlesque, significantly for this study,
as that pattern of making a mocking imitation of some
traditional and recognizable model of virtue. The discussion
of his festive, burlesque works points to the social value of
the entertaining counterfeit and, by inference, to the historical
foundations of the burlesque. In this sense, like with
Sancho's comments, the cousin's contentions are, burlesquely,
self-references about the nature and value of overall
burlesque mode in *Don Quixote* and, through extension, the
majority of texts labeled burlesque.

Parenthetically, it is of historical interest to point out some
of the various ways in which this section of the *Quixote* was
originally translated. The translations give us a clue as to
how burlesque literature was recognized and perceived by
other European communities, and to how peculiar burlesque
was to Spain.[41] The early English translation of *Don Quixote*
catches the essence of the burlesque mode: "for imitating
Ovid in it, by way of mocking," and indicates that the word
burlesque had not yet entered the Englishman's vocabulary.
The word *burlesque* did not enter the English vocabulary until
after 1640. One might suspect that romance language
translations come closer to the original use of *burlesco*
employed here by Cervantes.

The Portuguese translation is disappointing: "*porque
n'elle, parodiando Ovidio*" reverts to explaining burlesque by
means of parody. The Italian translation of 1625, however,
"*imitando Ouvidio, dipingo como per burla*" (my emphasis)
catches the jest but only signals the gist of mockery by
implication in the word *burla*: The French translation of 1618
"*A l'imitation d'Ovide, j'ay en bouffonnant dépeint que fut la
Giralda de Seville*" brings us closer to the connection of jesting
and mockery with the burlesque. The French and Italian
versions lose completely the notion of burlesque mode
however, as the jesting nature is attributed to the cousin and
not to the narrative itself. There is little doubt that the
conscious perception of burlesque mockery as a bonafide
mode of representation in art at this time in history was
peculiarly Spanish. In Spain, the burlesque had already

become a bonafide literary category, while in other literary traditions the notion of burlesque as a mode was not yet perceived as an authorized and official category with its own distinctive mode.

Cervantes's Spanish text is clear on the issue of the burlesque mode. The nature of what content is mocked is evident in the cousin's careful description of what sorts of things he covers and uncovers in these burlesque works which sport a *gentil estilo* (and what Murillo calls a joking avoidance of portraying the book for what it was: *"obra de erudición farragosa y pueril" (Don Quijote* 206 n13)):

> *Otro libro tengo, que le llamo* Suplemento a Virgilio Polidoro, *que trata de la invención de las cosas que se dejó de decir Polidoro de gran sustancia, las averiguo yo, y las declaro por gentil estilo. Olvidósele a Virgilio de declararnos quién fue el primero que tuvo catarro en el mundo, y el primero que tomó las unciones para curarse del morbo gálico, y yo lo declaro al pie de la letra, y lo autorizo con más de veinte y cinco autores. . ." (II:22 206).*

Within the narrative's "self-referential" pattern, the by now "burlesqued" cousin implies that he creates a false history by recording in an anecdotal fashion, everything that was left out of the true history. In fact, the cousin legitimates his counterfeit history by telling the hilariously gruesome details of the cure for the first person who suffered syphilis (*morbo gálico*). The cousin's history of origin and originality is, of course, both a burlesque and a model of how the burlesque turns on the propagator himself.

The whole episode is a burlesque imitation of some excesses by "humanist" scholars and their penchant for digging up the origins of even the most insignificant phenomena. Sancho's tease regarding the investigation of the first person to scratch himself is the completion of the burlesque and the awareness of it. The burlesque here relies on the apparently imbalanced inversion of ends and means. There must have been an original sufferer of the common cold or syphilis, but the perception of originality matters less than the illnesses themselves and the manner in which they are transmitted. These communicable social illnesses have origins that, for obvious reasons of anonymity, are obscured and hidden. Therefore, they can best be viewed only from the perspective of the receiver or the victim. That is, these illnesses--like madness and by extension, the burlesque mode in art--show *symptoms* in the victim and effect *admiratio*, amusement or disgust in the reader or spectator. The symptoms of the burlesque mode are the ways in which the burlesque distortion leaves its marks.

Symptoms of Burlesque: Burlesque Patterns in *Don Quixote*

Like a common virus that silently attacks the entire human body and leaves visible unsightly marks only on vulnerable parts of the skin's surface, the burlesque mode of representation is inherent throughout the *Quixote* and here too its symptoms are most obvious at the surface where the narrative is most fragile and vulnerable. Close examination of some of the *Quixote*'s notorious narrative games and burlesque patterns illustrates the mechanics of how the burlesque mode teasingly eats away at appearances to reveal a rather *unseemly* reality underneath.

To begin, Cide Hamete is a foreign, shoddy historian who cannot be trusted to narrate accurately what took place. The translators are unreliable not only because the nature of their business which puts any translation of a reliable original into question, but also because, in the *Quixote*, translators add their own comments and suspicions concerning the original Arab historian's qualms and beliefs. The clever appearance of shoddiness is due to a diffused sense of authorship which involves a series of relationships amongst those who have a hand in delivering readers the final textual versions of Book I and II. The text presents itself as a hand-me-down. The Arab's generated history is supposedly found, translated, and offered in translation to Spanish readers. Readers are distanced from the true origin of the history by the deliberate ambiguity and ironic ploys created between author, original text, and the text we hold in our hands. The mechanics of distance encourage readers to see that no matter what Cide Hamete or the translator writes, the history has become part of popular invention. In fact, there are many hands in the reporting of this story: Cide Hamete Benengeli who first wrote the story in Arabic, the Morisco who translated it into Spanish, and Cervantes who edited it and published it. The unreliable origins of the adventures of the mad hidalgo create a laughable situation because none of the writers have to take sole responsibility for what is written.

The diversification of responsibility creates an illusion of distances between the three writers and hence between readers and the "authentic" story of the hidalgo Don Quixote. The result is that the adventures are laughable because they are akin to common hearsay. In fact, readers are led to believe that they should suspect the "authenticity" of the storyteller as much as they question the seriousness of the manner in which the adventures are told. The example of the translator's interference in how the story of the hidalgo's adventures is told illustrates how burlesque mockery subverts the very notion of "authenticity." The translator makes a mockery of his own work by deciding to maliciously censor Cide Hamete's less interesting original:

> *Dicen que en el propio original desta historia se lee que llegando Cide Hamete a escribir este capítulo, no le tradujo su intérprete como él le había escrito, que fue un modo de queja que tuvo el moro de sí mismo, por haber tomado entre manos una historia tan seca y tan limitada como esta de don Quijote, . . .* (II: 44 366).

The translator's criticism of Benengeli's limited original is funny because readers have been entertained all along by the Arab's dry story. The irony is that here the Morisco translator is trying to gain some fame for himself by denouncing the Arab's dull story. Readers are burlesquely cajoled into believing that their hand-me-down has been critically altered to reflect the interpreter's interests. Whose text are readers reading? Where and what is original? Readers are encouraged to appreciate the translator's corrected narrative "*no por lo que escribe, sino por lo que ha dejado de escribir*" (II:44 36). The double-edged irony is pertinent to the burlesque narrative games: readers are asked to judge not what the translator has left for them to read but rather what he has not written or has left untold. The irony is that readers cannot judge what has not been recorded. Such narrative games are, ultimately, the underpinnings of a burlesque mode of narrating the story of social madness.

The narrative is written in such a fashion that the various meddlers interrupt the "historical" narration to add their own "two bits" as if translators were supposed to interpret and add to or subtract from what is or is not there to be translated with the purpose of sprucing up the story. The description of the episode in which Don Quixote and Sancho are stampeded by a horde of pigs emphasizes the destabilizing function of meddling. In Chapter 68 of the Second Part readers are told the details of a stampede of pigs and the resulting injuries of the mad hidalgo and Sancho Panza. The translator reports that: *"Don Quijote, arrimado a un tronco de una haya o de un alcornoque--que Cide Hamete Benengeli no distingue el árbol que era--"* (II:68 554, my emphasis). The translator adds what Cide Hamete left out: the superfluous distinction of whether the tree to which the hidalgo was clinging was a beech or an oak tree. He mocks the Arab's inability to distinguish between Spanish trees while emphasizing his own malicious attention to useless detail. The translator invents what isn't there and offers his inventions to readers to make up for gaps in the "original" text. Ironically, readers are encouraged time and again to believe that without the interference of the various hands in the reporting of the original history there might be very little information of interest. The translator suggests that the original story is dry and limited. Readers are led to believe that his playful additions and deletions have improved the story, that is, the burlesque narrative is matched at each step by another burlesque story of how the burlesque narrative was found and recomposed.

Unreliability in the narrative is tied to "authenticity" and burlesque imitation. Readers are told by another narrator that the original translator is also responsible for reporting comments written in the margin by the original author:

> *"Dice el que tradujo esta grande historia del original, de la que escribió su primer autor Cide Hamete Benengeli, que llegando al capítulo de la aventura de la cueva de Montesinos, en el margen dél estaban escritas de mano del mesmo Hamete estas mismas razones"* (II:24 223).

The translator's comments are a marvelous burlesque imitation of such narrative games regarding "authenticity":

> *Entra Cide Hamete, coronista desta grande historia con estas palabras en este capítulo: "Juro como católico*

*cristiano..."; a lo que su traductor dice que el jurar Cide
Hamete como católico cristiano siendo él moro, como sin
duda lo era, no quiso decir otra cosa sino que así como el
católico cristiano cuando jura, jura, o debe jurar, verdad, y
decirla en lo que dijere, así él la decía,como si jurara como
cristiano católico, . . . (II:27 249).*

The literary theatrics implied in the word *"Entra..."* mock
Benengeli's role as a reliable author: Arabs who swear as
Christians are liars. The translator makes fun of Cide
Hamete's presumptuous and dramatic entrance thus
systematically debunking Cide Hamete's authority for telling
readers anything that they might take for truth. The
repetition of variations on *"jura"* and *"decir"* highlight the
unreliability of what is now only supposedly "sworn" or
"said". According to the translator the first author of the
history is just another shoddy character in this account. He
points out that the Arab historian blasphemes by swearing
as a Catholic Christian, and burlesquely qualifies for readers,
that swearing as a Catholic Christian means little or nothing
to Cide Hamete, who indeed, was a lying Arab. Again, the
narrative marks the burlesque nature of its counterfeit
history.

   Underlying the bilingual translator's subversion of Cide
Hamete's authority is still another ambiguous mockery of
several common ideas about Arabs, Moriscos and Christians.
To read through the translator's mockery, readers must
accept the premise that Catholic Christians do not lie, while
Arabs, especially when they swear as Catholic Christians,
are not telling the truth. The translator attempts to clear up
the distinction between what Cide Hamete said and what he
meant to highlight the potential unreliability of Old and New
Christians within the already questionable context of an
Arab who swears as if he were someone he is not. The
problem of multiple narrators is thus compounded by the
unreliability of each, thus creating the burlesque
accumulation of imitators and impostors. Readers are told
that Cide Hamete is a liar and that the Morisco translator
translates on a whim and according to his own particular
interests. None of the storytellers can be trusted and readers
can never be sure who has stacked the deck against whom.
Clearly, readers are never quite certain who is telling them

the central story, or, absurdly who is responsible for the *story* of the story.

For example, in the episode following the ride in an enchanted boat, Don Quixote and Sancho come upon a very unusual sight characteristic of a chivalric romance: a noble lady dressed to the hilt, riding a pony and surrounded by her entourage. The narrator cannot be trusted when he tells readers what Don Quixote sees even though they know that what Don Quixote sees is usually unreliable: "*Sucedió, pues, que otro día, al poner del sol y al salir de una selva, tendió don Quijote la vista por un verde prado, y en lo último dél vio gente, y llegándose cerca, conoció que eran cazadores de altanería*" (268). Readers are encouraged to trust Don Quixote's judgment even though they know that he sees things askew. The trick is that the narrator offers the following description of what Don Quixote sees as truth:

> *Llegóse más, y entre ellos vio una gallarda señora sobre un palafrén o hacanea blanquísima, adornada de guarniciones verdes y con un sillón de plata. Venía la señora asimismo vestida de verde, tan bizarra y ricamente, que la misma bizarría venía transformada en ella. En la mano izquierda traía un azor, señalque dio a entender a don Quijote ser aquélla alguna gran señora, que debía serlo de todos aquellos cazadores, como era la verdad* (II:30 268).

The description of what the mad hidalgo sees (an elegant woman dressed elegantly and oddly, riding a palfrey) is an alarmingly faithful representation of what readers expect him to see through his madness. Readers don't expect to be sold his imaginations as narrative fact, however. The narrator pulls the reader's leg by narrating through the eyes of Don Quixote whose perception is often distorted. To enhance the joke, he chooses to narrate a scene of which readers must necessarily be suspicious. The words *palafrén* and *hacanea* have been marked narratively as chivalric inventions early on in Part One. The priest's mule is called a *palafrén* when Dorotea is atop it as Princess Micomicona, for example, and the enchanted Dulcinea rides a *cananea* or *hacanea* (II:10 111). The unreliability is increased when the narrator questions whether it is a *palafrén* or a *hacanea*, two words which have been marked systematically for getting Don Quixote off-track. The shifts on descriptive phrases are also a way of the burlesque mode. The final irony of the scene that the storyteller narrates *through the eyes of Don Quixote* comes in *"como era de verdad"* which may only refer to the woman's role as a *grand lady* who leads the band of hunters. If the ironic twists of the narrative's burlesque language were not confusing enough, the matter of unreliability is complicated further by drawing readers into the make-up of the history. In Part Two of the history readers of Part One also become characters. The lady atop the palfrey is the jesting Duchess who recognizes the mad hidalgo from her reading of the 1605 publication of Don Quixote's adventures. Here the narrator draws a parallel between the function of the readers of Part One who have now become representative, historical, opinionated characters in the 1615 Part Two and the diverse and sundry writers of the *original* history and *original* translation.

Burlesque imitation requires that illusions of historical reality meet the absurd reality of illusions: this is the basis for the counterfeit representation. The trappings of a counterfeit (a copy which is either a convincing, poorly convincing, or unconvincing fake) harks back to the original and often to other counterfeits, conjuring up the structure and content of these originals for comparative purposes, implicitly effecting a burlesque of the notion of (the) original. Cervantes's burlesque narrative is based on offering counterfeit(s) as original(s) which means that his burlesque mode of representing other narratives leads to a hilarious mockery of *communications*.

Don Quixote is more than just the amusing representation of a hilariously poor fake of bookish knight-errantry undertaken earnestly by a common fifty-year old hidalgo gone mad. This counterfeit of counterfeits employs a series of burlesque patterns and techniques of narrative games which can be identified within the text. In the following subdivisions some patterns and techniques of the burlesque mode are discussed. These are only patterns and techniques that, isolated from their narrative context might seem mechanical and void of their complex meanings, but studied within their textual environment they provide an illustrative examination of how the burlesque mocks--through laughter--weak material representations of ideological absolutes.

To illustrate, the counterfeit knight-errant becomes a counterfeit hero for a counterfeit history presented to seventeenth century readers who recognize the counterfeits for what they are. The fact is that recognizing a counterfeit as a counterfeit and/or recognizing the joke as a joke, or the jest as a jest has social implications. But there is another pressing issue concerning counterfeits and self-referentiality which is at the heart of burlesque in *Don Quixote*: the mock-heroic. Is *Don Quixote*'s burlesque just one more project of the counterfeit or is it more?

Don Quixote, Counterfeit and Mock-Heroic

Recently Roger Salomon focused particular attention on the "mock-heroic" mode in *Don Quixote*. His discussion is pertinent for this investigation of the burlesque mode because his discussion points out the very inadequacy of considering *Don Quixote* as a simple mock-heroic, parody, or what he calls *anti-climax*. Salomon suggests that even the declared intentions of invective against chivalric fiction are dubious in the *Quixote* since "the assumption against which all claims to heroic experience in the novel must be tested--namely, that knight errantry is untrue to the facts of empirical reality (for they are fabulous), unworthy of serious consideration (for it is absurd), and anachronistic and irrelevant to present conditions" of the 'social world' of *Don Quixote* (7). Chivalric romances are not solely fictive but inverisimilarly idealistic. They were considered entertaining and frivolous because of their erotic tendencies. Such romances were not worthy of earnest praise and emulation. Cervantes's narrative comic art depends on the disparity between the idealized chivalric heroism in chivalric romances and the hilarious, inadequate, counterfeit representation of the mad hidalgo. Salomon identifies the textual basis for the disparity: "the social world (of *Don Quixote*), moreover, from peasant to aristocrat, bears no serious resemblance to the society idealized in the chivalric romances" (8). What Salomon highlights is that in the mock-heroic narrative a fundamental technique of anti-climax uses the disproportion of the imaginary poles between two realms of existence, one imaginary and the other one "real," for the success of anti-climax.

Salomon's analysis of anti-climax reconfirms that the disparity basic to all mock-heroic narrative is due to the "radical disjunction between the heroic pretensions of the protagonist and the actual banality of his world" (8). He highlights that in Cervantes's *Don Quixote*, specifically, "the mock-heroic mode, in short, is both self consciously aware of fictions and grounded in an affirmation of gritty reality. Both his banal environment and his world of fictions mock the quixotic protagonist, however noble his values" (9). Salomon also identifies the social function of Cervantes's *Don Quixote* as mock-heroic literature: "Cervantine mock-heroic establishes an 'enabling' context that makes possible the transformation of nostalgia and despair into renewed engagement with the heroic values of the past" (9) *Mock-heroic* evokes transformations in ethos and *parody* becomes the means by which these target texts (e.g. chivalric romances, picaresque, pastourelle) are transformed. Salomon focuses on the mock-heroic mode in *Don Quixote* in order to demonstrate the pertinence of parody and anticlimax. Whereas parody "is committed to straight imitation," the writer of the mock-heroic "by contrast, is committed only to an imitative form that lays bare the pretensions of the more literal copyist and his model in the context of the same "real" world in which they must somehow function" (22). Parody is key to mock-heroic and, in the case of *Don Quixote*, to the burlesque mode of representation.

While analysis of mockery seems indispensable to Salomon's arguments, he attends to the mechanics of mock-heroic and to a general discussion of the concept of mode. His discussion of mock-heroic works successfully for the misadventures of the mad hidalgo and his treatment of the irreducible duality between seriousness and frivolity and the problems of genre and subgenre and hybridization is engaging, however, the analysis is incomplete. Salomon does not attend specifically to the narrative patterns and burlesque techniques that interact and which are part and parcel of the fundamental *humorous* disposition of the text. More concretely, he does not explore the particular interaction between ethos (the complex fundamental values, standards, and practices that underlie and permeate the *Quixote*), and mode (the technical vehicle of expression of those basic attitudes), even though the need for such an investigation is implicit in his conclusions.

Salomon is decidedly more concerned with determining the boundaries of the mock-heroic mode and its role in *Don Quixote*. There is no attempt to wrestle with the problems of mockery and comicality. His approach does not link the threads that stitch the loose text together. His arguments do not demonstrate how anti-climax might serve as the tapestry within which the variety of relations between narrator and readers, the hidalgo and madness, Sancho's gullibility and his popular wisdom, or amusement and an acute historical awareness are woven.

Don Quixote I and II provide the foundation for an analysis--not only the anatomy--of this *humorous* disposition. Salomon is correct in looking toward mode as the answer to the difficulties of interpretation. The mode used by Cervantes and often often referred to by critics as "cervantine" cannot be reduced only to techniques and patterns, however these can be conventionally isolated and analyzed for a variety of purposes. The isolation of these patterns and techniques of burlesque mockery locates systems of contemporary values, preconceived beliefs, standards, customs and practices, and a variety of contemporary means for dealing with them.

Paradox is often a key determinant of the humorous mode used by Cervantes in *Don Quixote*. The paradoxes of the *Quixote* carry out a plan that promotes mockery. These paradoxes require intellectual activity to strip away layers of preconceived and archaic notions governing sanctioned traditions and everyday behavior. The amusing excoriation of the externalities of society's body of discourses through mockery is a metaphorical strip-tease which leaves little more than skin on the mad hidalgo's weathered bones or the printed letters on the page of text. By the end of the narrative the hidalgo has been stripped of his social pretensions and of his social madness. He is stripped of life, and in death he is little more than a dry heap of bones. Does this mean that the story of the hidalgo's misadventures has only been an entertaining means to a serious end?

Cide Hamete (and his pen) are well aware that this heap of bones ("*los cansados y ya podridos huesos de don Quijote*") is of little interest to readers (II:74). Readers are encouraged to keep apocryphal writers from resurrecting them. The hidalgo's bones made up the infrastructure that gave him his unbecoming figure, that protruded his skin in ever-so-grotesque a manner and rubbed uncomfortably against the archaic armour of his forefathers. These bones, however, are of far less interest than the stripping of his inward and outward manifestations of perceived pretentiousness.

Mockery is key to the physical strip-tease of the mad hidalgo who attempts to leave his pseudo-pretentious armor hanging from a tree, and to the psychological strip-tease of his fiction-based madness (whose cure seems to be a result of constant hazing, jesting, hoaxing, and a feverish fit) which he leaves on his death bed. In short, what readers are left at the end of the second book is simply two volumes filled with printed pages that tell a funny story about how a good hidalgo, Alonso Quijano *el bueno*, became mad and how he was cured of his madness before he was put to rest. Or is that all that is left? By privileging the misadventures of an ordinary good hidalgo gone mad and an extraordinary madman's cure and death, one dangerously skirts the complex burlesque tapestry that holds the loosely knit threads of the *Quixote* together.

Alonso Quijano's rotting bones are of no interest to readers. Readers recall the jokes, the hoaxes, and the insults used to cure the madman, not his already rotted bones. As a rule in *Don Quixote*, means *seem* to outweigh ends. This apparent imbalance between ends and means haunts the *Quixote*. It is not only a thematic problem but a structural and semantic one as well. The manner by which the hidalgo transforms reality, for example, is more important than the conventionally distinct categories of illusion or reality. The means by which Sancho earns and looses his coveted island, Barataria--a hilarious, unconvincing, cheap, landlocked counterfeit--is conspicuously highlighted to point through the gimcrack show of the bogus squire. Sancho uses gullibility as the crux of his desire for gain.

On a more structural level the imbalance between ends and means is even greater. There seems to be undue attention paid to the untrustworthy Arab author of the history, and to an unreliable and pretentious translator. By highlighting the ignoble heritage attributed to the unreliable writer and contributors, and their particularly trifling and personal concerns in *reporting* the story, Cervantes draws attention to an apparent shoddiness in the telling of this *true history*. While the narrative is offered as *true* history readers are drawn to take this history for a mirth-provoking sham. Cervantes's narrative guides readers to recognize the unending tricks of appearance and illusion that taunt readers. This intentional sham is made possible by the assertion of means over ends.

The result of the narrative's apparent shoddiness is that the commonly accepted and recognized fame of an assortment of literary categories such as biographies, sermons, debates, bestiary, courtesy books, pastoral elegy, folktales, and exemplum is critiqued burlesquely. Likewise, familiar attitudes toward the social categories of marriage, friendship, prostitution, service, courtly and sexual lovemaking, for example, are rendered inadequate, unsightly or unseemly. The process of fraying the edges of preconceived notions of woebegone traditions and archaic ideologies is accomplished in an apparently harmless and thoroughly entertaining manner. The burlesque mode of representation makes readers laugh at what is potentially a critical review of everything they have taken for granted as serious reality.

Readers laugh because their attention has been drawn to certain absurdities which permit or favor the jesting with what is surely serious matter. Cervantes's burlesque narrative itself functions primarily on the basis of continually displacing accepted seriousness with undisguised, planned and well orchestrated comicality. Cervantes was well aware that the humorous disposition of the *Quixote* depended on maintaining the readers' sense of humor. Don Quixote's madness is of little consequence until its fabulous composition is tested in "real" social situations. Shakespeare wrote in *Love's Labour's Lost* "A jest's prosperity lies in the ear of him that hears it, never in the tongue of him that makes it" (V: 2). Don Quixote cannot appreciate a good joke since he does not have a humorous disposition. His humorous disposition is "all dried up." And the drier and more serious the narrative is, the louder and funnier the narrative about the hidalgo's dried up humor. Cervantes's burlesquing of so many discourses succeeds because he is well aware that for the jest to be successful he must divert the readers' attention to the process of jokes and hoaxes. Readers are continually reminded how hilariously silly everything is in this particular context. The effect is that the means of producing comicality are made more apparent than the ends of having produced that comicality.

The predominance of burlesque means over serious ends is the basis for the ideology of burlesque mockery. Burlesque permits the irreverence toward the mad hidalgo's moral system and the social codes of chivalric fiction enacted in everyday life. These codified systems of behavior are never dismissed, but they are simultaneously praised and admonished ambiguously. Likewise, mockery allows for an apparent irreverence toward the Spanish moral system and contemporary notions concerning codes for behavior. Again, these codified systems of behavior are not dismissed, but praised and admonished for the purpose of critical ambiguity. Readers are encouraged to broach the puzzling but very familiar factors of their society which, for one reason or another, seems to be in trouble. The crux of mockery is that readers confront historical meanings from perspectives which are both familiar and unfamiliar.

Bakhtin's study of *Rabelais and his World* provides a model for approaching the historical cultural significance of the often disregarded or little appreciated body of burlesque literature which drew on the carnivalesque. He offers a fundamental and provocative argument: "All popular-festive images were made to serve this historical awareness, from common masquerades and mystifications. . . to more complex carnival forms" (99). The historical awareness to which Bakhtin refers is the perception of change, a "carefully defined awareness of a great turning point, of a radical change of historical epochs" (98). *Don Quixote* must be read through extravagance and the absurd of an entertaining burlesque. Contemporary readers are guided toward viewing the puzzling factors of their day from a distanced, ambivalent perspective. The result is the exploration of effective ways for subverting official cultures, not primarily for sport, but for building a historical awareness of social accountability.

CHAPTER FIVE: BURLESQUE MOCKERY IN *DON QUIXOTE*

Locating Burlesque Patterns in *Don Quixote*: Stacking the Narrative

The following chapter includes analyses of several selections of the *Quixote*. Each one is exemplary of how the burlesque mode effects the peculiar travesties of the historical realities of both fiction and everyday life in *Don Quixote*. The purpose is not only to identify several of the many burlesque patterns and techniques found in the *Quixote*, but also to point out how these patterns and techniques work together to teasingly strip layers of archaic and inappropriate, although commonplace, interpretations of historical issues. The first is an analysis of the episode where the injured Don Quixote supposedly resists physical contact with Maritornes, a common whore, whom he takes for a princess. The nobility's pretensions of courtly love are stripped to physical combat, and the reputation of Cide Hamete's *true history* is sullied by his unseemly preoccupation with the watercarrier and rumors of his irreputable heritage.

The effect of this narrative stacked against the hidalgo, his fat squire, the sensually ugly Maritornes, the sexually anxious watercarrier and even against historians in general-- and Cide Mahamete Benengeli (sic) in particular--is not just laughter for and from readers. This tense narrative transition from Sancho's simple cover-up of past experiences to a hilarious situation which parallels the events that have been kept undercover is transmitted comicality at its receptive best. Readers are led to leer at the preparations of a lewd description of lovemaking in all its non-courtly and vulgar detail.

The narrative sequences are carefully contrived to enhance the burlesque: bruised and beaten after the misfortunes caused by Rocinante's poorly-timed instinctive sexual advances toward the yanguesan's mares, Sancho leads the uninjured Dapple, burdened by the dead-weight of the wounded Don Quixote, to an inn that the hidalgo--who converts historical realities into bookish fantasies--promptly mistakes for a castle. The narration of the accumulated nocturnal escapades at the inn is strategically farcical because readers are reminded by the intervening narrator that the hidalgo's mind, with all its noble, idealistic aspirations, is nevertheless the prisoner of his body and the body's common lodgings. The burlesque version of lover visitations is heightened by the seedy setting of the inn's "back room" which is an appropriate backdrop for the lewd activities readers expect to take place. Indeed, Cervantes provides an effective "narrative" stage for chronicling indecency.

In a rickety, make-shift bed set up in the open-air room of a Manchegan inn the hidalgo, having been fed, bandaged with plaster, and housed, imagines that he has nursed his body to the point where it is now ready to undergo sexual demands. In such a state of imaginary relations, the madman again mistakes the prostituting Maritornes for the young, beautiful princess residing in the castle who, as in chivalric romances, solicits his lovemaking; whereupon he too responds by making verbal and physical responses to her, but unbeknown to him, in front of her designated sexual partner, the muleteer, and the sleeping Sancho. His blindness to the social situation initiates a series of slapstick events that leads to another beating for him and Sancho.

Sancho, uncomfortably restricted by his plaster and oblivious to the pain that he acquired *through association* with Don Quixote, is fast asleep. Recall that Sancho denies that neither Don Quixote nor he had been beaten. He reports, falsely, that Don Quixote fell and he acquired his bruises through sympathetic association. The muleteer lies awake in sexual anticipation of the approaching promiscuous

Maritornes who sneaks into the room as per habit, quietly, although ready for action. Don Quixote, "mummified" by his bandages and plaster, is off in his imaginary world creating fantastic hallucinations which are funny to readers since, as in most circumstances, they expect that he will apply his nocturnal imaginations to a physical reality. The proper "bawdy" description of this episode is a good example of how the burlesque mode works to imitate mockingly the established expectations of certain traditions.

The burlesque here is not only a way to mock impractical traditional ideals concerning love but it is also a means to poke fun at writing histories in general and at writing a history of this episode in particular. The burlesque of writing histories is made when the narrator maliciously points out that Cide Hamete Benengeli chose to record this episode, among many others of course, because he knew the muleteer personally, and was perhaps even a relative. The narrator ridicules the historian by exposing his subjectivity, commends Benengeli burlesquely for his curiosity at a moment when readers expect to be told an erotic, if not pornographic tale, and then throws in an added slam against the relationship between Benengeli and the muleteer according to bloodline and occupation.

The narrator points out that Cide Hamete Benengeli was a very cautious historian who paid particular attention to details and that, unlike poor historians, he has not omitted the various and sundry petty points of the history. The suggestion is that other lesser historians might clean up these trivial points which are *"tan mínimas y tan rateras,"* but that their inclusion is commendable. The shady narrator's mockery of the inclusion of erotic material ambiguously praises and admonishes the not-so-serious original historian and, by extension, his artistic practices:

> *Benengeli fue historiador muy curioso y muy puntual en todas las cosas, y échase bien de ver, pues las que quedan referidas, con ser tan mínimas y tan rateras, no las quiso pasar en silencio; de donde podrán tomar ejemplo los historiadores graves, que nos cuentan las acciones tan corta y sucintamente, que apenas no llegan a los labios, dejándose en el tintero, ya por descuido, por malicia o ignorancia, lo más sustancial de la obra* (I:16, 201).

Readers are supposed to be entertained by the burlesquing of overly serious historians (*historiadores graves*). The narrator capitalizes on the mockery of such historians by interpolating Cide Hamete's personal interest in maliciously recounting the hidalgo's inept sexual prowess. The interruption seems to have little or nothing to do with the narration of events at the inn; however it does bring a grin to the lips of curious, anxious readers. While no real description of lewd activities is ever provided in essence, the mere intention to amuse readers with the suggestion of such material was risky. In an astute note to his edition of *Don Quixote* Luis Andrés Murillo points out a tidbit of historical interest: this section leads a lengthy portion which was censored in 1624 by the Portuguese Inquisition (I:16 201 n14). It is not inconceivable that the Inquisition saw this section for what it might be taken for with the burlesque: the preparation of a detailed account of lovemaking to whet the taste of "dirty" and curious minds; the suggestion of such an account would bring a malicious, sinful grin to the lips of readers. The seediness is part and parcel of burlesque.

There are at least two burlesque parodies at work in this particular mishap situated at the inn which was taken for a castle. First, there is the burlesque parody of the relationship between the damsel and her knight in imitation of chivalric romance that is somewhat analogous to the sensualist relationship between Góngora's Pyramus and Thisbe discussed in Chapter Three. As the short episode in which Maritornes--prepared for a quick sexual rendezvous with the familiar muleteer--creeps in on one of the mad hidalgo's fabrications, readers are provided with more, and less, than they expect. The hidalgo uses courtly language to declare his "good intentions" and moral obligations which preclude any sexual encounter, and hands-on experience with what would, according to the narrator, turn anyone's stomach--except for a muleteer. The burlesque parody of common bestiary in the the misadventure concerning Rocinante and the mares is another. The grotesque distortion of chivalric romance through its juxtaposition to the travesty of bestiary is a hilarious burlesque.

The comicality effected through parody, travesty, and grotesque distortion is enhanced by the narrative sequencing of Rocinante's mishap with the yanguesans and Don

Quixote's mishap with Maritornes at the inn. From the tragedy of Grisostomo (I:12-14) to the suit of Maritornes becomes a perfect example of the sublime ending up in the absurd--the staple of burlesque. The comicality is earned when what is surely going to happen--readers already suspect that the hidalgo's beating will parallel his horse's beating in the earlier episode--is devilishly delayed and thrown out of proportion. What is shown here is that the impact of burlesque depends upon markers and frameworks of markers which instruct and guide readers toward grasping comicality.

The writer of burlesque provides readers with recognizable experience (usually plucked from tradition) and a reasonable capability to deal with the notions and images involved in the mockery. In this sequence of events, for example, a mockery is made of the hidalgo's justification of his impotence and of the muleteer's poor taste and sense of smell. Other targets are grave historians who chose to tell uninteresting versions of *the seedy facts* and the process of amusement itself. Readers are amused because they sense the foolishness of the entire state of affairs. Surely the mad hidalgo should have known better than to attempt any sexual activity after the beatings he and Sancho received at Rocinante's aborted affair with the yanguesan mares. Yet Don Quixote could not have known better because of his madness. The narrative itself has stacked the deck, burlesquely, against him.

While readers get a good laugh at these misadventures, the burlesque outcome is not nearly so hilarious for the characters involved: Don Quixote, Sancho, Maritornes, the muleteer, the representative from the Holy Brotherhood, or the innkeeper. The trick is to create hilarious and riotous enjoyment at the expense of those who are the butts of the writer, and through them, the readers. The hidalgo's wrestling match with Maritornes is followed by a free-for-all and a domino effect of confusions and beatings. The narrative employs a violent slapstick sequence in the same way and toward the same end that slapstick was used in modern times by Laurel and Hardy, the Three Stooges, or the Marx Brothers. The beating only lasts as long as the narrator wishes it to. The victim, who never seems the worse for the wear, recovers quickly and is back to his mad activities. All the violent slapstick is an element of the burlesque mode of narrating episodes in *Don Quixote*. In fact, except for the

mitigating effects of the burlesque, the *Quixote* is one brawl
after another.

Timing is also crucial for burlesque. If the beatings and
joking are carried too far and too long the jest loses its power
of amusement. The mad hidalgo and Sancho, within the
typical self-referential process of *Don Quixote*, mention more
than once that in their opinion the joke has gone too far. For
burlesque to amuse there must be an appropriate tension
and accurate timing for breaking the tension to ensure the
desired amusing outcome. Timing in burlesque is equivalent
to the timing of the punch line of a joke. The comicality is
earned narratively when what is surely going to happen--
readers already suspect that the hidalgo's beating will
parallel his horse's beating in the earlier episode--is
provocatively delayed until the exact moment when the most
amusement can be assured.

The *ingenio* or wit involved in writing burlesque relies on
the visuality associated with theatricality for staging of
events which must be cleverly sequenced and timed, and
convincingly dramatized for the theater of the mind.
Theatricality relies on illusion. Readers are encouraged to
imagine the havoc created when "things that go bump in the
night" and when, necessarily, Don Quixote, Sancho,
Maritornes and the muleteer are tumbling about. The
nocturnal fumbling of these four characters at the inn is
nearly as available to readers as fumbling on stage is
available to spectators at a theater festival. Readers,
provided with the visual elements of theater, snicker as
though they were viewing the manhandling at the theater,
first-hand. The intimacy between text and reader here
mimics the intimacy between spectators and actors on stage.
This intimacy is tied to burlesque.

The intimacy between text and readers is rooted in the
narrative markings or clues which let readers in on what is
supposed to be funny and what is not. Narrative marking is
an economical effort to collapse different and apparently
separate sections or episodes of the narrative into one by
harking back to other "originals". Certain words, for example,
are marked for burlesque early on. Sometimes readers are
told that something is a *disparate*, a *pasatiempo*, or a *burla
pensada* or *pesada*.[42] However, much more often there is a
more subtly acute means of conjuring up the necessary

notions and sentiments that invoke a humorous reading. *Malferida*, for example, is a term which, used by anyone including Don Quixote, conjures up a smile because "malferida" is a clear burlesque imitation of archaisms. *Guardar* , *discreto, encantado* and *donaire* are others.

Caballero, coupled with the adjectives used to modify it, is perhaps the most ambiguously praised and ridiculed term in the entire text. Don Quixote is labeled a *caballero andante* or an *andante caballero*, for example, depending upon where he is in relation to Rocinante. He is also a *caballero armado* or an *armado caballero*, and a *caballero enamorado* or *enamorado caballero*, *caballero encantado* or *encantado caballero* depending upon his physical or mental state. The jest resides within the misplacing of *caballero* itself, and the initial jest of addressing the mad hidalgo in this fashion is only enhanced by the floating, descriptive, situational adjectives. The mad hidalgo is not a legitimate *caballero*. Nor is he a convincing counterfeit.

The narrative itself builds on an arsenal of words, situations, and patterns which, when recalled pertinently, enhance the humorous effect. What Cervantes accomplishes with all these small and large scale variations on an already funny theme is a method which strategically pushes comicality to burlesque. Repetition, and particularly absurd repetition, points to the artifice of the original and its more outrageous counterfeits. Don Quixote is not a very convincing hero of chivalric literature, but his outlandish representation of what he believes these heroes must have been encourages readers to question their sentiments toward entertaining chivalric fiction and toward the basic ideals underlying chivalric codes of conduct. Burlesque parody mocks an image of an original to create meaning. Readers laugh at the uncomfortable union of text against text because often the paradoxical relationship is ludicrous and absurd.

If a burlesque narrative is a jesting narrative structured by interrelating literary, situational and theatrical jokes, how is such a structure which relies on economical narrative reminders and cross-references sustained? There is no doubt that the jests of the narrative which keep on building on each other provide much of the comicality. The *Quixote* is a long narrative, however. Suspense must be built on episodic jokes, and narrative unity is determined by the continual reductions

and cross-references. Narrative marking is essential to
sustain the effectiveness of the burlesque in *Don Quixote*
because--like the appearance of physical sores that remind
the victims of syphilis of the disease that was otherwise
"silent"--the markings of *burlas* reminds readers that no
matter how serious or usual things seem to be the *veras* is
always matched by and enclosed in a joking framework.

Cervantes uses a variety of techniques of intimations that
build a jesting relationship between burlesque episodes. In
chapters I:16 and I:17 readers recognize the thematically
imitative relationship of Rocinante's misadventure with the
yanguesans and Don Quixote's misadventure at the inn when
the mad hidalgo, like his horse, deludes himself into believing
himself sufficiently equipped to handle sexual pursuit. More
specifically, readers are directed toward grasping the
burlesque correspondences in the very "equinesque" language
of I:16 which point and interact pertinently with I:15 in
which Rocinante is attacked for chasing the Yanguesan's
mares. Maritornes is described in equine terms: *"no tenía
siete palmos de los pies a la cabeza, y las espaldas, que algún
tanto le cargaban, la hacían mirar al suelo más de lo que ella
quisiera"* (I:16, 198). Similarly, the muleteer *trots* on the ribs
of the pretentious hidalgo:

> *pareciéndole mal la burla, enarboló el brazo en alto y
> descargó tan terrible puñada sobre las estrechas quijadas del
> enamorado caballero, que le baño toda encima de las
> costillas, y con los pies más que de trote, se las paseó todas
> a cabo a cabo* (I:16, 204).

The language used to describe the trampling of the hidalgo
is all narrative horse play. *"Quijadas"* is a pun which
highlights the relationship between *"Quijote"* and the flanks
of a horse. The description of the impulsive and violent
stomping of the *"enamorado caballero"* imitates mockingly the
ruthless trampling of the *enamored* horse, Rocinante, in the
previous chapter. The muleteer's cruel stampede on the
enamored horseman's ribs is burlesquely violent and funny.
The playfully horsy language is hilarious: the horseman's ribs
are stomped on at a gallop's pace by a common muleteer.
The absurd horseplay here anticipates the stampede of sheep
in I:18 and of pigs in II:68. Readers need not be overly
familiar with the imitation of chivalric romances or bestiary,

false historians or traditional notions concerning prostitution at inns to understand the jest because Cervantes inscribes the common knowledge necessary for them to appreciate the multi-leveled burlesques of related episodes. Narrative marking is key to narrating burlesque.

The analysis of I:16 indicates that there are some the patterns and techniques common to the burlesque mode of representation in *Don Quixote*. The salient functions of imitation, parody, the false indifference or the bogus impartiality of the historian, slapstick and violence, timing, theatricality, and narrative marking of words and textual units in terms of the burlesque mode are evident. These are but a few of the many techniques employed by Cervantes to narrate burlesquely. The prevalence of *narrating burlesquely* and the illustration of how one maintains the burlesque mode is best discussed in terms of other more Traditional Burlesques in *Don Quixote*.

There is no lack of what we might call traditional burlesques in the *Quixote*. A good example is Don Quixote's letter to Sancho while Sancho was governing Barataria "island" (II:51 428-30). His letter is a manual of instruction on how to behave, which burlesques the style and content of courtesy books. Another is the funeral homily offered in Sancho's verbal lament after the hidalgo has been thoroughly beaten (I:52 601). While Sancho's intention is to provide a proper official homily like those he may have heard while growing up, but the effect is that his very person mocks officiality. Sancho's gimcrack imitation is ludicrously off the mark when it comes to serious eulogies. On a more popular traditional scale, the friendship between Don Quixote and Sancho Panza is burlesquely compared and contrasted to the friendship between Rocinante and Dapple. The relationship is praised for its apparent closeness and debunked for its absurdity. The tale the mad hidalgo tells about meeting Montesinos and the enchanted Dulcinea after emerging from Montesinos's cave (II:23) and Sancho's story about sheep he sees while riding Clavileño (II:41) are tall stories within the popular-traditional fashion, however they offer more than just any tall tale. These tall tales rely on character-created illusions with which readers are quite familiar. Don Quixote's meeting with the begging, *enchanted* Dulcinea in Montesino's Cave is a good tall tale until readers recall or are reminded that Sancho is Dulcinea's enchanter. Sancho's tale about the sheep is a good tale until readers are reminded by the mad hidalgo of the tale of the Cave of Montesinos. In the context of *Don Quixote* these are unmistakable burlesques.

There seems to be an inexhaustible register of what might be called traditional burlesques in *Don Quixote*. Altisidora sings a burlesque parody of a dawn song to the forlorn hidalgo at the palace of the Duke and Duchess in order to force the mad hidalgo into making yet a bigger fool of himself. Sancho provides a burlesque description of Dulcinea including what she looks, sounds, smells and feels like (I:31 383-4). The mad hidalgo offers his opinions to a variety of audiences in apologies and debates, but the serious opinions within the discourse are always upstaged by the humorous circumstances under which they are presented. Readers are never allowed to take the word of a mimicking madman as anything but the words of a madman, or, those of any other jester even though they *seem* sound. The crowning blow of burlesque is unmistakable when what might have been a laudatory epilogue for a good dead man, Alonso Quijano *el bueno*, is a burlesque epilogue which has been reduced to the selfish markings of the writer's pen.

Comments concerning literary burlesque in *Don Quixote* have traditionally targeted the *pretext* of chivalric romances. The entire epic apparatus of chivalric romances including invocations, digressions, legends, folklore, magic tricks and descriptions of the supernatural, scenes of the underworld, eloquent speeches and perilous journeys and battles is grotesquely mimicked throughout the narrative by the hidalgo, his bogus squire, and many of the over-industrious and often malicious characters. The hidalgo addresses not only an absent but imaginary lady in delightfully amusing apostrophes. The "real" Don Quixote of Book II makes an ambiguously "real" don Alvaro Tarfe--who has come out of the apocryphal *Quijote* by Avellanda--sign a statement (an official document) that he has met the true, official Don Quixote after having met and housed an unofficial imposter whose history was told in the 1614 sequel written by the unreliable writer of the apocryphal *Don Quixote* (II:72, 578-79). The whole set-up is a mockery of the apparent reality and autonomy of fiction. The narrative itself is laden with false humility, false ambiguity, and false empathy. From the very beginning, *Don Quixote* offers itself as a *genuine* counterfeit.

The existence of a genuine counterfeit raises the problem of authenticity and originality in *Don Quixote*. The notion of authenticity is pertinent since lack of authenticity is the foundation of the burlesque mode of representation. To be understood and appreciated, burlesque imitations must interact pertinently and intimately with the prevalent popular and learned cultural patterns which are commonly recognized and accepted by readers. Burlesque mockery of the most intimate ideological experiences of readers is a means to promote the critical awareness of those very commonly accepted, but certainly idealistic expectations concerning authentic originality, selfless generosity, genuine sanctity, unprejudiced morality, sagacious innocence, excellent virtue, sincere simplicity, frank honesty, authentic integrity, unadulterated truth, uncompromised modesty, faultless continence, and impartial decency. Burlesque scopes the course of societal attitudes by challenging the absurd versions of realities that lie within them.

Creating a Burlesque Narrative

In *Don Quixote* the concept of quintessence is forced to share equal time and space with the essence of its inadequate material representation. Much of the puzzling fragmentation of the *Quixote* is explained by this curious flattening of the model and ideal concept against the counterfeit materiality. Below is a brief catalogue of the various literary and dramatic techniques of reduction, flattening, and leveling, and an operative analysis of how these techniques lead readers to develop a consciousness of the commonly accepted, but often unrealistic or unfaithful, representations of the sentiments, values, and attitudes of contemporary seventeenth-century Spanish society.

To illustrate, common proverbs strung together in an apparently meaningless harangue somehow evoke an acceptable sermon-like message of common and uncommon sense. Blunting and understatement increase comicality while they provide insights to truth. The mad hidalgo's lexical and grammatical archaisms which catch on with Sancho Panza and with those who desire to make fun of the two adventurers (including the narrator!), and his antiphrasis

(*doncella* for *mujeres mozas, destas que llaman del partido*,
castle for common inn [I:2, 82]) remind readers of details
which are important in reading for the humorous disposition.
Malapropisms like *presonas* for *personas* (II:3, 63) and *label
names* such as *Rocin*ante, Sancho *Panza*, and *Don* Quixote, or
the laughable but indecipherable *semidoncella* (I:43, 526) are
part and parcel of the burlesque's amusing manner of
praising and admonishing ambiguously. All these literary
and dramatic techniques help to effect a consistent mode of
representing critical issues. The employment of a variety of
these techniques can be observed in the following analysis of
the episode concerning the jest of the Dueña Dolorida at the
palace of the Duke and Duchess (II: 36-40).

It is a mid-summer night's eve when readers are told that
another game is afoot. Don Quixote and Sancho Panza have
just spent the day hunting and riding with the Duke and
Duchess, and just as the sun sets, the whole company is
surprised by unusual noises and a fiery light show in the
middle of the woods. The narrator points out that the woods
seemed to be afire, and that odd noises were emerging from
unidentified sources in the woods. The stage is set for
another hoax at the expense of the odd couple.

The narrator did not dismiss the power of music in
creating a scene. What is interesting here is the prominent
role of music in the initiation of the hoax:

> "*Luego se oyeron infinitos lelilíes, al uso de moros
> cuando entran en las batallas; sonaron trompetas y clarines,
> retumbaron tambores, resonaron pífaros, casi todos a un
> tiempo, tan contino y tan apriesa, que no tuviera sentido el
> que no quedara sin él al son confuso de tantos
> instrumentos*" (II:34, 309).

Time and again music marks the initiation of a new jest.
The narrative implements many elements of illusory
theatricality (script, sound, stage, props, costume, affected
speech patterns, director, actors, and spectators). The
narrator has already told readers that the Duke and Duchess
have planned a hoax for the mad hidalgo and his side-kick
squire, and here the intention is buttressed with a dramatic
setting and fitting musical accompaniment. The hoax is an
extravagantly organized set of mishaps which prepare Don

Quixote and Sancho Panza for a terrifying ride on Clavileño, the wooden horse stuffed with explosives.

The nature of these lighthearted mishaps is amusing. The function of stacking all these hilarious and absurd circumstances against Don Quixote and Sancho is to make readers laugh by providing them the perspective of the see-all, tell-all narrator. The major question that challenges the social function of burlesque is this: is the narrative so stacked for narrative hoaxes that readers do not take the time to analyze the jest on the basis of its social function or in terms of themselves, but instead pursue only its entertaining and aesthetic quality? Might reading the *Quixote* resemble attending a theatrical farce? Are readers only looking for a good smile or a malicious chuckle? The majority of *Quixote* criticism is an overwhelming argument to the contrary. Readers' expected laughter is a planned physical reflex action to protect, ambiguously, the sovereignty and authority of their own perspectives and attitudes concerning the familiar content of any cultural code in terms of the absurd and contradictory perspectives and attitudes offered in jest by the narrative. Guided reception for amusement short-circuits individual reactions that might find the jests too severe or unfair.

A close inspection of the reminders and clues for reading for and with a humorous disposition indicates how the application of the interlocking literary and dramatic techniques constitute the burlesque mode. Near the middle of the hoax at the Duke and Duchess's *pleasure palace* the narrator conjures up past jests in one adjective, reminding readers that this is a *dueñesco escuadrón*, that is, the group is unreliable and surely intends to "mess things up" (II:38 329). Recall that the nature of *dueñas* was inscribed and marked in the confrontation between Sancho Panza and the duchess's dueña Rodriguez.[43]

The Dueña Dolorida is particularly funny as the butt of the burlesque due to her flagrant improbity and expected unreliability. This *duenna* is less than convincing. She appears to be neither man nor woman, but sports the most abhorred characteristics of both. Readers are "in the know" about the joke, but the uninitiated Sancho has a difficult time believing there is a woman behind the beard. Her disguise is particularly important because while giving the illusion that sexual gender has been collapsed into one being, both genders are distorted, and thus emphasized for the purpose of amusement: "*Ella, puesta de rodillas en el suelo, con voz antes basta y ronca que sutil y dilicada, dijo: -- Vuestras grandezas sean servidas de no hacer tanto cortesía a este su criado, digo, a esta su criada*" (II:38 330). The Dueña Dolorida's disguise is not only a play on gender erasure, which on its own is rather ludicrous, but also a play on chivalric adventures, and on the mad hidalgo's not-so-convincing chivalric vestiture. Parody of chivalric fiction alone would not create the hilarious burlesque situation found here. Theatricality, grotesque caricature and imitation are accompanied by linguistic acrobatics to produce the burlesque.

Paired superlatives are used extensively in the Dolorida's speech (a means of narration later parodied hilariously by Sancho Panza) to emphasize each adjective--that is to increase, double, and triple the power of qualification; but when used extensively, persistently, and repeatedly by the Dolorida, the paired and tripled superlatives become counterfeit adjectives which allow readers to see the obvious machinery of verbal deception:

> *Confiada estoy, señor _poderosísimo_, _hermosísima_ mi* _cuitísima_ *en vuestros* _valerosísimos_ *pechos acogimiento, no menos* _plácido_ *que* _generoso_ *y* _doloroso_; *porque ella es tal, que es bastante a* _enternecer_ _los_ *mármoles, y a* _ablandar_ _los_ _diamantes_, *y a* _molificar_ _los_ _aceros_ *de los más endurecidos corazones del mundo; pero antes que salga a la plaza de vuestros* _oídos_, *por no decir* _orejas_, *quisiera que me hicieran sabidora si está en este* _gremio_, _corro_ *y* _compañia_, *el* _acendradísimo_ *caballero don Quijote de la* _Manchísima_, *y su* _escuderísimo_ *Panza* (II:38, 330, my emphasis).

The doubling and tripling of adjectives, nouns, and verbs as well as the ridiculous nonsense pairing of *oídos* and the more vulgar *orejas*, and, of course, the hilarious distortion of *Mancha* is all part of the burlesque. The distortion of a common complaint by a damsel to her knight with this preposterous version rendered even more unreliable by a rather unconvincing manly woman is at the foundation of burlesque. The extensive use of superlatives distracts from the message that the Dolorida wishes to impart, and masks, to a certain extent, the *real* complaint. The superlatives, in this sense, mediate the reception of the message.

The volleying back and forth and doubling of distortions makes this exchange between the Dueña Dolorida and spectators a spectacular burlesque. Immediately following the complaint, Sancho Panza cleverly mimics the Dolorida's manner of speech calling attention again to the doubling and distortion:

> "--*El Panza--antes que otro respondiese, dijo Sancho-- aquí está, y el don Quijotísimo asimismo; y así podréis dolorosísima dueñísima, decir lo que quisieridísimis; que todos estamos prontos y aparejadísimos a ser vuestros servidorísimos*" (II:38, 330).

The parallel distortion of Sancho's speech--akin to the modern burlesque of "tit-for-tat"--involves alliteration and the creation of "pretentious" superlatives, as did the Dolorida's. However, the spurious nonsense version of *quisiérais* in *quisieridísimis*, points up his impure, but even more absurd, imitation, which is only emphasized by the debunking hissing sound achieved by the repetition of the letter "s."

When Sancho imitates the curious narrative doubling characteristic of the *dueña's* speech he inadvertently perhaps, pokes fun at the false courtesy and grandiloquence of the *dueña's* discourse. This systematic verbal doubling effected through superlatives, alliteration, pairings and repetitions is carried on throughout the entire exchange which apans several pages. And, if the doubling of the *dueña's* own discourse were not obvious enough to guide spectators in the jest of antonomasia, the jokester Dolorida adds, with a clever appearance of gratuitousness, a choice story of the princess Antonomasia, heir to the kingdom of Candaya.

Verbal ambiguity created by antonomasia (using superlatives to deride the mad hidalgo, his bogus squire, and their "good" intentions) is mirrored theatrically by the costuming and disguises which jestingly blur the distinction between what is characteristically male and female. Disguised male representers carry on in nearly female roles exposing male "parts" (beards) which, to the glee of spectators "in the know," become a bargaining tool with the mad hidalgo. The bearded Dueña Dolorida bills her/himself as the *medianera* (II:38 334) as s/he becomes the crux of an obvious joke. The superlatives in the *dueña*'s complaint constitute false praise.

The emasculation of the *dueña* and her entourage is part of the narrative blurring of traditional sexual roles initiated with the defrocking of the priest who, to fool the mad hidalgo, dressed in drag. The blurring continued with the enchanted Dulcinea's man-like vault onto her *palafrén* (II:10). Later on in the Clavileño hoax readers recognize the narrative's playful "unisexing," and laugh when, to protect his tender bottom, Sancho rides Clavileño *a mujeriegas* (II:41, 348). The blurring of sexual distinction continues to haunt the narrative systematically until its explosion in this Dueña Dolorida-Clavileño hoax effected by the Duke, Duchess and company.

This insistent use of caricature is a key element of burlesque. The caricature of a manly woman or a womanly man is immoderate, immodest, and immoral (in terms of decency). The narrator's description of the Dolorida is reminiscent of medieval caricatures like the grotesque mountain girl (*la serrana*) in Juan Ruiz's *El libro de buen amor*. The mountain girl is a hideous sight with her out of proportion, oversized, and grotesque male and female features. Androgyny is monstrous and ugly because it mocks what men and women hold inviolable about gender.

Caricature is an indispensable element of burlesque: burlesque mockery employs caricature because through the exaggeration of features and mannerisms or ludicrous imitation and the deliberate distortion of what is held sacred--or at least as accepted shared experience--it exposes the most salient and obvious elements of those universal sacrosanct experiences. The exposure of façades, especially in *Don Quixote*, is socially relevant: mockery is not intended to change opinions, but instead to incite the reflection of the nature of cherished myths propagated as absolutes. Does the beard make the man, does the skirt make the lady, does the laughter make a *good* joke? (Or perhaps a more accurately: does the long beard make the real man, does the thicker skirt make the real lady, does loud and raucous laughter make the joke a really *good* one?) There is no such thing as *kindly* burlesque. Burlesque is never sexless. Its mockery is never indifferent, nonpartisan, or impartial. And herein lies the potential fallacy of most traditional critics: no one doubts their analysis of the *Quixote* as a funny book; it is their failure to account for the social function of the burlesque that undermines their analyses.

In the *Quixote*, burlesque is pervasive. Its mockery taints even the most solemn of categories. As Anthony Close suggests in his introduction to the *Romantic Tradition, Don Quijote* is *every sort of burlesque* (19). Readers can easily identify the several traditional burlesque categories in *Don Quixote*: burlesque verse, dramatic burlesque, and narrative burlesque. The burlesque as a mode of representation in the *Quixote* cannot be discussed in terms of the categories of high or low burlesque, per se. These are traditional categories of burlesque that were established a century after the writing of *Don Quixote*. The burlesque mode of representation in *Don Quixote* can be discussed in terms of both the learned and popular-traditional elements. In fact, burlesque mocks both popular and learned *pretexts* with the intention of testing attitudes and sentiments surrounding these *pretexts*.

The investigation of a more traditional literary burlesque provides a case in point. Altisidora's burlesque ballad sung in jest outside the mad hidalgo's window at the Duke and Duchess's palace appears to be little more than a delightful diatribe against an entertaining complaint in the *amour courtois* tradition. The diatribe is carried out by a young woman who presents herself not only as a young, love-stricken, worthy damsel of the palace but also as a shameless hussy who wants to get in for a little leg rubbing. Her very words turn the codes of the *amour courtois* tradition topsy-turvy: "*Más vale vergüenza en la cara que mancilla en el corazón*" (II:44 372). What the burlesque effects here is ambiguous praise of two separate but fused traditions: the learned tradition of courtly love and the popular ballad tradition are associated with an improper sexual advance. The social relevance of the burlesque mode of representation is that an awareness of the extremes of sensualism and chastity is raised through laughter. The historical relevance of the burlesque representation of courtship is that the burlesque raises an awareness about historical realities concerned with courtly and sexual love, and absurd interpretations of myths about them.

Altisidora mimics the acceptable dawn-song tradition with less than acceptable equipment. She lays no claim to beauty;

her self description reminds us of the ugly Asturian wench Maritornes: "*Y aunque es mi boca aguileña / y la nariz algo chata, / ser mis dientes de topacios / mi belleza al cielo ensalza*" (II:44 374). Her words are those of a low-class woman who suggests bartering her sexual wares along with an extra skirt: "*Trocárame yo por ella, (y diera encima una saya / de las más gayadas mías*" (II:44 373). Perhaps she is far less than deserving of the sexual endeavors of a heroic knight, but she is not necessarily out of line for the impoverished and deluded madman. Her burlesque romance strips away the rhetoric of courtly love to reveal the sensualist drive within it. Her mockery of chivalric matters seems just as mad and outlandish as the hidalgo's burlesque representation of them. Just as the ecclesiastic questioned the sanity of the Duke and Duchess, here the narrative suggests, ever so subtly, that Altisidora may be no *saner* than the madman. The appearance is that the categorical distinctions between madness and sanity are overlapping. The tease is that while Altisidora *appears* to be mad she is only mocking and ridiculing a madman (*de burlas*). Don Quixote not only appears mad but, from the time that his brains dried up, he is to be considered mad (*de veras*). The tease does not keep readers from contemplating--at least for a moment or so--the possibility of Altisidora being as mad as the hidalgo for playing into his madness.

The young woman's gaming works, and Don Quixote laments his misfortune for being once again the object of unsolicited desire. He responds with a *romance* of his own. The hidalgo's ballad is anything but original. It relies exclusively on common proverbs and clichés which are nothing more than embellished ordinary advice. He offers several verses of his ballad to cure the enamored Altisidora: "*Suelen las fuezas de amor sacar de quicio a las almas, tomando por instrumento la ociosidad descuidada*" (II:46 384). Here the hidalgo attributes the cause of obsession, based on madness, to boredom. The irony is that the madman pinpoints the cause of his own madness and then offers <u>business</u> as a possible cure for love melancholy: "*Suele el coser y el labrar, y el estar siempre ocupada, ser antídoto al veneno de las amorosas ansias*" (384). The mad hidalgo suggests that love sickness is a *social illness* caused by idleness and that it has a social cure: love sickness can be thwarted by keeping *busy*.

In addition he adds a short advisory warning against lewd behavior and social deviance by praising decency (*honestidad*), and admonishing a quick toss in the hay ("*el amor recién venido que hoy llegó y se va mañana*") (384). The hidalgo's use of the popular *refranero* is pertinent since it is with the knowledge treasured in these short and economical phrases that he summarizes unwittingly and ironically his own plight and solves his own difficulties.

The commonality and acceptability of these popular sayings in the hidalgo's earnest *romance* are not funny when they stand alone. The burlesque rests on the speaker of the verses, the uncanny situation, and the readers' knowledge of the overly serious intentions of the hidalgo in relation to the corny situation: a lovesick madman recites common proverbs as part of what he believes to be an educated, literary romance to thwart the vulgar *sexual advances* of what he believes to be a *fine lady*. The hidalgo's hilarious common ballad is socially pertinent since the poor counterfeit is offered to cool the passions of a counterfeit wanton damsel waiting in pseudo-sexual distress. Cervantes distorts the popular traditional *refranero* here just as he uses other traditional learned categories within the burlesque mode. The popular-traditional materials seem to be as rich a source for burlesque pretexts as materials from learned traditions. The burlesque is steeped in the traditions of both popular and learned sources; it preys on both. Little seems to escape its harsh mockery.

Principles of Mockery

To this point many components of the burlesque mockery in *Don Quixote* have been examined: the fundamental principles of the burlesque mode which are based on paradox; the entertaining nature of burlesque mockery; the isolable patterns which make up the safeguarded laughable method of besieging the puzzling factors which concerned Cervantes and his contemporaries. What has not been examined is the gimcrack nature of mockery itself. Several questions haunt the data so far. Is the burlesque mode necessarily funny? If burlesque mockery requires intimacy and confidence, and it deals with familiar and comfortable sentiments in a harsh and nasty fashion, how is it that it is so marketable to so many? What indeed distinguishes hilariously amusing mockery such as the Duke and Duchess' mockery of a gullible Sancho in the governorship of the Island Barataria from the apparently serious mockery of the holy sacrament of marriage in *El curioso impertinente*? The following analysis focuses on these questions.

While readers might not expect to find any elements of burlesque in the more serious *El curioso impertinente* there are important parallels between this serious *novela* and the overall burlesque mode of representation in the *Quixote*. To begin, the tale radically breaks up the narrative as a sort of after-dinner entertainment. In another instance of self-reference, the reading of the *novela* follows a lengthy discussion of the purpose and value of reading, and focuses specifically on an issue relevant to the burlesque: the value of reading as an end in itself for the sake of entertainment. Such entertainment relaxes tensions, wistfully *quita canas*, amuses, keeps everyone busy and out of trouble, and most importantly, keeps the mind from wandering by entertaining idle thoughts. In *Don Quixote*, such discussions are related to the social function of burlesque art.

According to the innkeeper the manuscript of eight *pliegos sueltos* written in long hand is one of two manuscripts abandoned in the inn's trunk. The ironic uniqueness of this particular short story in terms of the overall structure of the *Quixote* is that it is read and criticized autonomously as entertaining fiction by characters within the *Quixote* and by readers outside the pages of the narrative who must respond, simultaneously, both to the story read and the readers reading it. The story read from the *pliegos sueltos* appears to be completely estranged from the *Quixote*. The *novella*'s autonomy is due to the fact that none of its characters appear in the principal story of the mad hidalgo and his misadventures. The *novella*'s characters are independent and alien to the principal story. The characters of the *fictional novella* are consequently viewed in contrast to the *real life* characters (Dorotea, Fernando, Cardenio, Lucinda, innkeeper and family, priest, and barber) who gather around to be entertained, but exemplarily, at the expense of the *curioso impertinente*. What is potentially burlesque is the unlikely connection of a tragic story to daily amusements.

As the story unfolds readers read and *overhear* the priest as he reads the story aloud to the audience gathered at the inn. There is little doubt that this story is very different from the *true* history of the mad hidalgo--different characters, a different setting, etc., but as far as the teasing and trickery concerned with its unusual history (left in a trunk at an inn with another *novela* by Cervantes) it has quite a bit of kinship with the story about a mad hidalgo in which it is couched. The title is marked by the Italian word *novella* which generically denotes something new, a novelty, or a singular piece of news or tidings woven into an entertaining tale of a shorter length that might cause *admiratio* in readers. The word *novella* points up the category of fiction to which this narrative belonged, on the one hand, and designates a category of Italian fiction that exemplified an extraordinary case worthy of note. Cervantes used the *novella* to spin a not-so-common tale of unusual events which, within a burlesque imitation of hyperbole, served to warn against the dangers of extremism. The *novella*, thus, necessarily departs from straight truth and delights in the extreme consequences of exemplarity. Exemplarity highlights the hazards of obsessive and uncanny human behavior through extremely ridiculous and absurd cases.

El curioso impertinente is centered upon a reversal of fortune, a reversal that tragicomically is caused by those involved. In Florence the perfect friendship between Anselmo and Lotario, two young men of rich and noble stature, commonly recognized in the city as *los amigos*, and the exemplary marriage between the young, respectable and locally famous Florentine youths Anselmo and Camila are destroyed by Anselmo's quirky, mad obsession to prove the excessive value and uncommon virtue of his new wife Camila. There are no obvious motives for Anselmo's madness, as with Don Quixote, except his own impertinence in pushing his curiosity to absurd ends. However, his madness, like Don Quixote's mania, seems to be an exceptional and absurd interpretation of proving honor and virtue.

Once crazed by the mania of testing his wife's fidelity, he refuses to accept the dictates of society that determine how he, Lotario, and Camila must live and behave. The epitome of the dutiful and responsible nobleman, friend, and husband becomes an enemy to honorable duties and marital responsibilities. To test his wife's fidelity he puts his friendship with Lotario on trial, and threatens the honor of his own household. Anselmo's ludicrous test pits the sanctity of friendship and marriage against each other. Herein lies the fundamental relationship between laughter and serious concern: there is a precarious borderline between the serious and the burlesque; that is, both farce and tragedy emerge from dire conflicts and clashes. Anslemo's *mad* request to Lotario is unacceptable, frightening, and loathsome because it makes a mockery of what men and women hold inviolable about marriage and friendship.

The mad Anselmo is both a pathetic and laughable character. Like Don Quixote, Anselmo is certain of and even obsessed by his ideal. Don Quixote believes in the reputed virtue of fictional knight errants. Anselmo believes in the potential virtue of his yet untested wife. Unless her virtue and fidelity are tested in society, he argues, they are of no value, at least as far as his obsessive suspicions are concerned. Just as the mad hidalgo is told that fictional knight errantry is at best little more than entertaining fiction and that it cannot survive the test of common sense or verisimilitude, let alone in everyday social reality, Anselmo is told that woman is made of glass and that she will not withstand the ludicrous experiment. These parallels and analogous problems are taking place within a decidedly burlesque imitation of bookish ideals ranging from heroism to love.

Before the parallels between Anselmo's madness and the insanity of the hidalgo can be isolated and discussed, the pertinence of the *tragic* of the *Curioso* in a *funny* book like *Don Quixote* needs to be examined. The irony of the *Curioso Impertinente* is that the narrator of the tale cannot be Benengeli, yet, it is--burlesquely--told in Arabic by him and read in Spanish by the priest. Readers cannot ignore the burlesque results of the insertion of a serious tale in a burlesque book: according to the rules of the narrative game of *Don Quixote*, the situation is recorded in la Mancha by an Arab who wrote a version of it in Arabic. The Spaniard Cervantes found the Arab's version, had it translated by a bilingual Morisco into Spanish and then had his version edited and published under the name of Cervantes. The tease is that, according to the narrative, the *Curioso Impertinente* was left in the trunk at the inn described by Cide Hamete Benengeli with another *novela* by Cervantes,

Rinconete y Cortadillo. Thus, the *Curioso* which was originally recorded by Benengeli was translated from Spanish to Arabic, translated back into Spanish by a Morisco, and read by the priest, as a retranslation into Spanish. Such is the burlesque pertinence of the *tragic* story of the *Curioso Impertinente*.

There are other parallels of exemplarity and madness that are salient to the discussion of the burlesque mode and the inclusion of the *Curioso Impertinente*. Anselmo desires to discover truth by means of truth itself. However, he fails to recognize that truth can only be discovered through its relationship with a lie, life through its relationship with death, faithfulness through its relationship with adultery. The narrator of the *Curioso* interrupts his story to highlight Anselmo's foolish impertinence with a few insulting remarks and warns him with a pertinent poem:

> *Busco en la muerte la vida,*
> *salud en la enfermedad,*
> *en la prisión libertad,*
> *en lo cerrado salida*
> *y en el traidor lealtad.*
> *Pero mi suerte, de quien*
> *jamás espero algún bien,*
> *con el cielo ha estatuido*
> *que, pues lo imposible pido,*
> *lo posible aun no me den.* (I: 33 416).

The poem mocks the fool who, metaphorically speaking, seeks virgins in a brothel--indirectly, a definition of the mad hidalgo. The only means by which Anselmo's extreme mental construct can be carried out in appearance and in essence is through deception. Anselmo's madness leads him to put himself in the position of being one of the greatest targets of social mockeries of all time: he orchestrates his own cuckoldry, thereby making an exemplary fool of himself. Parallel to the hidalgo's burlesqued imitations, Anselmo becomes a tragic version of *el pintor de su deshonra* but within the burlesque context of the *Quixote*.

Anselmo's exemplary madness sets in place the codes for behavior within which Lotario and Camila must act. Thus, Anselmo authors his own dishonor by establishing excessive rules of behavior, and his dishonor is contagious. The appearance of social stability in such a topsy-turvy world requires deception. Just as madness determines deception, deception determines the topsy-turvy order of things. Lotario and Camila deceive Anselmo in word and in deed thereby making a mockery of his companionship, friendship, marital intimacy, and the institution of marriage. The borderlines between burlesque theatricality and serious moral and social consequences are precariously close.

Anselmo also makes a mockery of himself by requesting that Lotario write suggestive love poems to entertain and possibly *seduce* Camila. The two sonnets that Lotario composes at Anselmo's request make a mockery of Anselmo's foolish desire to be entertained by his best friend's seduction of his own wife. Both sonnets, although well woven into the high-style sonnet tradition, are marked with a past sexual encounter and cuckoldry. The first sonnet parodies a love sonnet in the tradition of courtly love but makes clear the physical encounter behind the elevated language. Lotario's sonnet tells of the lover's melancholy evenings when he must only dream of the lovemaking he experiences during the day. Although he sighs in Clori's nocturnal absence, in her presence his *cries* and *groans* increase.

> *En el silencio de la noche, cuando*
> *ocupa el dulce sueño a los mortales,*
> *la pobre cuenta de mis ricos males*
> *estoy al cielo y a mi Clori dando.*
> *Y al tiempo cuando el sol se va mostrando*
> *por las rosadas puertas orientales,*
> *con suspiros y acentos desiguales*
> *voy a la antigua querella renovando.*
> *Y cuando el sol, de su estrellado asiento*
> *derechos rayos a la tierra envía,*
> *el llanto crece y doblo los gemidos.*
> *Vuelve la noche, y vuelvo al triste cuento,*
> *y siempre hallo, en mi mortal porfía,*
> *al cielo sordo; a Clori, sin oidos.* (I:34 422).

The sonnet mocks the cuckold who cannot see through Lotario's declaration of satisfaction with daytime physical love and dissatisfaction with having to forgo lovemaking in the evening when husband and wife sleep together. The poet's *melancholia* is sincere and serious. The specific context in which it is recited, however, makes this lover's lament a mockery of the unwitting cuckold husband.

The second sonnet, read at the dinner table as part of the evening's entertainment, is a greater mockery and demonstrates how Lotario--by mocking the sanctity of marriage with the *burla* of adultery--makes a mockery of his own enviable position in Italian society. He is considered the very best of friends, the most honorable and virtuous of young Florentines. The sonnet, although offered as seductive entertainment, predicts danger and tragedy. The speaker in the poem complains that he would rather be dead (a common poetic *metaphor)* than repent for loving his illicit beloved.

> Yo sé que muero; y si no soy creido,
> es mas cierto el morir, como es mas cierto
> verme a tus pies, ¡oh bella ingrata!, muerto,
> antes que de adorarte arrepentido. (I:34 423).

In the second quatrain the poet claims that even if he is eventually rejected, the memory of the moments they spent in embrace is a keepsake sculpted eternally on his breast.

> Podré yo verme en la región de olvido,
> de vida y gloria y de favor desierto,
> y allí verse podrá en mi pecho abierto,
> como tu hermoso rostro está esculpido. (I:34 423).

In the first tercet the poet concludes that the memory of their sexual encounter maliciously labeled *esta relíquia* will both comfort him and threaten his life, and laments, in the second tercet, his uncomfortable plight of navigating dangerous waters without direction or harbor.

> Que esta relíquia guardo para el duro
> trance que me amenaza mi porfía,
> que en tu mismo rigor se fortalece.
> Ay de aquél que navega, el cielo escuro,
> por mar no usado y peligrosa via,
> adonde norte o puerto no se ofrece. (I:34 423).

The poet in the poem recognizes the danger in which he has put himself with this illicit love although, ironically, Lotario does not necessarily realize the serious implications of the sonnet he wrote to make fun of Anselmo. The sonnet outlines the fate of a social deviant who is marked by one pleasurable, but immoral act.

Lotario and Camila are trapped within the confines of the ludicrous codes of conduct imposed on them by Anselmo who conspires against the accepted social rules of proper conduct. By attempting to keep Anselmo's flagrant social misjudgment and obvious indiscretion from becoming public knowledge, Lotario and Camila logically and necessarily fall prey to Anselmo's self-created and perpetuated shackles of dishonor to which they are linked *eslabón a eslabón a la cadena.*

The consequences of social madness are, in this case, serious. Anslemo's mad obsession mocks the sacred sacrament of marriage and the inviolable bonds of friendship, and the outcome of this defiance of acceptable and familiar social codes can only be tragic. And so it is: Camila dies miserable and forlorn in a convent. Lotario dies honorably as a soldier in a battle, but miserably as a shamed and lonely man. Anselmo, informed of his public disgrace by a commoner on the road, contemplates his personal misfortune, and arranges his own death.

What distinguishes the mockery in the *Curioso Impertinente* from the mockery of the rest of *Don Quixote?* Burlesque mockery establishes a set-up for a critical review of absolutes. This critical review forbids a choice between absolutes, while instead, fusing conventionally separate categories such as history and fiction, appearance and reality, spirit and matter, or ends and means. In the example of *Don Quixote*, the mad hidalgo establishes--discursively, and enacts physically--an apparently fine defense of preconceived chivalric notions which might have been considered morally and socially noble, and virtuous for his contemporaries if their defense relied on contemporary guides for behavior instead of their accordance with a fictional guide set out in the chivalric romances. Thus, for those both familiar and unfamiliar with literary chivalric guidelines, the hidalgo's defense of fictional chivalric behavior as a functional code of behavior for his contemporary world often seems to make sense and seems even to have substance.

Unlike Anselmo, the mad hidalgo spouts arguments that seem reasonable and that possess apparently valuable information. In fact, close examination of his seemingly reasonable discourses is key to perception of many of the serious issues of morality, human values, and social orders of the day. To summarize, then, a contemporary hidalgo (1605-1615), one of many like him, imitates fabulous fiction and is mocked routinely with everyday jokes, and some fantastic, out-of-the-ordinary hoaxes, which recreate and reproduce, burlesquely, an air of the fabulous and fantastic. This is where the social function of jokes lies because the social and historical types consistently debunk putting ideals into practice when the fellow who is doing so is an Alonso Quijano *el bueno*, gone mad and dressed to prove it. The burlesque, however, is greater since, while the mouthed ideological and utopian notions are not mocked directly, but hailed as sound and acceptable by the hidalgo's contemporaries, they are mocked consistently by the narrative frame.

The mad Anselmo is not only unreasonable but socially dangerous. His *burla* or mockery of the inviolable social codes for behavior is taken too far. Anselmo's motive seems to be based on the desire for amusement and entertainment. However, he takes the amusement to its logical conclusion. A *good* joke should never be at the expense of a third party. The *Quixote* text defines, in an exemplary novel, what is meant by *"no son burlas las que duelen, ni hay pasatiempos que valgan si son con daño de tercero."* (II:62 509) Anselmo does not forgive Lotario, the instrument of his dishonor, for hurting an innocent. He recognizes that Camila cannot be held responsible for his impertinent curiosity which leads him to act indecently, irresponsibly, and unreasonably.

The fictive readers of the tale as well as those of *Don Quixote* do not laugh at Anselmo. He is not a woebegone figure like the mad hidalgo, but instead, an exemplary community figurehead who has gone awry. His private mockery of fidelity, marriage, loyalty, and friendship becomes the object of public gossip. The *Curioso Impertinente* is too farfetched for the priest who reads the tale to the group of listeners gathered at the inn while the burlesqued madman is asleep. Ironically, of course, the madman does manage to interrupt the tale during his wild, violent dream and sleep walking.

The account of Anslemo's irreverence of venerated social principles and standards, that is, his impertinence, is pertinent to *Don Quixote* for thematic and schematic reasons.

The exemplary novel provides a model of misguided behavior which results in public scorn of private social deviance from social norms. The unattractive model guides the outcome of Fernando's impertinent mockery of friendship, loyalty to Cardenio, and fidelity and promise of marriage to Dorotea. The *Curioso* focuses on mockery as one of many mediating factors between individuals and the society in which they live. The *Curioso* also provides an exemplary model of mockery taken too far. Anselmo's jest fails and it must be read and accounted for as a serious transgression of commonsensical social interaction and reasonable moral judgment. Anselmo's undiscerning excessive mockery of the social codes of behavior occasions shrewd scorn and contempt.

What is the essential connection between the mockery characteristic of the narration of the mad hidalgo's misadventures in contemporary Spanish society and that of the *Curioso Impertinente*? The essential connection is the humorous disposition of the first, and the distempered disposition of the second. Burlesque mockery forces an apparent irreverence toward moral systems, social codes and virtuous life without ever destroying those systems, codes and standards. In burlesque mockery absurd versions of morality, proper behavior and reputation are exposed and laughed at. Burlesque mockery is necessarily both jesting and serious but never only jesting or only serious.

The Seriocomic and the Economy of Burlesque Mockery

The notion of *serio ludere* has been defined as "exercises of wit designed to amuse an audience sufficiently sophisticated in the arts of language to understand them" (Colie 5). In the *Autoridades* (1732) *jocoserio* is defined as an adjective which is applied to *el estilo que mezcla las chanzas con lo sentencioso y sério*. In this chapter the patterns and techniques in *Don Quijote* that make up these *exercises of wit* are highlighted in terms of some of the shared values and sentiments concerning learned and popular conventions which readers must handle to be able to appreciate the humorous disposition of the burlesque mode in *Don Quixote*. The analysis of specific textual examples illustrates *how* Cervantes was able to identify and mock the most salient intellectual incompatibilities, influential moral anomalies,

and perplexing social factors of his age in a very amusing but
critical way.

The economy of burlesque mockery is that it builds a
critical awareness of the limitations and rigidity of everyday
idealistic, impractical and archaic ideals by testing the
interpretation of an ideal against the social reality in which it
is *supposed* to function successfully. As suggested earlier,
Cervantes's burlesque mode of representation has been tied
exclusively to an age of sordid and miserable realities: the
decadence of Imperial Spain. Through the method of
burlesque representation extreme pity, leniency, sympathy
and compassion toward social madness are slated against
excessive severity, rigor, inclemency and stringency. Certainly,
as in the *Curioso*, the result of flattening an ideal against its
material representation has the potential for being tragic.
However, the result of testing any socially generated ideal
against its faithfully unconvincing counterfeit representation
in fiction and everyday reality is amusing because true
feelings of pity or compassion are inhibited by the bogus
manner in which these very feelings are construed.

Readers are amused when they are continually encouraged
to operate these potentially alarming contradictions between
ideal and reality, spirit and matter, or history and fiction in
an apparently frivolous and playful fashion. The critical
review of absolutes appears harmless because there is no
obvious infraction against what Cervantes's contemporaries
held inviolable. The essence of the ills inherent in the
perception of Imperial Decadence is essential to the mockery
made of those ills. To be certain: the serious gist of
representation, *is*, paradoxically, in the jest; that is, in terms
of *Don Quixote* modern readers are constantly dealing with
the critical functions of the burlesque mode.

The Serious Determinants of Burlesque: *Don Quixote* and the Spanish Golden Age

It happens that the serious dimension of the burlesque
lies in the very mode of burlesque imitation which produces a
contrast by going beyond the superficial appearance of things
ridiculed and mocked: the hidalgo's emulation contrasts with
the superficial appearance of chivalric heroes. Obviously the
"externals" of burlesque heroism and the essence of heroism
coincide by contradicting each other. But going underneath

the superficial appearances of burlesque is no simple task. First, the serious elements which lie within the burlesque are not simply there waiting to be found. In the case of *Don Quixote*, for example, the narrative (re)presentation of the complex world of madness as well as the existing scholarly attempts to understand this fictional world demand the task of producing the literary and critical concepts appropriate to the serious determinants hidden within the burlesque mode. Furthermore, conceptualizing the burlesque is not enough: the task is to show how seriousness determines and gives rise to burlesque which is, necessarily, apparent and observable in everyday life.

To understand the burlesque mode of representation consists in going beneath the appearance of the society of the crazy hidalgo to the reality underlying it (i.e. the false values or pretensions of chivalry and glory). Although the burlesque seems in many ways like parody, caricature and especially travesty, there are three specific proposals about the relationship between burlesque appearances and serious dimensions that allow burlesque to stand apart: first, the burlesque appearance or the mocking imitation conceals beneath its threadbare appearance of counterfeit the authenticity of seriousness and history. Certainly, the *hero* Don Quixote conceals in this manner the serious hidalgo Alonso Quijano. Secondly, the burlesque appearance is best explained--and determined by--the serious reality that *appears* in the mock-imitation. The conduct of Don Quixote is understood because it is determined by the discreet manner of the hidalgo who is the one that *appears* as the ridiculous version of chivalric heroism. And thirdly, the burlesque appearance is often lively and convincing and in this sense *real*: the amusing antics of Don Quixote are much more attractive than the miserable reality of the common hidalgo of Alonso Quijano *el bueno*, yet one cannot be divorced from the other.

The burlesque mode of representing the *character* Alonso Quijano dramatizes hilariously the discrepancy between the model and the imitation, or else between appearance and reality. No one will deny that the hidalgo does not merely imitate chivalric heroes but instead the ethos of nobility by reconstructing, through fiction, the particular way of life of heroic and magnanimous men. His burlesque representation of all chivalric details including noble lineage, worthy ancestors, social hierarchy, high rank, strong, respectable and honest males, combat, duels, refined language; beautiful damsels and good riders, and so on, is laughed at, ridiculed and degraded. His main preoccupation is with distinguishing himself to fame. Yet, his idealism and claim to fame involve a false perception of *true* virtue. The burlesque representation obtains because his *excellence*, which can only be proven through deeds which, hilariously and grotesquely, mimic heroic deeds by fictional knights errant, needs to be appreciated by others. His reputation relies on what others think of him. The irony is that there is nothing more degrading than to be ridiculed and laughed at.

The strategies of burlesque in *Don Quixote* allow readers to develop fresh associations and correspondences between idealism and reality which produce often amusing rational insights that uncover ready-made, but overtly (in)adequate and already worn-out solutions offered time and time again in history. Thus the hoax or *burla* is the classic illustration of the *distinction and connection* between burlesque and seriousness, illusion and reality, fiction and history. Burlesque obtains when the so-called *hero* is degradingly mocked. However, the ironic dimension of the narrative suggests that this burlesque appearance is also misleading since the sane exploit the crazy hidalgo by taking advantage of the madness that leads to burlesque representation. The burlesque appearance is inseparable from the seriousness of hoax.

CONCLUDING REMARKS

There is an implied premise in Anthony Close's provocative rejection of most *Don Quixote* studies as *untrue* to the author's plans and imitations: modern readers are products of what the major modern appraisals of the *Quixote* have propagated; and, similarly, Cervantes scholars should be aware of the cultural and academic conditions that have shaped, in one way or another, modern readings of the Spanish classic. Close provides a historical survey of radical changes in reading (and understanding) the burlesque narrative about a local madman: from its publication to modern times, he charts the ways in which that reading has changed as the history of ideas in which readings of literature are rooted, kept on changing. The modern ways in which readers and critics have read the *Quixote* text have profoundly influenced the interpretation of the work: the interpretations of the *Quixote* text range from that of a funny burlesque to a serious, even tragic view of lost illusions. The shifts in interpretations are of interest now because scholars are in the midst of reexamining all literary categories and also because the over-serious interpretations of the *Romantic critics* and their tradition have never laced all the loose threads of the *Don Quixote* text together.

The Close premise, for example, leads to some stark implications for all Hispanic historiography. In terms of *Don Quixote* readers have been trained within two planes of understanding on which the form and meaning of the two-part narrative burlesque (1605, 1615) have been perceived. There is the plane of the *textual* or *literary* sense of the

burlesque in the *Quixote* as revealed commonsensically from
the author's declared intentions concerning the parodic or
invective aspect of the burlesque; but there is simultaneously,
a series of interpretations of that same textual or literal
reality. The supposed deeper *meanings* and *interpretations*
have been produced, maybe even *invented* or *imposed*, within
Cervantine studies and expostulated repeatedly in hundreds
of ways by some of the most respected scholars in the field.
Now, so far removed from each other, are these two readings
of the same burlesque narrative, or, even, of *perceived*
burlesque, that the diametrically opposed interpretations
derived from them, *funny* or *serious*, appear to be those of
wholly different burlesques or burlesque modes.

  What is the burlesque, then, not only in *Don Quixote*, but
in other *Golden Age* texts? Lest anyone think the question
obvious or superfluous, one might point to the on-going
polemics, which range from savage, wistful or amusing
regarding every aspect, surrounding the theory and practice of
Don Quixote as a *burlesque imitation of the serious romances
of chivalry*. In parallel, the same applies to Quevedo's
frivolous attacks. The functions of the burlesque mode in
Golden Age literature are open to inquiry. The question of
various readings or diverse and often contradictory
interpretations as well as provocatively ambiguous
historiography of the period are often relevant to one, and
only one factor: the mode of burlesque representation of
critical issues in Spanish Golden Age burlesque texts.

  No one to my knowledge has ever denied (for they cannot)
the fact that the burlesque permeates the narrated episodes
of *Don Quixote*, I and II, or the situations in Góngora's
Píramo y Tisbe, Lope de Vega's *Gatomaquia* or Quevedo's
burlesque sonnets. The burlesque mode of representation is
pervasive, explicit, inhering in most descriptive details,
phrases, images, proverbs, characters and actions. Each
element of the burlesque mode qualifies and is qualified by
every other. Yet, despite the global agreement of the
burlesque presence and dominance, wherever has there been
a single burlesque situation sufficiently explicated without
debates and controversies regarding its art, and function in
history? Most investigations concerning the burlesque of *Don
Quixote* and of other Golden Age texts (with the possible
exception of Valle-Inclán's unknown or scandalously ignored

observations) are usually only suggestive, indicating, therein, possibilities or tokens and not definitive explanations.

Although the theory of burlesque (like parody or satire) and its applicability to Golden Age texts include discussions which appear to be abstract, they are ultimately meant to be relevant to the analysis of concrete works. The long reappraisal of *Don Quixote* in terms of the burlesque (which is used here not as an end but as a pretext in terms of the burlesque) grew out of reviewing the contradictions and confusions not only of the *Quixote* but of the *Quixote* experts who have tried to disentangle the enigmas posed by the consistently elaborated burlesque patterns of the narrative. In this sense, the two chapters on the *Quixote* serve to highlight it as a paradigm of what burlesque is and what its diverse functions might be. When scholars reexamine the *canon* and other orthodox interpretations it is necessary to consider the *foundations* of burlesque--in other burlesque texts. Although only a few literary texts of the Golden Age have been studied here, the thesis implies that other forms could be included (texts such as burlesque paintings, music, and all cultural productions) as Linda Hutcheon has done with *A Theory of Parody*. The contribution of such investigations and explorations is that the analysis of the *burlesque mode* becomes a means to open ways of solving diverse problems concerning the burlesque literary examples although it cannot claim to be a definitive interpretation of those texts.

The aim has been to address certain theoretical and historical issues of evaluation by presenting practical expositions of certain representative examples of the burlesque mode. The ultimate purpose was to expose both the burlesque and the controversy that surrounds it to do a thorough critique. There have also been some excursions into the literary and cultural history of burlesque works as well as their reception. It happens that the various burlesque genres (especially during Spain's Imperial growth and decadence-- from Cervantes to Quevedo) have often been bypassed or dealt a rough treatment in terms of equitable representation in the Hispanic canon. This explains my focus on the critique of burlesque rather than its detailed history or development. Works by Cervantes, Góngora and Quevedo--and, in particular, the very controversial *Don Quixote* text--have been taken as paradigms of the burlesque mode of representation rather than as subjects for detailed analyses.

Thus, in method, this study on the burlesque of the Spanish Golden Age combines practical analysis and some theory: on the one hand, letting some decidedly burlesque works themselves explain and define the burlesque mode of representation; and on the other, providing as much critical or theoretical discussion of the burlesque as possible. The purpose was to evaluate most of the intrinsic and social factors of burlesque production, and, in particular, their applicability to the study of all Spanish literary genres connected with or depending on the burlesque. In order to analyze the dense episodes of the *Quixote*, for example, the implications of the burlesque mode of representation had to be developed through several levels of discussion and history until it was ultimately able to grasp and explain the complexities of what is obviously a very funny book about very critical issues. Cervantes's own view of the burlesque mode within *Don Quixote* and the *entremeses* (like Valle-Inclán's later view of the grotesque and the *esperpentos*) is at the level of the *comic*, and as demonstrated here the analysis of the burlesque mode is an indispensable basis for the development of new ways with which to analyze burlesque texts. It is from this angle that the few works chosen, especially *Don Quixote*, treated in some detail as burlesques, are enough.

The central point of this study about the burlesque mode of literature has been the identity of burlesque laughter and serious concern. The majority of serious motifs of Western civilization are mockingly burlesqued in the representative texts analyzed here or at least they have mockery, laughter or travesty for the mode of articulation. The question for these Spanish Golden Age burlesque texts is how far and to what effect the burlesque articulation of serious matters is, functionally or narratively speaking, carried out. As an illustrative example, just exactly what readers are to understand by burlesque (and its related modes) is explained and illustrated throughout *Don Quixote* with remarkable clarity: Cervantes is not confused; in historiography the reading of the burlesque narrative has been confused. The burlesque representations of the fictive situation make up the comic, even distant and disrespectful, point of view which mocks and debunks utopian and glorious chivalric idealism for denying foolishly and pathetically that the daily realities and the present social world of La Mancha have importance-- or even true reality. *Don Quixote's* idealism about history, which is burlesqued as foolish madness, consists in nothing else (just as in the original source, the romances of chivalry) than in assuming that present social realities including those of the insignificant fifty year old hidalgo or the credulous peasant have no veritable substance or importance.

Chivalric idealism transcends the reality of inns, prostitutes, peasants, landowners, merchants, traders, windmills, shepherds, and barber's basins. Don Quixote's idealism ascribes these same things to castles, maidens, squires, gentlemen, warriors, giants, armies and military gear. Social realities are *meta-realized*, and transformed into ideals. It happens that these specific transcendences of reality are consistently and rigorously burlesqued for all the ridicule and laughter that can be squeezed out of their *reductio-ad-absurdum*. In *Don Quixote*, what is burlesqued (and hence parodied, satirized, travestied, inveighed, criticized, and laughed at) is what has already, by itself, become an absurd version of how things should be but are not. The burlesque imitation of chivalric values, in which a local hidalgo extends the identity of his concerns for nobility and the current decadence (*oro/hierro*) to the identity of seriousness and burlesque, heroism and mock-heroism, follows logically and never flags.

This pattern is probably also true of the classic split regarding the comic and tragic. Yet the burlesque mode of representation is special because, on all counts, it carried the *split and convergence* to all its logical ends. Nothing is as *disparatado* as the serious attempt to perform what comes out as a burlesque act in origin, execution, reception and even in memory or articulation. To put it in modern terms, heroic idealism does not recognize historical events as a veritable reality, as something ultimate and absolute or as something ideal or eternal. Consequently, the opposition in chivalric romances, of real and ideal or ideal and verisimilar, has no significance. It never enters into the equation of narrative structure. It is the function of the burlesque mode in *Don Quixote* to point out, at all turns of the narrative, that the opposition of hero and hidalgo or ideals and concrete reality or, finally, serious intents and comic results do have significance.

Any literary study, therefore, which ascribes often exclusively *ultimate*, *absolute*, or *philosophic* meanings to burlesque mockery without considering the split inscribed within the narrative's burlesque mode, (that is, bypassing the burlesque as such), would not deserve the name of objective, historical or unbiased literary scholarship. Perhaps there is a need for a disclaimer. Such an attitude may carry Anthony Close's onslaught to the level of a scholarly slum-clearance, but it may well be that, eventually, an all out rejection of the *Quixote* canon is the only inevitable result of a study of the *Quixote* strictly for what it is: on the artistic level, a burlesque of representing traditional narratives, whereby the formal apparatus is as important as the episodic contents. The novel is, burlesquely, *how* the novel came about to be as it is, on the reading or social level and on the historical level of reception or reading. It is a laughable representation of traditional values of chivalry and heroism, whereby idealistic messages, themes and ideas of traditional values are hilariously mocked for their pretentiousness and inauthenticity. As an example, the function of the burlesque is to preserve the hidalgo and the peasant from the knight errant and the squire. Throughout the *Quixote* idealism says that history *seems* to be, but is not. The cases of the prostitutes, Juan Haldudo, the cage, the walled library are a testimony to the problems of appearance and reality, fiction and history. The burlesqued idealism shows that history *seems* to be only because it *is*. In other words, Don Quixote is the ridiculous, laughable figure he seems to be. Thanks to the burlesque prism, what is for the idealist an illusion of historical reality is, simultaneously, the historical reality of an *absurd* illusion of the world. In this key issue of the ironic interplays between appearance and reality--perhaps the key theme of Western culture--the burlesque mode of elaborating the problem is the catalyst for the entire novel.

Finally, the apparent *innocence* or *spontaneity* or even simplicity and frivolousness of the burlesque in *Don Quixote* make up the foundation of the historical function of the burlesque madness of the hero and its radical potential. The burlesque mode of representation in the *Quixote* provides the one irony of the novel that gives a serious coherence to all the episodes and hence a serious cause and effect to the narrative: what the fictive madman most desires is to become, like Amadis, the hero of a *romance*, and the fictional hero of a prose narrative. What the hero gets in this burlesque novel is just what he desires: the chance to be the protagonist of a long prose narrative, thanks to the burlesque. For the *Quixote* is, as all critics agree, just that: a burlesque representation of chivalric romances.

NOTES

Chapter 1 Notes

[1] The cultural age of the Baroque as a historical concept was redefined recently by José Antonio Maravall in *La cultura del barroco*. Maravall situated the cultural age of Spanish Baroque within the first two-thirds of the seventeenth century and more specifically, the period encompassing the years 1605-1650. Maravall broadened the concept of baroque culture from a purely artistic style-denomination to a period concept that encompasses a culture, history, and social life in the early seventeenth century Spain that was perceived to be in crisis and transition. The significance of Maravall's study of the perception of crisis in the cultural age of the Baroque is clear for an investigation of the burlesque: the burlesque mode is a harmless and amusing way of representing the transformations of sensibility tied to changing social conditions.

[2] The term Golden Age refers to a corpus of texts produced in Spain during the sixteenth and seventeenth centuries. A more precise definition of the Spanish Golden Age is offered by Wlad Godzich and N. Spadaccini: "In Spanish literature, a cluster of such masterpieces came to be identified quite early and constituted what the Spaniards call the *siglos de oro*, which we have rendered by the singular but collective English term: the Spanish Golden Age" (Introduction *Literature Among Discourses* xii).

[3] The social and economic crisis of the reign of Philip III is well documented. For this study, however, it is more important that there was a awareness or perception of social, economic, political and moral crises among Spaniards that has been recorded and documented in letters and memorials by *arbitristas* like Sancho de Moncada, F. de Navarrete or G. de Cellorigo as well as through fictional representations of crisis in books and poems.

[4] Festive literature is used here to represent those Spanish works called "obras festivas." The adjective "festivo" suggested "lo que es de fiesta y de plazer" (*Autoridades*). "Festivo" is also provided as a synonym for "jocoso." (*Autoridades*) In fact, "alegre", "festivo", and "chancero" are given as definitions for "jocoso." (*Autoridades*).

[5] *Obras festivas* have traditionally been associated with "obras de pasatiempo" or works that passed the time by entertaining with frivolities, "de vanidad en vanidad" (*Autoridades*).

[6] Some studies which stand out in the sociology of amusement are by Gregory Bateson, Mikhail Bakhtin, Henri Bergson, Anthony J. Chapman, Clinton-Baddeley, H. C. Foot, Keir Elam, Desiderius Erasmus, R. Flemming, Michel Foucault, Sigmund Freud, Northrop Frye, Ed Galligan, J. H. Goldstein and P. E. McGhee, Morton Gurewitch, J. Henderson, Gilbert Highet, Johan Huizinga, Linda Hutcheon, Wolfgang Karrer, Edith Kern, A. Kernan, Walter Kerr, Harry Levin, G. Meredith, John Morreall, Margaret Rose, Michael Seidel, Enid Welsford and David Worcester. See *Bibliography*, especially the works included under the heading "Humor Theory and Practice."

[7] Most of the names of writers included here and in the following paragraphs are part of a unique study concerning the possible authors of the apocryphal *Don Quixote* by J.B.S.P. (*Avellaneda*. Madrid-Cadiz: Escelicier, S.L., 1940). The short study investigated the historical accusations concerning the authorship of the apocryphal *Quixote* (Part I), provided an alphabetical listing of 177 contemporary writers (Part II), and argued quite convincingly that Salas Barbadillo was indeed the author of the apocryphal *Don Quixote* (Part III). Part II is a rare compilation of the names, occupations, interests and writings of Cervantes's contemporaries.

[8] This discussion of amusement is based on the essays concerning amusement by Morreall and Scruton in *Philosophy of Humor* (Morreall ed.). Morreall and Scruton agree that to appreciate a jest one must be able to operate those categorical concepts in a non-practical, non-theoretical and amusing way to avoid any violation of conceptual patterns that might evoke negative emotions or disorientation.

[9] Spadaccini and Godzich *Literature among Discourses* xi. Spadaccini and Godzich highlight the importance of the Spanish *Golden Age* in terms of the development of the *literary canon*. They explain that "the strategic location of Spanish literature in the validation of the construct at the time of its emergence suggests that we begin with it" (xi).

[10] Scholars such as Forcione, Maravall, J. Caro Baroja, Spadaccini, C. Sullivan, Nerlich, Russell, Close have rediscovered that the so-called masterpiece literature of the sixteenth and seventeenth century Spain was rich in inscribing popular-traditional elements and not only steeped in learned traditions.

[11] F. Sanchez and N. Spadaccini summarized what Maravall considered the role of picaresque literature in terms the perception of change and crisis: "*Desde la perspectiva de la historia social de las mentalidades, la literatura picaresca vendría a ser un testimonio de una situación de alta conflictividad y un exponente de primer orden de la crisis que atravesará la sociedad española a lo largo de su transición a una plena sociedad de clases y, por lo tanto, un índice de las profundas contradicciones sobre las que se asentaba la construcción del Estado Moderno.*" ("*La picaresca desde el pensamiento de Maravall.*" *Ideologies and Literature.* 3:1 (Spring 1988) 2).

¹² Some of my arguments have already been set forth in my article "The Backbone of Burlesque: Vertebral Jokes and Hoaxes in Cervantes' *Don Quixote*".

Chapter 2 Notes

¹³ Markiewicz. 'On the Definitions of Literary Parody,' *To Honor Roman Jakobson* 1:266, qtd. in *Parody//Meta-fiction* 39.

¹⁴ My entire discussion of Gypsy Rose Lee and American Burlesque Shows is rooted in the information offered in the following books concerning American Burlesque: *Gypsy* Rose Lee's *A Memoir* and her novel, *The G-String Murders* (a novel which later became the basis for the 1943 movie *Lady of Burlesque*). I also used Morton Minsky and Milt Machlin's *Minsky's Burlesque* (New York: Arbor House, 1986), and John E. Dimeglio's *Vaudeville U.S.A.* (Bowling Green, OH: Bowling Green University Popular Press, 1973) for general information concerning popular entertainment in the Depression Era.

¹⁵ See especially chapter one "Judgements, allusions et reminiscences la préciote et le burlesque 1620-1660" and chapter three concerning *Don Quixote* and burlesque realism.

¹⁶ The *Autoridades* defines chanza as "dicho burlesco, festivo, y gracioso, à fin de recrear el ánimo ù de exercitar el ingenio."

¹⁷ All citations are from the Luis Andrés Murillo edition of Don Quixote (*El ingenioso hidalgo don Quijote de la Mancha* I, II. Madrid: Castalia, 1978).

Chapter 3 Notes

¹⁸ *Obras de Góngora.* (Brussels, 1659).

¹⁹ Both N. Spadaccini and E. Asensio referred to the "óptica burlesca" in the introductions to their editions of Cervantes's *Entremeses*.

²⁰Francisco Madrid *La Vida altiva de Valle-Inclán* 104 and reproduced in Cardona and Zahareas *Visión del esperpento* 237

²¹ See Wright, Thomas. *A History of Caricature and the Grotesque in Literature and Art* (New York: Frederick Ungar, 1986) and M. Eastman's Exaggeration as Weapon: Caricature, Burlesque, and Parody" (*Enjoyment of Laughter* New York: 1936, 156-162) for more detail on the nature of caricature.

²² *Obras de Góngora* (Brussels, 1659, Sonnet V). The Carreira version (*Luis de Góngora: Antología poética*) reads:

> Llegué a Valladolid; registré luego,
> desde el bonete al clavo de la mula,
> guardo el registro, que será mi bula
> contra el cuidado del señor don Diego.

> Busqué la orte en él, y yo estoy ciego,

o en la ciudad no está, o se disimula.
Clelebrando dïetas vi la gula,
que Platón para todos está en Griego.

La lisonja hallé y la ceremonia,
con luto, idolatrados los caziques,
amor sin Fe, interés con sus virotes.

Todo se halla en esta Babilonia
Como en botica grandes alambiques,
Y mas en ella títulos que botes.

23 The version in the edition from Brussels reads "*Haziendo Penitencia vi à la bula*" while the Carreira edition reads "*Celebrando dïetas, vi a la gula.*"

24 For a discussion of *medro* see Maravall's *La aspiración social de 'medro' en la novela picaresca* or his recent book on the picaresque.

25 For a useful study of tricksters in general and particularly in the work of Cervantes see Ruth El Saffar's study "Tricking the Trickster in the works of Cervantes" (*Symposium.* 1983 Summer; 37 (2) 106-124).

26 All citations are from Carreira's *Luis de Góngora Antología poética* (Madrid: Castalia, 1986). For the reader's ease I have included the line number of the verses and not the page number of the Carreira edition.

27 In a study of *Cervantes and the Spanish Comedia* N. Spadaccini highlighted the parallel discourses concerning *arte, gusto,* and *vulgo* in the notorious *Arte nuevo* and the theatre of Cervantes. According to Spadaccini "In his *Arte nuevo* Lope defends the primacy of pleasing and entertaining ("*dar gusto*") over what was right artistically, in the traditional Aristotelian sense ('*lo justo*')" (*Cervantes and the Spanish Comedia.* 55).

28 Góngora was not the only writer to make a mockery of Ovid's tragic version. An early example of burlesque in England might be the "play of Pyramus and Thisbe" performed by the character Bottom and his hilarious companions in *A Midsummer Night's Dream.* It seems that Shakespeare may have been making fun, through the legend, of the Interludes of earlier generations.

29 Arguments concerning the social consequences of burlesquing the ideology of pedigree were set forth in my article "Ideology of Pure Blood".

30 Américo Castro is still considered the foremost critic of Spain's identity crisis that involved *Old* and *New* Christians, Jews and Moors.

31 Spadaccini 220. All the following citations of the *Retablo* are from the Spadaccini edition of Cervantes's *Entremeses.*

32 Gonzalo de Cellorigo's Memorial (Microfilm of original,1600). In this section of the memorial Cellorigo discusses the social and ideological distractions from holding down legitimate occupations. He explains that since there is little value placed on agriculture, commerce, trade and manufacturing of products that Spaniards go against the divine Natural Order and God who desires that they work the land and not remain idle: "Lo que más ha destraido a los nuestros de la legítima ocupación que tanto

importa a esta republica, ha sido poner tanto a honra y la authoridad en el huir del trabajo: estimando en poco, a los que siguen en la agricultura, los tratos, los comercios, y todo cualquier género de manifactura contra toda buena política. Y llega a tanto, que por las constituciones de las ordenes militares, no parece sino que se han querido reduzir estos Reynos, a una república de hombres encantados, que vivan fuera del orden natural" (25).

Chapter 4 Notes

[33]*Divertir, desocupar: Don Quixote* was also considered to be part of the "*literatura de pasatiempo*". Such literature was "*diversión o entretenimiento en que se passa el tiempo*" (Autoridades). Perhaps the most obvious argument for reading *Don Quixote* as a purely entertaining book is the fact that from the seventeenth to the present century *Don Quixote* has been a book read by children and youth.

[34]*Don Quijote I* "*Prólogo*" 58. All citations are from the L. A. Murillo edition. *El ingenioso hidalgo don Quijote de la Mancha. I, II.* Madrid: Clásicos Castalia, 1973. For the ease of reading the references to citations from the *Quixote* text will be as follows: Book I or II: Chapter number, page number.

[35]Capmany *Teatro de la elocuencia española* IV 62, qtd. in the Bradford's edition of Clemencín's *Indice de notas* 105.

[36]M. Foucault was one of the first to argue that the history of madness was also the history of sanity in *Madness and Civilization*. Trans. Richard Howard. New York: Vintage Books, 1973.

[37]See studies listed in the bibliography by T. McCallum, B. Creel, J. H. Elliot, J. A. Maravall, A. Domínguez Ortíz, Vicente Lloréns, J. Lynch and P. Vilar for discussions of, contemporary seventeenth century Spaniards' perceptions of crisis.

[38]I have summarized here the ideas expressed in "Laughter" *Philosophy of Laughter and Humor*. New York: State University of New York Press, 1987 170. Scruton's propositions are essential to my arguments concerning the function of burlesque as a mode.

[39]It is well documented that the finances of many young men were ruined by their attentions to women. Quevedo, for example, burlesques the wanton waste of money in the *Buscón* when Pablos ends up spending his friends' savings trying to impress a young woman.

[40]Laughter as cure is elaborated especially in Burton's early seventeenth century English treatise on melancholia *The Anatomy of Melancholy* (New York: Vintage Books, 1977).

[41]Translations used for analysis of *burlesco* are Lorenzo Fransciosini Fiorentino's translation into Italian, *Dell ingenioso Cittadino Don Chisciotte della Mancia*. Venetia: Andrea Baba, 1625.; F. de Rosset's translation into French, *Seconde partie de L'Histoire de l'Ingendeux, et redovituble Chevalier, Don Quichot de la Manche*. Paris: Iacques do Clos and Denis Moreau, 1618; the translation into Portuguese by Viscondes de Castilho e de Azevedo, *O engenhoso fidalgo Dom Quijote de la Mancha*. Porto: Companhia Litteraria, 1876-78; and two early English translations:

The History of the valoroys Knight Errant Don Quixote of the Mancha.
Rans. William Stansby. London, 1612 and *The history of Don Quixote de la Mancha with an account of his exploits and adventures.* London: Milner and Sowerby. I also consulted early translations into Catalonian, Dutch and German but the French, Italian and Portuguese seem, for now, enough.

Chapter 5 Notes

[42]The *Autoridades* defines *disparate* as akin to *dislate* "*cosa despropositada, la qual no se hizo o dixo con el modo devido y con cierto fin, y assí disparar es hazer una salida sin intento, dezir a lugar cierto; y los arcabuzes y las pieças de artillería se disparan quando tiran no a puntería, sino al ayre y que dé la pelota donde diere. Dislate: Un hecho despropositado, que a nadie puede parecer bien. Esta contraydo de la palabra disparate, la qual se dixo de dispar, por no tener paridad ni igualdad con la razón*" (477, my emphasis and italics).

[43]The prejudice against *Dueñas* and *Doncellas* in contemporary Spanish society has been established by C. H. Marianella. (*Dueñas' and 'Doncellas.*" She illustrated that *dueñas* were anything but reliable servants.

INDEX

SELECT BIBLIOGRAPHY

Burlesque, Theory and Practice

Angell, Olva. Burlesk. Dikt. Oslo: Gyldendal, 1966.

Ashton, John. Humour, Wit, and Satire of the Seventeenth Century. London, 1883. Reprint: New York: Dover, 1968.

Bar, Francis. Le genre burlesque en France au XVIIe siècle. Etude de style. Paris: Editions d'Artrey, 1960.

Bec, Pierre. Burlesque et obscenité chez les troubadours: pour une approche du contre-texte médieval. Paris: Stock, 1984.

Bond, R.P. English Burlesque Poetry 1700-1750. Cambridge: Harvard University Press, 1932.

Boothe, W.W. A Study of the Major Burlesque Works of Charles Cotton (1630-1687). Diss. (Masch.) Nashville, IN. 1965.

Brun, P.A. "Masque de Burlesque, Charles Coippeau, Sieur Dassoucy, et son Ovide en belle humeur" Autour du Dix-Septième. Siècle. Grenoble: 1901.

Brunetière, F. "La maladie burlesque" Etudes critiques sur l'histoire de la litérature française, 8 Bde. Paris, 1917, VIII, 57-94.

Burlesque et formes parodiques dans la littérature et les arts. Seattle-Tubingen: Actes du Colloque de l'Universite du Maine,1987.

Caldicott, C.E.J. "Baroque or Burlesque? Aspects of French Comic Theatre in the Early 17th Century." Modern Language Review, 1984. Oct. 79(4) 797-809.

Mockery in Spanish Golden Age Literature:
Analysis of Burlesque Representation

Clinton-Baddeley, V.C. The Burlesque Tradition in the
English Theatre after 1660. London: Methuen, 1952.
Dimeglio, John E. Vaudeville U.S.A. Bowling Green, Ohio:
Bowling Green University Popular Press, 1973.
Eastman, M. "Exaggeration as Weapon: Caricature,
Burlesque, and Parody." Enjoyment of Laughter. New
York: Simon and Schuster, 1936, 156-162.
Flibbert, Joseph. Melville and the Art of Burlesque.
Amsterdam: Rodopi, 1974.
Flögel, C.F. Geschichte des Burlesken. Leipzig: hg. F.
Schmidt, 1794.
Fournel, V. "Du burlesque en France et en particulier du
Virgile Travesti de Scarron." La littèrature indépendante
et les écrivains oubliés. Paris, 1862,   277-329.
Gosse, E. "Burlesque." Selected Essays. First Series. 2 vol.
London: W. Heinemann,1928, 181-190.
Gruber, J.G. "Burlesk" Allgemeine Encyklopädie der
Wissenschaft und Künste. Leipzig: J.S. Ersch und J.G.
Gruber. I:14 (1825): 114-118.
Havens, Raymond Dexter. "Epic and Burlesque Poetry." The
Influence of Milton on English Poetry. New York: 1961,
315-322.
Hawkins, John. Travesty. New York: New Directions, 1976.
Hébert, Chantal. Le burlesque au Québec: un divertissement
populaire. Ville La Salle: Hurtubise HMH, 1981.
Iffland, James. "'Antivalues' in the Burlesque Poetry of
Góngora and Quevedo." Neophilologus. 63 (1979) 220-
237.
Joly, Monique. "La bourle et son interprétation: recherches
sur le passage du XVIIe siècle." Lille: Atelier National
Reproduction des Thèses, Université de Lille III;
Toulouse: Diffusion France-Ibérie Recherche, Univ. de
Toulouse-le-Mirail, 1982.
Jump, John J. Burlesque. London: Methuen. 1972.
Keeble, T.W. "Some Mythological Figures in the Golden Age
Satire and Burlesque" Bulletin of Spanish Studies. XXV
(1948) 238-46.
Kitchen, George. A survey of burlesque and parody in
English. New York: Russell and Russell, 1967.

Kral, Petr. Le burlesque ou Morale de la tarte à la crème.
Paris: Stock, 1984.
Kurak, A. Imitation, Burlesque Poetry, and Parody. A Study
of Some Augustan Critical Destinations. Diss. University
of Minnesota, Minneapolis, 1963.
Lee, Gypsy Rose. Gypsy, A Memoir. New York: Harper,
1957.
---. The G-String Murders. New York: Simon and Schuster,
1941.
Leeble, T.W. "Some Mythological Figures in Golden Age
Sature and Burlesque." Bulletin of Hispanic Studies.
XXV (1948) 238-246.
Lioni Ullman, Pierre. "The Burlesque Poems which Frame
the *Quijote*." Anales Cervantinos. 9 (1961-2).
Martín, Adrienne L. "Cervantes and the Burlesque Sonnet."
DA 48 (1987): 880-817. Harvard University.
Mathec, C.K. "Parody and Burlesque of Heroic Ideals in
Wycherley's Comedies: A Critical Reinterpretation,"
Papers on Language and Literature 8 (1972), 273-283.
McElroy, John F. Parody and burlesque in the tragicomedies
of Thomas Middleton. Salzburg: Institüt für Engl.
Sprache u Literatur, Univ. Salzburg, 1972.
Minsky, Morton and Milt Machlin. Minsky's Burlesque. New
York: Arbor House, 1986.
Morillot, P. Scarron et le genre burlesque. Paris: Lecène et H.
Oudin, 1888.
Nestle, W. "Anfänge einer Götterburleske bei Homer"
Griechiosche Studien. Untersuchungen zur Religion,
Dichtung, und Philosophie der Griechen. Stuttgart
1948,1-31.
Newlin, Keith. Hardboiled Burlesque: Raymond Chandler's
Comic Style. San Bernardino, CA: Bongo Press, 1986. c.
1984. Revision of Thesis Col. State U.
Rence, Robert Irving. "The Burlesque Techniques employed
by James Planché in his dramatic works and their
relation to the English burlesque tradition between
Fielding and W.S. Gilbert." Diss. University of
Minnesota, Minneapolis, 1967.

Replogle, C. "Not Parody, Not Burlesque: The Play within the Play in Hamlet." Modern Philology. 67 (1969/70), 150-159.

Richards, Edward Ames. Hudibras in the Burlesque Tradition. New York: Columbia UP, 1937.

Rogers, F.R. Mark Twain's Burlesque Patterns as seen in the Novels and Narratives 1855-1955. Dallas: Southern Methodist University Press: 1960.

Rubbi, A. ed. Satiri e burleschi del secolo XVI. Venezia: A. Zatlo e figli, 1787.

Salomon, Roger B. Desperate Storytelling: Mock-Heroic Mode. Athens, Georgia: University of Georgia Press, 1987.

Schlötke-Schroer. "Die französische burleske Kunst des 17. Jahrhunderts in geistesgeschichtlicher Bedeutung." Zeitschrift für französische Sprache und Literatur 64 (1942), 321-347 u. 65 (1943/44), 477-511.

Shepperson, A.B. The Novel in Motley: A History of the Burlesque Novel in English. Cambridge, Massachusetts: Harvard University Press, 1936.

Sobel, Bernard. A Pictoral History of Burlesque. New York: Putnam, 1956.

Stoppard, Tom. Travesties. London: Faber, 1975.

Sypnicki, Josef. "La continuation des procédés du comique verbal de Rabelais chez les burlesques: la formation des mots." Le comique verbal en France au XVIe Siècle. Warsaw: Eds. de l'Univ. de Varsovie, 1981. 187-197.

Toldo, P. "Etudes sur la poésie burlesque française de la Renaissance" Zeitschrift für romanische Philologie 25 (1901), 71-93, 215-229, 257-277, 385-410, 513-532.

Topazio, V.W. "Voltaire's Pucelle: a Study in Burlesque," Studies on Voltaire and the 18th Century 2 (1956) 207-223.

Trussler, S. "Introduction" Burlesque Plays of the Eighteenth Century, London: hg. S. Trussler, 1969, VII-XIV.

Weisstein, U. "Parody, Travesty, and Burlesque: Imitations with a Vengeance." Proceedings of the IVth Congress of the International Comparative Literature Association. 2 vols. The Hague: F. Jost, 1966, 802-811.

Werner, D. Das Burleske. Versuch einer
literaturwissenschaftlichen Begriffs-bestimmung, Diss.
Berlin, 1966.

West, Albert Harvey. L'influence française dans la poésie
burlesque en Angleterre, entre 1660 et 1700. Paris: H.
Champion, 1931.

Wilson, Robert F. "Their Form Confounded" Studies in the
Burlesque Play from Udall to Sheridan. The Hague:
Mouton, 1975.

Wortley, Richard. Skin Deep in Soho. London: Jarrods Publ.,
1969.

Watters, George M. Burlesque. New York: S. French, 1935.

Humor, Theory and Practice

Apte, Mahadev L. Humor and Laughter: An Anthropological
Approach. Ithaca: Cornell University Press, 1985.

Bakhtin, Mikhail. Rabelais and His World. Trans. Helen
Iswolsky. Cambridge, Massachusetts: M.I.T. Press,
1968.

---. The Dialogic Imagination. Ed. Michael Holquist. Trans.
Caryl Emerson and Michael Holquist. Austin: University
of Texas Press, 1983.

Barthes, Roland. Mythologies. New York: Hill and Wang,
1973.

Bateson, Gregory. "A Theory of Play and Fantasy." Steps to
an Ecology of the Mind. London: Intertext, 177-93.

Baudelaire, C. The Essence of Laughter. Introduction. New
York: Meridian Books, 1956.

Bentley, Eric. "Farce." Comedy: Meaning and Form. Ed.
Robert W. Corrigan. 2nd ed. New York: Harper & Row,
1981, 193-211.

Bergson, Henre. Laughter: An Essay on the Meaning of the
Comic. New York: Macmillan, 1911.

Berlezne, D.E. "Humor and its Kin." Psychology of Humor.
New York: Academic Press, 1972.

Bertin, Giovanni Maria. Disordine esistenziale e instanza
della razione: tragico e comico: violenza ed eros. Bologna:
Cappelli, 1981.

Booth, Wayne C. The Rhetoric of Irony. Chicago: The
University of Chicago Press, 1974.
---. The Rhetoric of Fiction. Chicago and London: The
University of Chicago Press, 1961.
Bristol, Michael D. Carnival and Theatre: Plebian Culture
and the Structure of Authority in Renaissance England.
New York and London: Methuen, 1985.
Burke, Kenneth. Attitudes Toward History. Los Altos, CA:
Hermes, 1959.
---. A Grammar of Motives. Berkeley: University of California
Press, 1962.
---. A Rhetoric of Motives. Berkeley and London: University of
California Press, 1969.
Brooke, Nicholas. Horrid Laughter in Jacobean tragedy.
London: Open Books, 1979.
Caputi, Anthony Frances. Buffo: the Genius of Vulgar
Comedy. Detroit: Wayne State University Press, 1978.
Cardona, Rodolfo, and Anthony N. Zahareas. Visión del
esperpento: teoría y práctica en los esperpentos de Valle-
Inclán. Madrid: Castalia, 1970.
Caro Baroja, Julio. Carnaval. Madrid: Taurus, 1969.
Carpenter, R. "Laughter, a Glory in Sanity." American
Journal of Psychology, 33, (1922) 419-22.
Chapman, A. J. and H. C. Foot, eds. Humor and Laughter:
Theory, Research and Applications. London, New York:
Wiley, 1976.
---. It's A Funny Thing, Humour. Oxford, New York:
Pergamon Press, 1977.
Charney, Maurice. Comedy High and Low: An Introduction to
the Experience of Comedy. New York: Oxford University
Press, 1978.
Cherry, Charles Maurice. "The Nature of Comedy in Early
Drama of Lope de Vega." Diss. Northwestern University,
1980.
Collins, Anthony. A discourse concerning ridicule and irony in
writing. London. 1729.
Cornford, Francis. The Origin of Attic Comedy. Cambridge:
Cambridge University Press, 1934.

Crane, W.G. Wit and Rhetoric in the Renaissance.
Gloucester, Massachusetts: Peter Smith, 1964. (orig.
publ. 1937).

Crespo Matellan, Salvador. La parodia dramática en la
literatura española y análisis de *Los amantes de Teruel,*
comedia burlesca de Vicente Suarez de Deza. Salamanca:
Universidad de Salamanca, 1979.

Darst, David H. Imitatio. (Polémicas sobre la imitación en el
Siglo de Oro). Madrid: Orígenes, 1985.

Davis, Jessica M. Farce. London: Methuen, 1978.

Elam, Keir. Shakespeare's Universe of Discourse: Language-
Games in the Comedies. Cambridge, London and New
York: Cambridge University Press, 1985.

Elgin, Suzette Haden. The Gentle Art of Verbal Self-Defense.
Englewood Cliffs, New Jersey: Prentice Hall, 1980.

Elliot, Robert E. The Powers of Satire: Magic, Ritual, Art.
Princeton: Princeton University Press, 1960.

Erasmus, Desiderius. Praise of Folly. Trans. Betty Radice.
Hamondsworth: Penguin Books, 1971.

Fine, G.A. "Obscene Joking across Culture." Journal of
Communication, 26, 134-140, (1976).

Flemming, R. "Of Contrast Between Tragedy and Comedy."
Journal of Philosophy, 36, (1939) 543-553 .

Fischer, Seymour. Pretend the World is Funny and Forever:
A Psychological Analysis of Comedians, Clowns and
Actors. Hillsdale, New Jersey: L. Erlbaum
Association, 1981.

Foucault, Michel. Madness and Civilization. (3rd imp)
London: Tavistock Publishing Ltd., 1982.

---. The Order of Things. An Archeology of Human Sciences.
New York: Vintage Books, 1973.

Frazier, Harriet C. A Babble of Ancestral Voices.
Shakespeare, Cervantes, and Theobald. The Hague:
Mouton, 1974.

Freud, Sigmund. Jokes and Their Relation to the
Unconscious. Trans. James Strachey. New York and
London: W.W. Norton and Co. 1963.

Frye, Northop. Anatomy of Criticism. Princeton: Princeton
University Press, 1957.

---. A Natural Perspective: The Development of Shakespearean Comedy and Romance. New York: Harcourt, Brace and World, 1965.

Galligan, Edward L. The Comic Vision in Literature. Athens: University of Georgia Press, 1984.

---. "True Comedians and Flase, Don Quixote and Huckleberry Finn" Sewanee Review 86 (Winter 1978) 66-83.

Goffman, Erving. Frame Analysis: An Essay on the Organization of Experience. New York: Harper and Row, 1974.

Goldstein, J.H. and McGhee, P.E., eds. The Psychology of Humor. New York: Academic Press, 1972.

Grant, Mary A. The Ancient Rhetorical Theories of the Laugable. The Greek Rhetoricians and Cicero. Madison: University of Wisconsin Studies in Language and Literature. 21, 1924.

Grant, H.F. "The World Upside-down." Studies in Scottish Literature. (1973) 103-35.

Gruner, C.R. Understanding Laughter: The Workings of Wit and Humor. Chicago: Nelson-Hall, 1978.

Gurewitch, Morton. Comedy: The Irrational Vision. Ithaca and London: Cornell University Press, 1975.

Hazlett, W.C. Studies in Jocular Literature. Detroit: Gale, 1969. (Orig. 1890)

Henderson, J. The Maculate Muse: Obscene Language in Attic Comedy. New Haven: Yale University Press. 1975.

Herrick, Marvin T. Comic Theory in the Sixteenth Century. Urbana: University of Illinois Press, 1964.

---. Italian Comedy in the Renaissance. Urbana: University of Illinois Press, 1966.

---. Tragicomedy; Its Origin and Development in Italy, France and England. Urbana: University of Illinois Press, 1955.

Hirst, David L. Tragicomedy. London and New York: Methuen, 1984.

Huarte de San Juan, Juan. Examen de ingenios para las ciencias. Esteban Torre, ed., Madrid: Editora Nacional, 1976.

Highet, Gilbert. The Anatomy of Satire. Princeton: Princeton University Press, 1962.

Huizinga, Johan. Homo Ludens: A Study of the Play Element
    in Culture. Boston: The Beacon Press, 1962.
---. The Waning of the Middle Ages: A Study of Life, Thought
    and Art in France and the Netherlands in the XIV and
    XV Centuries. Trans. F. Hopman. Garden City:
    Doubleday Anchor Books, 1954.
Hume, Kathyrn. Fantasy and Mimesis: Responses to Reality
    in Western Literature. New York and London: Methuen,
    1984.
Hutcheon, Linda. A Theory of Parody: The Teachings of
    Twentieth Century Art Forms. New York: Methuen,
    1985.
Jauss, Hans Robert. Aesthetic Experience and Literary
    Hermeneutics. Trans. M. Shaw. Minneapolis: University
    of Minnesota Press, 1982.
---. Toward an Aesthetic of Reception. Minneapolis:
    University of Minnesota Press, 1982.
Kaiser, Walther. "The Last Fool" Praisers of Folly: Erasmus,
    Rabelais, Shakespeare. Cambridge: Harvard University
    Press, 1963.
Karrer, Wolfgang. Parodie, Travestie, Pastiche. München:
    W. Fink, 1977.
Kern, Edith. The Absolute Comic. New York: Columbia
    University Press, 1980.
Kernan, A. The Cankered Muse. New Haven: Yale University
    Press, 1959.
Kerr, Walter. Tragedy and Comedy. New York: Da Capo
    Press, 1967.
Klapp, O.E. "The Fool as Social Type." American Journal of
    Sociology. 55, (1950) 157-62.
Klotz, Volker. Burgerliches Lachtheater: Komodie, Posse,
    Schwank, Operette. München: Deutscher Taschenbuch-
    Verlag, 1980.
Lachmann, Renate. Bakhtin and Carnival Culture as
    Counter-Culture. Minneapolis: Center for Humanistic
    Studies, University of Minnesota, 1987.
Larsen, Egon. Wit as Weapon. London: Frederick Muller,
    1980.

Legman, G. No Laughing Matter: Rationale of the Dirty
    Joke. Second Series. Breaking Point, New Jersey:
    Wharton, 1975.
---. Rationale of the Dirty Joke. New York: Grove, 1968.
---. "Toward a Motif Index of Erotic Humor." Journal of
    American Folklore, 75, (1962) 227-248.
Lever, K. The Art of Greek Comedy. London: Methuen,
    1956.
Levin, Harry. "The Example of Cervantes." Contexts of
    Criticism. New York: Atheneum, 1963.
---. Veins of Humor. Cambridge, Massachusetts: Harvard
    University Press, 1972.
Maddox, Donald. Semiotics of Deceit: The Pathelin Era.
    Lewisburg, PA: Bucknell University Press, 1984.
Mahony, P. Barbed Wit and Malicious Humor. New York:
    Citadel, 1956.
Mandel, O. "What's So Funny: The Nature of the Comic."
    Antioch Review. 30, (1970) 73-89.
McCarther, H. "Tragic and Comic Modes." Criticism. 3, 36-45
    (1961)
Mc Ghee, P. and Jeffrey Goldstein, eds. Handbook of Humor
    Research. New York: Springer-Verlag. 1983.
McGhee, P. E. Humor, Its Origin and Development. San
    Francisco: W.H. Freeman, 1979.
Meredith, G. An Essay on Comedy. New York: Charles
    Schribner's Sons, 1918.
Mikhail, E.H. Comedy and Tragedy: A Bibliography of
    Critical Studies. New York: Whitston, 1972.
Milner, G.B. "Homo ridens: Towards a Semiotic Theory of
    Humor and Laughter." Semiotica. 1, 1-3 (1972)
Morreal, John., ed. The Philosophy of Laughter and Humor.
    New York: State University of New York Press, 1987.
---. Taking Laughter Seriously. Albany: State University of
    New York, 1982.
Nevo, R. "Toward a Theory of Comedy." Journal of Aesthetics
    and Art Criticism. 21, 338 (1963)
Olson, E. Theory and Comedy. Bloomington: Indiana
    University Press, 1970.
Palmer, D.J., ed. Comedy, Development in Criticism: A Case
    Book. London: Macmillan, 1984.

Paulos, John Allen. I Think Therefore I Laugh. An
    Alternative Approach to Philosophy. New York: Columbia
    University Press, 1985.
Petr, Pavel, David Roberts, and Philip Thomson, eds. Comic
    Relations: Studies in the Comic, Satire and Parody.
    Frankfurt am Main. New York: P. Lang, 1985.
Raskin, Victor. Semantic Mechanisms of Humor. Dordrecht
    and Boston: D. Reidel Publ. Co., 1985.
Reinhold Grimm, Walter Hink. Zwischen Satire und Utopie.
    Zur Komik Theorie und zur Geschichte der europäische
    Komödie. Frankfurt am Main: Suhrkamp, 1982.
Rey, Henri-François. La Parodie. Trad. María Paricio.
    Esplugues de Llobregat, Barcelona: Plaza y Janés, 1983.
Rey-Flaud, Bernadette. La farce, ou la machine à rire: théorie
    d'un genre dramatique,1450-1550. Geneve: Droz, 1984.
Rickonen, H.K. Menippean Satire as Literary Genre: With
    Special Reference to Seneca's *Apocolocyntosis*. Helsinki:
    Societas Scientiarum Fennica, 1987.
Risa y sociedad en el teatro del Siglo de Oro. Actes du 3e
    colloque du Groupe d'Etudes Sur le Théâtre Espagnol.
    Toulouse: C.N.R.S., 1980.
Romero-Navarro, Miguel. "El humorismo y la sátira de
    Gracían." Hispanic Review X, (1942) 126-146.
Rose, Margaret. Parody//Metafiction: An Analysis of Parody
    as a Critical Mirror to the Writing and Reception of
    Fiction. London: Croom Helm, 1979.
Sareil, Jean. L'écriture comique. Paris: Presses
    Universitaires de France, 1984.
Scholburg, Kenneth. Sátira e invectiva en la España
    medieval. Madrid: Gredos, 1971.
Seidel, Michael. Satiric Inheritance: Rabelais to Sterne.
    Princeton: Princeton University Press, 1979.
Shershow, Scott C. Laughing Matters: The Parodox of
    Comedy. Amherst: University of Massachusetts Press,
    1986.
Simon, R.K. The Labyrinth of the Comic: Theory and
    Practice from Fielding to Freud. Tallahassee: Florida
    State University Press, 1985.

Steig, Michael. "Defining the Grotesque: An Attempt at
    Synthesis." Journal of Aesthetics and Art Criticism 29
    (1970-71): 259.
Sontag, Susan. Illness as Metaphor. New York: Farrar,
    Straus and Giroux, 1978.
Stolz, Christiane. Die Ironie in Roman des Siglo de Oro:
    Untersuchung zur Narrativik im *Don Quixote*, im
    Guzmán de Alfarache und im *Buscón*. Frankfurt am
    Main: Peter D.L. Lang, 1980.
Swain, Barbara. Fools and Folly during the Middle Ages and
    the Renaissance. New York: Columbia University Press,
    1932.
Torrance, Robert. The Comic Hero. Cambridge,
    Massachusetts: Harvard University Press, 1978.
Todorov, Tzvetan. Mikhail Bakhtin: The Dialogical Principle.
    Trans. Wlad Godzich. Minneapolis: University of
    Minnesota Press, 1984.
Vasquez de Prada, Andrés. El sentido del humor. Madrid:
    Alianza Ed., 1976.
Viñas, David. Grotesco, inmigración y fracaso. Armando
    Discépolo. Buenos Aires: Corregidor, 1973.
Welsford, Enid. The Fool: His Social and Literary History.
    New York: Doubleday, 1961.
Willeford, W. The Fool and his Scepter: A Study in Clowns
    and their Audience. Evanston, Illinois: Northwestern
    University Press, 1969.
Wilson, J.H. Court Wits of the Restoration. New York:
    Octagon, 1967.
Worcester, David. The Art of Satire. Cambridge,
    Massachusetts: Harvard University Press, 1940.
Wright, Thomas. A History of Caricature and the Grotesque
    in Literature and Art. New York: Frederick Ungar, 1968.
Ziomeck, Henryk. Lo grotesco en la literatura española del
    siglo de oro. Madrid: Alcalá, 1983.

"Don Quijote" and Related Cervantine Studies

Translations and Adaptations: Below is a list of
translations and adaptations of <u>Don Quixote</u> consulted
concerning the translations of *burla* and *burlesco*. I have
included the complete bibliographical information for the
Biblioteca Nacional, Madrid (in parentheses) whenever
possible:

Catalan
Cervantes Saavedra, Miguel de. <u>L'Enginyos Cavaller Don</u>
<u>Quixot de la Manxa</u>. Trans. Antoni Bulberoy. Tusell.
(1891) (R 32387).
Dutch
Cervantes Saavedra, Miguel de. <u>Den Verstandigen Vroomen</u>
<u>Ridder Don Quichot de la Mancha</u>. 2 vol. Trans. Door
L.V.B.- Dordrecht: Jacubuy Savry. 1657. (Cerv. 3434).
English
Cervantes Saavedra, Miguel de. <u>Don Quixote de la Mancha</u>.
Trans. Charles Jarvis. Illust. Arthur Boyd Houghton and
Coi. Ltd. (S.a.) (Cerv. Sedó 1.755).
---. <u>The history of Don Quixote de la Mancha: with an</u>
<u>account of his exploits and adventures</u>. London. Milner
and Sowerby, (S.a.) (Cerv. Sedó 301 or R 419.387).
---. <u>The History of the valoroys Knight Errant Don Quixote of</u>
<u>the Mancha</u>. Trans. William Stansby. London. 1612.
(Cerv. Sedó 8.673/74).
Flemish
Cervantes Saavedra, Miguel de. <u>De Aveonturen van der</u>
<u>Roemruchte Ridder Don</u> <u>Quichote de la Mancha</u>. adapt.
de C. Wilkeshuis para la juventud. 194pp. (Cerv. 839;
16-VII-3435).
French
Cervantes Saavedra, Miguel de. <u>L'Ingénieux Don Quixote de</u>
<u>la Manche</u>. Trans. César Oudin. Paris: Foüet, 1614,
(Cerv. 1568) [First edition in French]
---. <u>Seconde partie de L'Histoire de l'Ingenieux, et redoutable</u>
<u>Chevalier, Don Quichote de la Manche</u>. Trad. F. De
Rosset. Paris: Jacques do Clov & Denis Moreau. (1618) 4
hoj. 878pp. 4 hoj. (Cerv. 2703).
German

Cervantes Saavedra, Miguel de. Don Kichote de la Mantscha.
1669. (Cerv. Sedó 8.848).
---. Don Kichote. Trans. Johann Ludwig du Four. Basel u.
Franckfurt, 1682. (Cerv. 3297) 1st complete German
translation.

Italian

Cervantes Saavedra, Miguel de. L'ingegnoso Cittadino Don
Chisciotte della Mancia. Trad. Lorenzo Franciosini
Florentino. Venecia: Andrea Baba. 1622. (Cerv. Sedó
8670). [The second part was first published in 1625]
---. Dell ingenioso Cittadino Don Chisciotte della Mancia.
Trans. Lorenzo Franciosini Florentino. Venetia: Andrea
Baba, 1625. (Cerv. Sedó 8. 662-63). [Second Italian
edition]

Portuguese

Cervantes Saavedra, Miguel de. Don Quixote de la Mancha.
4 vols. 2ª ed. Lisboa: Ferreira & Oliveira: Limitada
Editores, 1907. (Cerv. Sedó 8485-88).
---. O engenhoso fidalgo Dom Quijote de la Mancha. 6 vols.
Lisboa, 1794. (Cerv. 3341-6).
---. O engenhoso fidalgo Dom Quijote de la Mancha. 6 vols.
Traduzido em vulgar. Lisboa: Na Typografia
Bollandiana, 1794, (R 92533-8).
---. O engenhoso fidalgo Dom Quijote de la Mancha. 2 vols.
Trad. Viscondes de Castilho e de Azevedo. Com os
desenhos de Gustavo Dorê gravadas por H. Pisan.
 Porto: Companhia Litteraria, 1876-1878. (R
420.060).

"Quixote " Studies

Allen, John J. "Don Quijote and the Origins of the Novel."
Cervantes and the Renaissance. (Papers of the Pomona
College Cervantes Symposium 16-18, 1978) Ed. Michael
D. McGalia. Easton, PA: Juan de la Cuesta, 1980, 125-
140.
---. Don Quijote, Hero or Fool. Gainsville: University of
Florida Press, 1971 (second printing).
Aguirre Bellver, Joaquín. El borrador de Cervantes. Como se
escribió el Quijote. Madrid: Rialp, 1992.

Antolín, Teófilo. "El uso de la Sagrada Escritura en
Cervantes" Cuadernos de Literatura, 3 (1948) 109-37.
Auerbach, Erich. "The Enchanted Dulcinea." Mimesis: The
Representation of Reality in Western Literature.
Translated by Willard R. Trask. Princeton: Princeton
University Press, 1953.
Avalle-Arce, J.B. "Cervantes and the Renaissance." Cervantes
and the Renaissance. (Papers of the Pomona College
Cervantes Symposium 16-18, 1978) Ed. Michael D.
McGalia. Easton, PA: Juan de la Cuesta, 1980, 1-10.
---. Don Quijote como forma de vida. Madrid: Fundación
Juan March, 1976.
Aylward, E.T. Cervantes, Pioneer and Plagiarist. London:
Tamesis, 1982.
Bardon, Maurice, ed. Critique du livre de Don Quichotte. By
Perrault, Pierre. Paris: Les Presses Modernes, 1930.
---. Don Quichotte en France au XVIIe èt au XVIIIe siècle.
1605-1815. Genève: Slatkine Reprints, 1974.
Barriga Casalini, Guilhermo. Los dos mundos del Quijote:
realidad y ficción. Madrid: José Porrúa Turanzas, D.L.,
1983.
Bradford, Carlos F., ed. Indice de las Notas de Diego
Clemencín de El ingenioso hidalgo don Quijote de la
Mancha. Madrid: Fundación de Manuel Tello, 1885.
Byron, William. Cervantes: A Biography. New York:
Doubleday and Co., 1978.
Casalduero, J. Sentido y Forma. Madrid: Insula,1966, 1970,
1975.
---. Sentido y forma del "Quijote". Barcelona-Madrid: Insula,
1970.
Castro, Americo. El pensamiento de Cervantes. Barcelona-
Madrid: Editorial Noguer, 1972.
---. "Cervantes y Pirandello." Hacia Cervantes. Madrid:
Taurus, 1924.
---. "Los prólogos al Quijote." Hacia Cervantes. Madrid:
Taurus, 1924.
---. Cervantes y los casticismos españoles. Madrid: Alianza-
Alfaguara, 1974.

Close, Anthony J. Romantic Approach to Don Quijote. A Critical History of the Romantic Tradition in 'Quijote' Criticism. London: Cambridge University Press, 1977.
---. "Sancho Panza: Wise Fool" Modern Language Review, 63 (1973), 344-57.
Coburn, William L. "In Imitation of the Manner of Cervantes. Don Quijote and Joseph Andrews." Diss. University of California Davis, 1969. UMI.
Combet, Louis. Cervantes ou les incertitudes du désir. Une approche psychostructurale de l'oeuvre de Cervantes. Lyon: Presses Universitaires de Lyon, 1980.
Contag, Kimberly. "The Backbone of Burlesque: Vertebral Jokes and Hoaxes in Cervantes' Don Quixote." Critical Essays on the Literatures of Spain and Spanish America. Boulder, Colorado: Society of Spanish and Spanish-American Studies, Winter 1992, 65-75.
Corley, Ames Haven. "A Study in the Word-play in Cervantes' "Don Quijote." Diss. Yale 1914. Published as Word-Play in the "Don Quixote". New York: 1917.
Creel, Bryant L. "Don Quixote", Symbol of a Culture in Crisis. Valencia: Albatros Hispanófila, 1988.
Criado Costa, Joaquín. La Dulcinea de don Quijote. Córdoba: Facultad de filología y letras. Dept. de literatura española, 1978.
Criado del Val, M. Análisis verbal del estilo. Indices verbales de Cervantes, de Avellaneda y del autor de "la tia fingida." Madrid: Consejo Superior de Investigaciones Científicas. Instituto Miguel de Cervantes, 1953.
De la Fuente, Patricia A. Mock-heroic narrative techniques in Ariosto and Cervantes. Diss. University of Texas at Austin, 1976.
Del Toro, Frances Magaret Bothwell. "The Quixotic and the Shandean: A Study of the Influence of Cervantes' Don Quijote on Stern's Tristam Shandy. Diss. Florida State University, 1980.
Drake, Dana B. Don Quijote in World Literature: A Selective, Annotated Bibliography. New York: Garland Publishing, 1980.
Durán, Manuel. "El Quijote a través del prisma de M. Bakhtine: Carnaval, disfraces, escatalogía y locura."

Cervantes and the Renaissance. Ed. Michael D.
MacGaha. Newark, New Jersey: Juan de la Cuesta,
1980, 71-86.
Efron, Arthur. "Don Quixote" and the Dulcineated World.
Austin and London: University of Texas Press, 1971.
Eisenberg, Daniel. "Don Quijote and the Romances of
Chivalry: the Need for a Reexamination." Hispanic
Review, 41(1973), 511-23.
---. "Who Read the Romances of Chivalry?" Kentucky
Romance Quarterly, 20 (1973), 209-33.
El Saffar, Ruth. "Cervantes and the Games of Illusion."
Cervantes and the Renaissance. (Papers of the Pomona
College Cervantes Symposium 16-18, 1978) Ed. Michael
D. McGalia. Easton, PA: Juan de la Cuesta, 1980, 146-
156.
---. Distance and Control in "Don Quixote: A Study in
Narrative Technique. North Carolina Studies in Romance
Languages and Literatures, Chapel Hill: University of
North Carolina Press, 1974.
---. Novel to Romance: A Study of Cervantes' "Novelas
ejemplares." Baltimore and London: Johns Hopkins
University Press, 1974.
---. "Tricking the Trickster in the Works of Cervantes."
Symposium. 1983 Summer; 37 (2):106-124.
Entwistle, William J. Cervantes: 1547-1616. Oxford: The
Clarendon Press, 1940.
Flores Arroyuelo, Francisco, J. Alonso Quijano, el Hidalgo
que encontró el tiempo perdido. Madrid: Alcala Ediciones,
1982
Flores, Robert M. Sancho Panza Through Three hundred
Seventy-five Years of Continuations, Imitations and
Criticism, 1605-1980. Newark [Delaware]: Juan de la
Cuesta, 1982.
---. The Compositors of the First and Second Madrid Editions
of Don Quijote, Part I. London: The Modern Humanities
Research Association, 1975.
Fonte, Thomas Gilbert. "The Evolution of Humor in Don
Quijote." Diss. University of Wisconsin, 1975. DAI, 36A.

Forcione, Alban K. Cervantes and the Humanist Vision: A
   Study of Four Exemplary Novels. Princeton, New Jersey:
   Princeton University Press, 1982.
---. Cervantes and the Mystery of Lawlessness: A Study of
   "El casamiento engañoso" y "El coloquio de los perros".
   Princeton, New Jersey: Princeton University Press, 1984.
---. Cervantes, Aristotle and the Persiles. Princeton:
   Princeton University Press, 1970.
Frazier, Harriet C. A Babble of Ancestral Voices:
   Shakespeare, Cervantes and Theobald. Mouton: The
   Hague, 1974.
Friedman, Edward. "An Archetype and Its Modifications:
   Cervantes' Dramatic Theory and Practice." The American
   Hispanist 4, xxviii 9-11.
---. "Dramatic Structure in Cervantes and Lope. The Two
   Pedro de Urdemalas Plays." Hispania 60, 486-97.
---. "The Unifying Concept: An Approach to the Structure of
   Cervantes' Comedies." Diss. Johns Hopkins, 1974. DAI
   35A 3678-79. Publ.: York, S.C.:Spanish Literature
   Publications Co., 1981.
García Gomez, Amparo. Cervantes: Cuatro siglos en la
   literatura universal. Valencia: Corona, 36, 1984.
García Martín, Manuel. Cervantes y la comedia española en
   el siglo XVII. Salamanca: Universidad, 1980.
Gella Iturriaga, José. Flor de refranes cervantinos: un millar
   de proverbios del que más de quinientos son del Quijote.
   Madrid: Gella Iturriaga, 1978.
---. Los pensamientos populares en las obras de Cervantes.
   Madrid: Instituto de España, 1981.
Gonzalez Lopez, E. "La actualidad político-social de España
   en el Quijote. Los Saavedras, el conde de Lemos y los
   vizcaínos." A Cervantes XI, 1972. 141-6.
Gorfkle, Laura Jeanne. "The Grotesque-Comic in Don
   Quixote." Diss. University of Wisconsin-Madison. 1988.
Gruber, Vivian Mercer. "François Rabelais and Miguel de
   Cervantes: Novelists of Transition." Diss. Florida State
   University, 1960.
Gump Stewart, Marilyn. "The Festive Irony of Carnival:
   Comic Affirmation in "Don Quixote, The Brothers
   Karamazov, and The Reivers." Diss. Dallas, 1980.

Gutierrez Noriega, Carlos. Significado y trascendencia del humorismo en Cervantes. Lima, Peru: 1948.

Haley, George, ed. El Quijote. Madrid: Taurus, 1984.

---. "The Narrator in *Don Quijote*, Maese Pedro's Puppet Show." Modern Language Notes, 80 (1965) 145-65.

Heiple, Daniel Louis. "Cervantes' Wise Fool: A Study of Wisdom and Fortune in "El licenciado Vidriera." Diss. University of Texas at Austin, 1977. Ann Arbor: UMI 712.

---. "Renaissance Medical Psychology in Don Quijote." Ideologies and Literatures, 2, No. 9 (1979).

Homes, Alan B. "Laurence Sterne, Rabelais and Cervantes: The Two Kinds of Laughter in Tristam Shandy." Laurence Sterne: Riddles and Mysteries. Myer, Grosvenor, (Eds.). London: Vision; [1984]. Totowa, N.J.: Barnes and Noble, 1984, 39-56..

Ihrie, Maureen. Skepticism in Cervantes. London: Tamesis Books, 1982.

Lacarta, Manuel. Diccionario del Quijote. Madrid: Alderabán, 1995.

Lloréns Torres, Vicente. "Don Quijote y la decadencia del hidalgo." Aspectos sociales de la literatura española. Madrid: Castalia, 1974.

Madariaga, Salvador de. Guía del lector del Quijote, ensayo psicológico. Madrid: Espasa-Calpe, 1926 and Buenos Aires: Ed. Sudamericana, 1943.

Mancing, Howard. "Cervantes and the tradition of chivalric parody." Forum for Modern Language Studies. 11 (1975) 177-191.

---. The Chivalric World of Don Quixote: Style, Structure and Narrative Technique. Columbia: University of Missouri Press, 1982.

Manuel García, Martín. Cervantes y la comedia española en el siglo XVII. Salamanca: Universidad de Salamanca, 1980.

Maravall, José Antonio. Utopía y Contrautopía en el *Quijote*. Santiago de Compostela: Pico Sacro, 1976.

Marianella, Conchita Herdman. Dueñas" and "doncellas": A Study of the "Doña Rodriguez" episode in "Don Quijote".

Chapel Hill: University of North Carolina, Dept. of
Romance Languages, 1979.
Martínez Val, José María. El sentido jurídico en el "Quijote".
Madrid: José Vicente Hernandez, 1960.
McGalia, Michael D. ed. Cervantes and the Renaissance.
(Papers of the Pomona College Cervantes Symposium 16-
18, 1978) Easton, PA: Juan de la Cuesta, 1980.

Molho, Mauricio. Cervantes: raíces folklóricas. Madrid:
Gredos, 1976.
Murillo, Luis Andrés. Cervantes and the Renaissance. Ed.
M.D. McGaha. Easton, PA: Juan de la Cuesta, 1980, 51-
70.
---. ed. El ingenioso hidalgo don Quijote de la Mancha. I, II,
III Madrid: Castalia, 1978.
---. The Golden Dial. Oxford: Dolphin, 1975.
Neuschapfer, Hans Jörg. Der Sinn die Parodie in *Don Quijote*.
Carl Wintes-Universitätsverlag. Güngberg. Gustav
Jantech. 1963.
Orozco Díaz, Emilio. Cervantes y la novela del barroco.
Granada: Universidad de Granada, 1992.
Ortega y Gasset, José. Meditaciones del Quijote. Madrid:
Revista del Occidente, 1970.
Osterc, Ludovik. El pensamiento social y político del Quijote.
México: UNAM, 1988.
Parker, Alexander A. "Fielding and the Structure of Don
Quijote." Bulletin of Hispanic Studies. 33 (1956) 1-16.
Percas de Ponseti, Helena. Cervantes y su concepto de arte.
Madrid: Gredos, 1975.
Predmore, Richard L. An Index to Don Quijote. New
Brunswick: Rutgers University Press, 1938. (New York:
Kraus Reprint Co. 1970).
---. El mundo del Quijote. Madrid: Insula, 1958.
---. The World of Don Quijote. Cambridge: Harvard
University Press, 1967.
Riley, E. C. Cervantes' Theory of the Novel. Oxford: Clarendon
Press, 1962.
---. Don Quixote. London: Allen and Unwin. 1986.
---. "Don Quijote and the Imitation of Models." Bulletin of
Hispanic Studies. 31 (1954), 3-16.

---. "Who's who in Don Quijote? or An Approach to the Problem of Identity." Modern Language Notes. 81 (1966) 112-130.

Riquer, Martín de. Cervantes, Pasamonte y Avellaneda. Barcelona: Sirmio, 1988.

---. Aproximación al "Quijote". Barcelona: Teide, 1967. Estella [Navarra]: Salvat, 1970.

---. Cervantes y el Quijote. Barcelona: Teide, 1960.

Rosenblat, Angel. La lengua del "Quijote." Madrid: Gredos, 1971.

Russell, P.E. Cervantes. Oxford and New York: Oxford University Press, 1985.

---. "Don Quijote as a Funny Book." Modern Language Review, 64 (1969), 302-26.

--- Spain: A Companion to Spanish Studies. Ed. P.E. Russell. London and New York: Pitman Publishing Co., 1973.

Salazar Rincón, Javier. El mundo social del "Quijote". Madrid: Gredos, 1986.

Sanchez, Alberto. Cervantes: Bibliografía fundamental, 1900-1959. Madrid: CSIC, 1961.

Santos, Guilherme G. de Oliveira. Ao redor de duas edições do "Dom Quixote de la Mancha." Lisboa: Livraria Portugal, 1980.

Sieber, Harry. "On Juan Huarte de San Juan and Anselmo's *Locura* in El Curioso impertinente." Revista hispánica moderna, 36 (1970-71) 1-8.

Sobre, J.M. "Don Quijote, the Hero Upside Down." Hispanic Review, 44 (1976) 127-41.

Spitzer, Leo. "Perspectivismo lingüistico en el 'Quijote'. Lingüistica e historia literaria. Madrid: Gredos, 1955. 135-187.

Syverson-Stork. Theatrical Aspects of the Novel: A Study of "Don Quixote". Valencia: Albatros Hispanófila. 1986.

Torrente Ballester, Gonzalo. El Quijote como juego. Madrid: Guadarrama. 1975.

Ugalde, Victoriano. "La risa de Don Quijote." Anales Cervantinos 15 (1976, publ. 1978), 157-70.

Unamuno, Miguel de. Vida de Don Quijote y Sancho según Miguel de Cervantes Saavedra. 6a ed. Madrid: Espasa Calpe. 1938 (15a ed. 1971)

Urbina, Eduardo. El sin par Sancho Panza: Parodia y
creación. Barcelona: Anthropos, 1991.
Wardropper, Bruce W. "Cervantes' Theory of Drama."
Modern Philology. 52 (1955) 217-21.
---. "Don Quijote: Story or History?" Modern Philology. 63
(1965) 1-11.
---. "The Pertinence of El Curioso Impertinente." Publications
of the Modern Language Association. 72 (1957) 587-600.
Weigir, John G. "Don Quijote: The Comedy In Spite of Itself."
Bulletin of Hispanic Studies. 60: 4 (Oct. 1983) 283-92.
Welsh, Alexander. Reflections on the Hero as Quixote.
Princeton University Press, 1981.
Willis, Raymond S.J. The Phantom Chapter of the *Quijote*.
Boulder: Miner and Journal Press, 1953.
Zimic, Ztanislav. "Sobre la clasificación de las comedias de
Cervantes." Acta Neophilologica. 41 (1981) 63-83.
---. "El gran teatro del mundo y el gran mundo del teatro en
Pedro de Urdemalas de Cervantes." Acta Neophilologica.
10, 55-105.
Ziomek, Henryk. Relexiones del Quijote. Madrid: Gráf.
Molina, 1969.

**Spanish Baroque Humorous and Popular Festive
Works (Selected Studies and Editions)**
Alziev, Pierre and Robert James. Floresta de poesías eróticas
del siglo de oro. Toulouse: France-Ibérie Recherche.
1975.
Arrellano, Ignacio. "Elección y expresividad en la poesía de
Quevedo: Algunas variantes burlescas." Thesaurus.
1983 May-Aug: 38 (2): 385-95.
---. Poesía satírica burlesca de Quevedo. Pamplona:
Universidad de Navarra. 1984.
Asensio, Eugenio, ed. Entremeses. Miguel de Cervantes.
Madrid: Castalia, 1980.
Astrana Marín, Luis, ed. Obras completas. Versos.
Francisco de Quevedo y Villegas. Madrid: Aguilar, 1943.
Aubrun, Charles Vincente. La comedia española (1600-
1680). Trans. Julio Lago Alonso. Madrid: Taurus, 1968.

Ball, Robert Frances. "Góngora's Parodies of Literary Convention." Diss. Yale, 1976. Ann Arbor: UMI.

Bergman, Hannah E., ed. Entremeses. By Luis Quiñones de Benavente. Entremeses. Madrid, Barcelona: Anaya, 1968.

Bergua, José. Refranero español. 8th ed. Madrid: Ediciones Bergua, 1977.

Bernard, Mary E. "Myth in Quevedo: The Serious and the Burlesque in the Apollo and Daphne Poems." Hispanic Review. 52: 4 (Autumn) 499-522.

Blecua, José Manuel, ed. Obra poética I. By Francisco de Quevedo y Villegas. Madrid: Editorial Castalia, 1969.

Ciplijauskaité, Biruté, ed. Sonetos. By Luis de Góngora y Argote. Madison: The Hispanic Seminary of Medieval Studies, 1981.

Carreira, Antonio, ed. Antología poética. Polifemo, Soledad primera, Fábula de Píramo y Tisbe y otros poemas. By Luís de Góngora. Madrid: Castalia, 1986.

Chevalier, Máxime. "El aldeano cómico en la comedia Lopesca." Risa y sociedad en el teatro del Siglo de Oro. Actes du 3e colloque du Groupe d'Etudes Sur le Théâtre Espagnol. Toulouse: C.N.R.S., 1980, 197-207.

---. Sur le public du roman de chevalerie. Bordeaux: Institut d'Etudes Ibériques et Ibéro-américaines de l'Université de Bordeaux, 1978.

---. Tipos cómicos y folklore. Madrid: Edi-6, 1982.

Cros, Edmond. Ideología y genética textual: el caso del Buscón. Madrid: Cupsa, 1980.

Crosby, James O. En torno a la poesía de Quevedo. Madrid: Castalia, 1967.

---. Guía bibliográfico para el estudio crítico de Quevedo. London: Grant and Cutler, Ltd. 1976.

Dominguez, Frank. ed. Cancionero de obras de burlas provocantes a risa. Valencia: Albatros Hispanófila,1978.

Esqueva Martínez, Manuel. La colección teatral "la Farsa." Madrid: Consejo superior de investigaciones científicas, 1971.

Espinosa, Aurelio M. Cuentos populares españoles. 3 vols. Madrid: CSIC Instituto "Antonio de Nebrija" de Filología, 1946.

Estruch, Juan. Literatura fantástica y de terror española del siglo XVII. Barcelona: Fontamara, 1982.

Fernandez de Avellaneda. El Quijote. Illust. Cobos. Barcelona: Marte, 1972.

Floresta de poesías eróticas del siglo de oro. Comp. Pierre Alzieu, Robert Jammes, and Ivan Lissorgues. Toulouse: France-Ibérie Recherche, 1975.

Ford, Robert Martin. Text, Carnival, Palimpsest: A Stylistic and Semiotic Reappraisal of Góngora's Humorous Verse. Diss. State University of New York, Stony Brook. 1982. DAI 43 (2) 461A

Galaz Vivar Welden, Alicia. "Análisis estilístico de la Fabula de Píramo y Tisbe de don Luis de Góngora y Argote." Memoria de los egresados. Santiago de Chile, II: 1 (1958) 241-332.

---. "Perrenidad de la poética innovadora de Luis de Góngora: las burlas y las veras de la "Fábula de Píramo y Tisbe." Diss. University of Alabama, 1980.

Góngora y Argote, Luis de. Delicias del Parnaso en que se cifran todos los Romances Líricos, Amorosos, Burlescos, Glosas y Décimas Satíricas del regocijo de las Musas del prodigioso Don Luis de Góngora. Pedro Verges, Pedro Esquer, 1643.

Góngora y Argote, Luis de. Obras de Don Luis de Góngora. Brusselas: Francisco Foppens, 1659.

González, Elroy R. "Carnival on the Stage: Céfalo y Pócris, a "comedia burlesca." Bulletin of the Comediantes 30: 3-12

Gracián, Baltasar. Agudeza y arte de ingenio. 2 vol. Madrid: Clásicos Castalia, 1969.

Herrero García, Miguel. Oficios populares en la sociedad de Lope. Madrid: Castalia, 1977.

Hurwood, Bernhardt J. The Golden Age of Erotica. Los Angeles: Sherbourne Press, 1965.

Iffland, James. "'Antivalues' in the Burlesque Poetry of Góngora and Quevedo." Neophilologus. 63 (1979) 220-237.

---. Quevedo and the Grotesque. London: Tamesis Books, 1978-82.

Iturriaga, José Gella. ed. Flor de refranes cervantinos: un millar de proverbios del que más de quinientos son del "Quijote." Madrid: José Gella Iturriaga, 1978.

---. Los pensamientos populares en las obras de Cervantes. Madrid: Instituto de España, 1981.

Jammes, Robert. Etudes sur l'oeuvre poétique de Góngora y Argote. Bordeaux: Institut d'Etudes Ibériques et Ibéro-Americaines de l'Université, 1967.

---. "Notes sur la Fábula de Píramo y Tisbe de Góngora." Les Langues Néo-Latines. LV (1961) 1-47.

---. La obra poética de Don Luis de Góngora y Argote. Madrid: Castalia, 1987.

---. Retrogongorismo. Toulouse: France-Ibérie Recherche. U. de Toulouse-Le Mirail, 1978.

J.B.S.P. Avellaneda. Madrid, Cadiz: Escelicier, S.L., 1940.

Lerner, Lía Schwartz. Metáfora y sátira en la obra de Quevedo. Madrid: Taurus, 1984.

Maurer, Christopher. Interpretación de la "Epístola satírica y censoria" de Quevedo. Madrid: Cuadernos Hispánicos, 1980.

Merino Quijano, Gaspar. Los bailes dramáticos del siglo XVII. 2 vol. Madrid: Universidad Complutense, 1981. (Facsimile)

Nuñez Ramos, Rafael. Poética-semiológica: "El Polifemo de Góngora." Oviedo: Universidad de Oviedo: Servicio de publicaciones, 1980.

Olivares, Julian Jr. The Love Poetry of Francisco de Quevedo. Cambridge: Cambridge University Press, 1983.

Orozco, Emilio. Góngora y Quevedo: poetas. Madrid: La Muralla, 1975.

---. Introdución a Góngora. Barcelona: Crítica, 1984.

Parker, Alexander A. The Humour of Spanish Proverbs. London: Hispanic and Luso-Brazilian Councils, 1963.

Periñan, Blanca. Poeta ludens: Disparate, perque y chiste en los siglos XVI y XVII. Pisa: Giardini, 1979.

Pou, Pablo Jauralde and Juan Alfredo Bellón Cazabán eds. Cancionero de obras de burlas provocantes a risa. Madrid: Akal Editor, 1974.

Quevedo, Francisco de. Poemas satíricos y burlescos. Ed. José Manuel Blecua. Barcelona: Sinera, 1970.

Rodriguez, Evangelina and Antonio Tordera. eds.
Entremeses, jácaras y mojigangas. Madrid: Clásicos
Castalia, 1982.

Rodríguez Marín, Francisco. Burla burlando. 2nd ed. Madrid:
Tip. de la "Revista de Archibos." 1914.

Salomón, Noël. Recherches sur le thème paysan dans la
"comedia" au temps de Lope de Vega. Madrid: Castalia,
1985.

Soons, Alan. Haz y enves del cuento risible en el siglo de oro.
London: Tamesis Books, 1976.

Snell, Ana María. Hacia el verbo: signos y transignificación
en la poesía de Quevedo. London: Tamesis Books, 1982.

Varo, Carlos. Carajicomedia. Madrid: Playor, 1982.
(Facsimile.)

Zahareas, Anthony. "The Historical Function of Art and
Morality in Quevedo's Buscón." Bulletin of Hispanic
Studies. 61 (3) (July, 1984) 432-443.

Zahareas, Anthony N. and Thomas R. McCallum. "Towards
a Social History of the Love Sonnet: the Case of Quevedo's
Sonnet 331." Ideologies and Literature. 2 (1978) 90-100.

Spanish Baroque: Cultural History

Bataillon, Marcel. Erasmo y España: estudios sobre la historia espiritual del siglo XVI. Trans. Antonio Alatorre. Mexico City and Buenos Aires: Fondos de Cultura Económica, 1950.

Blanco Aguinaga, Carlos, and Julio Rodriguez-Puértolas, and Iris Zavala. Historia social de la literature española. 2 vols. Madrid: Castalia, 1979.

Cardona de Gilbert, Angeles. La innovación teatral del barroco. Madrid: Cincel, 1981.

Castro, Américo. An Idea of History. Trans. S. Gilman and Edmund L. King. Columbus: Ohio State University Press, 1977.

Contag, Kimberly. "Cervantes' Retablo de las maravillas and the Ideology of Pure Blood." The Resurgence of Learning: Proceedings of the Cameron University RENAISSANCE CONFERENCE. Vol 1. 1993.

---. "Imaginary Representations of Historical Ills: Analysis of the Body Politic and the Decadence of Imperial Spain." Torre de papel. Summer 1995 volume V, number 2. 109-118.

Defourneaux, Marcelin. Daily Life in Spain in the Golden Age. Trans. Newton Branch. New York: Praega Publishers, Inc., 1971.

Diez Borque, José María. Sociología de la comedia española del siglo XVII. Madrid: Cátedra, 1976.

Dominguez Ortíz, Antonio. The Golden Age of Spain: 1516-1659. Trans. James Casey. New York: Basic Books,1971.

Elliot, J.H. Imperial Spain: 1469-1716. Hamandsworth: Penguin Books, 1970.

---. "Monarchy and Empire (1474-1700)." Spain: A Companion to Spanish Studies. Ed. P.E. Russell. London: Pitman Publishing Co., 1973.

---. "Self-Perception and Decline in Early Seventeenth-Century Spain." Past and Present, 74 (1957) 41-61.

---. "The Decline of Spain." Past and Present, 21 (1961) 52-75.

Fernández de Navarrete, M. Vida de Miguel de Cervantes Saavedra. Madrid: [s.n.] 1819.

Ferández de Navarrete, Pedro. Conservación de monarquías
  y diversos políticos. Madrid. 1626.
Fernández Mosquera, Santiago; Azaúste Galiana, Antonio.
  Indice de la poesía de Quevedo. Barcelona:
  PPU/Universidade de Santiago de Compostela, 1993.
Fernández Oblanca, Justo. Literatura y sociedad en los
  entremeses del siglo XVII. Oviedo: Universidad de
  Oviedo, 1992.
Gilman, Stephen. "An Introduction to the Ideology of the
  Baroque in Spain." Symposium, 1 (1946): 82-107.
Green, Otis H. "On the Attitude Toward the Vulgo in the
  Spanish Siglo de Oro." Studies in the Renaissance. IV
  (1957) 190-200.
---. Spain and the Western Tradition. The Castilian Mind in
  Literature from "El Cid" to Calderón. 4 vols. Madison:
  University of Wisconsin Press, 1963-66.
Herrero García, M. Estimaciones literarias del siglo XVII.
  Madrid: Voluntad, 1930.
Jones, Royston O. A Literary History of Spain. The Golden
  Age: Prose and Poetry. The Sixteenth and Seventeenth
  Centuries. New York: Barnes and Noble, 1971.
Leavitt, S.E. Golden Age Drama in Spain. Chapel Hill:
  University of North Carolina Press, 1972.
Llorens, Vicente. Aspectos sociales de la literatura española.
  Madrid: Castalia, 1974.
Lynch, John. Spain under the Habsburgs. 2 vols. New York:
  Oxford University Press, 1964-1969.
Mandrou, Robert. De la culture populaire au XVIIe siècle.
  Paris: Stock, 1964.
Maravall, José Antonio. El humanismo. Madrid: Institutos
  de estudios políticos [S. Aguirre], 1948.
---. Estado moderno y mentalidad social (siglos XV a XVII).
  Madrid: Revista de Occidente, 1972.
---. Estudios de historia del pensamiento español: siglo XVII.
  Madrid: Ed. Cultura Hispánica, 1975.
---. La cultura del barroco: análisis de una estructura
  histórica. Esplugues de Llobregat: Ariel, 1975.
---. Teatro y literatura en la sociedad barroca. Madrid:
  Seminario y Ediciones, 1972.

---. Utopía y contrautopía en el "Quijote." Santiago de
  Compostela: Pico Sacro, 1976.
Moncada, Sancho de. Restauración política de España. Jean
  Vilar Ed. Madrid: Clásicos del pensamiento económico
  español, 1974.
Montoto y Rautenstrauch, Luis. De Cervantes y Sevilla.
  Crónica. 1616-1916. Sevilla: Tip. de Girones, 1916.
Parker, Alexander A. "Approach to the Spanish Drama of the
  Golden Age." Tulane Drama Review, 4 (1959) 42-59.
Rico, Francisco, ed. Historia y crítica de la literatura
  española. Vol. III: Siglo de oro: Barroco. Barcelona:
  Crítica, 1983.
Rodríguez Moñino, Antonio. La transmisión de la poesía
  española en los siglos de oro. E.M. Wilson, ed. Barcelona:
  Ariel, 1976.
Ruggerio, M.J. "Dramatic Conventions and Their
  Relationship to Structure in the Spanish Golden Age
  "Comedias.'" Revista Hispánica Moderna, 37 (1972-
  73), 137-54.
Salomón, Noël. "Algunos problemas de sociología de las
  literaturas de lengua española. " Creación y público en la
  literatura española. Madrid: Castalia, 1974.
---. La vida rural castellana en tiempos de Felipe II. Trans.
  Francesc Espinet Burunat. Barcelona: Planeta, 1964.
---. Lo villano en el teatro del Siglo de Oro. Madrid: Castalia,
  1985.
Salstad, M. Louise. The Presentation of Women in Spanish
  Golden Age Literature. Boston: G.K. Hall, 1980. Sanchez,
  F. and Nicholas Spadaccini. "La picaresca desde el
  pensamiento de Maravall." Ideologies and Ltierature. 3:
  1 (Spring 1988)
Shergold, N.D. A History of the Spanish Stage. Oxford:
  Clarendon Press, 1967.
---. Representaciones palaciegas, 1603-1699: estudio y
  documentos. London: Tamesis, 1982.
Silverman, Joseph H. "Some Aspects of Literature and Life
  in the Golden Age of Spain. "Estudios de literatura
  española ofrecidos a Marcos A. Morínigo. Madrid: Insula,
  1971.

Spadaccini, Nicholas, ed. Entremeses. By Miguel de
    Cervantes. Madrid: Cátedra, 1982.
Spadaccini, Nicholas and Anthony N. Zahareas. Vida y
    hechos de Estebanillo González, hombre de buen humor.
    2 vols. Madrid: Castalia, 1978.
Terry, Arthur. "An Interpretation of Góngora's Fábula de
    Píramo y Tisbe." Bulletin of Hispanic Studies, 4 (1956),
    202-217.
---. "The Continuity of Renaissance Criticism: Poetic Theory
    in Spain Between 1535 and 1650." Bulletin of Hispanic
    Studies, 31 (1954) 27-36.
Valbuena Prat, Angel. Historia de la literatura española. 4
    vols. Barcelona: Gustavo Gili, 1968.
Vicens Vives, Jaime. Approaches to the History of Spain.
    2nd ed. Trans. Joan Connelly Ullman. Berkeley, Los
    Angeles, and London: University of California Press,
    1970.
---. Aproximación a la historia de España. Barcelona:
    Editorial Vicen-Vives, 1952.
Vilar, Jean. Literatura y economía: La figura satírica del
    arbitrista en el Siglo de Oro. Madrid: Revista del
    Occidente, 1973.
Vilar, Pierre. "El tiempo del Quijote." Crecimiento y
    desarrollo, economía e historia: reflexiones sobre el caso
    español. Trans. Emilio Giralt y Raventós. Barcelona:
    Ariel,1964.
---. Historia de España. Trans. Manuel Tuñón de Lara.
    Paria: Librairie Espagnole, 1975.
---. "Le Temps du Quichotte." Europe, 121-22 (1956) 3-16.
---. Spain: A Brief History. Trans. Brian Tate. Oxford: The
    Pergamon Press, 1967.
---. "The Age of Don Quixote." New Left Review. 68 (1961)
    59-71.
Wallerstein, Immanuel. "The 'Crisis of the Seventeenth
    Century'." New Left Review. 110 (1978) 65-73.
Wilson, E.M. and Duncan Moir. The Golden Age: Drama
    1492-1700. Vol III. of A Literary History of Spain. Ed. R.
    O. Jones. London: Ernest Benn, 1971.

Dictionaries and Lexical References

Alonso Herneandez, José Luis. Léxico del marginalismo del siglo de oro. Salamanca: Universidad de Salamanca, 1977.

Bradford, Carlos F. ed. Indice de las Notas de Diego Clemencín de *El ingenioso hidalgo don Quijote de la Mancha*. Madrid: Fundación de Manuel Tello, 1885.

Casares y Sánchez, Julio. Diccionario ideológico de la lengua española. Barcelona: Gustavo Gili, 1959.

Corominas, Joan. Diccionario crítico-etimológico de la lengua castellana. 4 vols. Madrid: Gredos, 1954.

Correas, Gonzalo. Vocabulario de refranes y frases proverbiales. Madrid. 1617. Louis Combet, ed. Bordeaux: Féret et Fils, 1967

Covarrubias y Orozco, Sebastian de. Tesoro de la lengua castellana o española. Madrid: Luís Sánchez, 1611. Ed. M. de Riquer. Barcelona: S.A. Horta, 1943.

Diccionario de autoridades. 3 vols. Facsimile ed. Madrid: Gredos, 1969.

Fernán Gómez, Carlos. Vocabulario de Lope de Vega. 3 vol. Madrid: Real Academia Española, 1971.

Hidalgo, Juan. Romances de germania. Madrid: Antonio de Sancha, 1779.

Sentencias de Don Quijote y agudezas de Sancho. Madrid: G. Blazquez, 1981 (facsimile of Madrid 1863 edition).